THE STORY OF
MUSIC
FROM ANTIQUITY TO THE PRESENT

Editor: Ritu Malhotra
Design: Mallika Das
DTP: Neeraj Aggarwal
Project coordination: Daniel Fischer
Cover: All images: © Lebrecht Music & Arts, except for:
Front Cover: top far right: © MaxJazz / Lebrecht Music & Arts
top right: © JazzSign / Lebrecht Music & Arts
middle left: © Tristram Kenton / Lebrecht Music & Arts
bottom left: © ColouriserAL / Lebrecht Music & Arts
Back Cover: bottom right: © Laurie Lewis / Lebrecht Music & Arts
Cover design: Simone Sticker
Overall responsibility for production: h.f.ullmann publishing GmbH, Potsdam, Germany

Printed in China, 2013

ISBN 978-3-8480-0561-1

10 9 8 7 6 5 4 3 2 1
X IX VIII VII VI V IV III II I

www.ullmann-publishing.com
newsletter@ullmann-publishing.com

Maria Lord

with John Snelson

THE STORY OF MUSIC

FROM ANTIQUITY TO THE PRESENT

h.f.ullmann

Contents

ANCIENT MUSIC

RITUAL TRADITIONS (UP TO 800 AD)

Since the beginning of human presence on earth it is thought that people have made music, either through singing or playing instruments. Music has played a part in almost all the important stages of human life, from adolescence to marriage, childbirth and death. It has accompanied religious rituals, work, dance and entertainment. The sound itself has been produced by the voice or by any one of a number of idiophones (instruments that produce the sound from their own body, usually by being struck, shaken or scraped), membranophones (drums with skins), aerophones (instruments that are blown) or chordophones (stringed instruments that are either plucked, bowed or struck).

PREHISTORY

Little evidence remains of very earliest music-making in western Europe, and what there is comes either from iconography (for example, cave paintings) or archaeological finds. The contexts in which music was performed are a matter of conjecture, although it is likely that they would have included life-cycle rituals and religious settings, and it is suspected that many artifacts have been lost through the decay of organic materials. The Lower Paleolithic (c. 40000–8000 BC) gives the first items that may be tentatively described as instruments; perforated shells may have acted as rattles and animal bones drilled with holes are

Painting in the tomb of Inherkha,
Deir el-Medina, West Thebes; Ancient Egypt, 19th dynasty/1295–1186 BC

A detail showing a harpist entertaining the deceased and his wife.

MESOPOTAMIA
3000 BC: City-states, including that of Ur, are established in the Tigris–Euphrates basin.

2600–2400 BC: The Standard of Ur shows one of the earliest depictions of music-making at the Sumerian court.

2334 BC: The Akkadians unify the whole region into a single kingdom. From this point on, cuneiform records are kept in both Sumerian and Akkadian.

1794 BC: The Amorites take over and make Babylon their important city. Musical instructions begin to be written down.

1200 BC: The Assyrians conquer the region and establish their capital at Nineveh.

609–539 BC: Neo-Babylonians take control under Nebuchadnezzar II and rule until the Persian conquest in 539 BC.

EGYPT
2755–2255 BC: The Old Kingdom
The pharaoh is the absolute ruler and considered the incarnation of Horus and later Ra, the sun god. The pyramids at Saqqara and Giza are built. The indigenous arched harp is in use.

2134–1786 BC: The Middle Kingdom
The unification of upper and lower Egypt by Mentuhotep of Thebes. Construction of vast temple complexes in Karnak to Amon, the principal deity of Egypt. The earliest surviving example of an ancient Egyptian drum.

1570–1070 BC: The New Kingdom
Egypt grows in power, reaching the peak of its rule under Queen Hatshepsut and greatest extent under Tuthmosis III. Temple complexes are built at Karnak, Luxor and Abu Simbel. New chordophone types arrive from Mesopotamia.

525–332 BC: The Late Dynastic Period
Egypt is conquered by the Macedonians (under Alexander) in 332 BC.

GREECE
2100–1200 BC: First the Minoans on Crete and then the Myceneans on the Peloponnese form Bronze Age kingdoms.

1100–750 BC: Dorians begin to establish city-states, including Athens and Sparta, on the Greek mainland.

550 BC: Pythagoras establishes the numerical basis of acoustics.

500 BC: The dramas of Aeschylus, Euripides, Sophocles and Aristophanes are first performed.

490 BC: The Athenians defeat the Persians at Marathon, marking the beginning of the ascent of Athens as the dominant power in Greece.

478 BC: The naval Confederation of Delos is formed as a protection against further attacks from Persia.

443–429 BC: The age of Pericles; the Acropolis in Athens is rebuilt and the Parthenon erected.

431–404 BC: The Peloponnesian Wars; Athens capitulates and Sparta

emerges as the strongest Greek city-state.

368 BC: Aristoxenus proposes a new theoretical basis for musical tuning.

338 BC: Philip of Macedonia takes control of all Greek city-states except Sparta, later incorporated into the Macedonia Empire by Philip's son Alexander.

ROME
750 BC: The foundation of Rome.

509–265 BC: The Early Republic.

168 BC: Rome conquers Macedonia and takes control of Syria and Egypt.

45 BC: Julius Caesar becomes sole ruler of the Roman Empire.

27 BC: Emperor Augustus becomes the Senate-approved *Princeps*.

1st century AD: Musicians and dancers arrive in Rome from West Asia and North Africa.

54 AD: Nero becomes emperor.

79: Vesuvius erupts and destroys Pompeii and Herculaneum.

161–80: Marcus Aurelius becomes the Roman emperor.

*A woman playing a lyre
(Wall painting in the tomb of Zeserkaresonb; Ancient Egypt; 18th dynasty/c. 1420–11 BC)*

313: Constantine's Edict of Milan ensures religious freedom for Christians.

330: Byzantium is renamed Constantinople and from 395 becomes the capital of the Eastern Roman Empire.

likely to have been used as flutes. Animal jawbones with serrated edges have been discovered that some researchers take to be Paleolithic scrapers. The Paleolithic cave paintings in France and Spain contain little of direct relevance to music-making or dance, though the odd figure may show people playing flutes or frame drums. Finds of a similar nature become a little more regular with the Mesolithic (c. 8000–5000 BC) and by the time of the Neolithic (c. 5000–2500 BC) finds of new items such as rattles, drum vessels and flutes made of pottery become increasingly widespread.

With the onset of the Bronze and Iron Ages (from 2300 BC to 500 BC and 800 BC onward) the histories of northern Europe and the areas bordering the Mediterranean follow radically different patterns: Greece and Anatolia (and later Italy) in particular were greatly influenced by literate cultures to south and east, while those areas to the north and west of the Alps were largely divorced from these developments and did not form literate cultures until much later. Among the most characteristic items dating from the metal ages to the north of the Alps are a wide variety of trumpets and horns, generally curved and made of bronze. Examples of these have been found in Ireland, Scandinavia and in central Europe, famous types being the *lur* of northern Germany and Scandinavia, of which there are numerous surviving examples, and the *carnyx* with its animal-head bell, associated with the widespread La Tène culture. However, as for earlier periods, there are no written sources describing musical practice and very few examples of musical iconography.

MUSIC IN ANCIENT CIVILIZATIONS

Mesopotamia

The emergence of urban settlements around 3000 BC in the Middle East, along the Indus river and down the Nile, coincided with the rise of the first literate societies, and from these we have a great deal of evidence for music-making, not only from written sources but also surviving instruments and iconography. Both the civilizations of ancient Egypt and Mesopotamia, as well as the slightly later developments in Anatolia, were influential on ancient Greece and Rome, and thus on the direction that Western music history took after the fall of the Roman Empire in 476 AD. This was through not only musical theory but also the development of instruments.

Mesopotamia is the area between the Euphrates and Tigris rivers in present-day

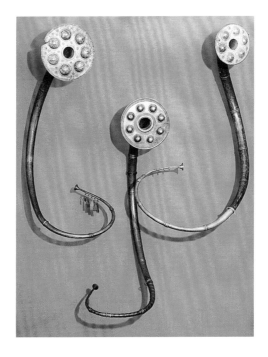

Iraq, during the fourth millennium BC. It was settled by the Sumerian people who, by around 3000 BC, established a series of city-states, including the well-known site of Ur. Between c. 3300 and 2500 BC, a writing system developed, known as cuneiform, which remained in use until around the first century AD. The many thousands of clay tablets bearing cuneiform inscriptions that have been excavated, and subsequently deciphered, have yielded a vast amount of information on musical practice. The Sumerians were conquered by the Akkadians—a people from the city of Akkad to the north of Ur led by Sargon—in c. 2334 BC and the region became unified into a single kingdom. The Sumerians became dominant again after 2154 BC until new peoples moved into the kingdom in around 1794 BC. Chief among these were the Amorites who were responsible for making Babylon the most important city in the region. In around 1200 BC the Assyrians to the north moved down into the lower Euphrates and Tigris and conquered the entire area. From their capital at Nineveh they ruled until they too were overthrown by the Babylonian king Nebuchadnezzar II in 609 BC. This Neo-Babylonian dynasty ruled until the Persian conquest in 539 BC, and after Alexander's conquest of the Persians in 330 BC, Mesopotamia became part of the Seleucid Empire until it was absorbed by Rome in 64 BC.

For all this complex exchange of rulers and dynasties there was a remarkable continuity in cultural identity and dual record keeping in Sumerian and Akkadian over much of the period outlined above. Early tablets tell of the importance of music-making at both the royal court and in the temple, for which the musical rituals were lavish

Standard of Ur, British Museum, London; Sumer; Early dynastic, 2500 BC; Wood, lapis lazuli and shell

This is one of the earliest representations of music-making at the Sumerian court. On one side of the object is a depiction of a war; this side, however, shows a banquet scene with the feasting accompanied by a harpist. The exact function of this decorated box dating from around 2600–2400 BC has never been satisfactorily explained.

and involved. The prominence of instruments, as well as vocal performance, in religious settings is attested to by the use of the same terms in Sumerian for a hymn type and specific instruments. For example, *BALAG* (Akkaddian *balaggu*) was the Sumerian word for both a drum and a hymn-type; the terminologies applied to the different hymn types, and other categories of song including laments and epic poetry, also seem to have denoted the mode, rhythm and formal structure of the performance. Temples had reserved spaces for large ensembles of instruments that would play during the long rituals presided over musically by the *GALA* (*kalu* in Akkaddian), the chief lamentation singer, and *GALA.TUR* (*kalaturru*), an assistant. The form and melody of the litany seems to have been prescribed in exact detail and the training was rigorous; that the goddess INANNA (Ishtar) was patron of the litany suggests that its form and transmission was divinely sanctioned. During the Early Sumerian period instruction was passed on through oral tradition but by the Old Babylonian much of this was being written down on clay tablets. The instructions suggest that there was a degree of heterophony, with descants, antiphonal responses and part singing.

Music was performed in many other contexts and numerous tablets discuss performances at court. Although there is no one word for "music" in Sumerian or Akkadian, one of the commonly used terms, *I.LU* or *nigutu*, also refers to happiness and revelry, suggesting that music was in some way associated with enjoyment. Seals depict shepherds playing flutes and tablets have been deciphered containing everything from the lyrics of love songs to the instruction that musicians should travel with the army on its campaigns. One of the earliest and most striking depictions of the musical entertainment at the Sumerian court is found on the so-called Standard of Ur dating back to 2600–2400 BC, while a much later relief of around 668–626 BC shows a large court orchestra of harps, drums and oboes. Many of the instruments used were recorded in some detail in texts and iconography (from seals, reliefs); they include sistra and clappers, cymbals and drums (some extremely large, as used in the temple rituals), flutes and oboes. Among the best-known instruments, however, are the lyre and harp. Examples of Sumerian harps survive, again from Ur, and are among the most elaborate artifacts to have been found from such an early period. A lyre was also found along with the harps, and it was the lyre that became the instrument associated with the exposition of musical theory.

A number of the technical terms for tuning and stringing not only the lyre but also the harp and lute, are known from a text of around 2070 BC, and from around the same period there exists a large corpus of material that discusses tuning systems through the mathematical proportions of string lengths. From these it is evident that the cycle of fifths was well-known and that the scale-types used were heptatonic diatonic modes akin to the Greek modes which later became the foundation of the eight principal modes of Gregorian chant.

Ancient Egypt

The impressive cultural achievements of Mesopotamia have a parallel in those of ancient Egypt, a similarly long-lasting society and culture, with a remarkable homogeneity over

The "Garden Party" relief, British Museum, London; Assyria, Ancient Iraq; 645 BC; Stone

This panel from the North Palace of Ashurbanipal, Nineveh (*c.* 645 BC) clearly shows a harpist accompanying the meal of King Ashurbanipal. The Standard of Ur shows a similar context from around 2,000 years earlier, and if this relief emphasizes the importance of music and musicians within the later Assyrian court it also demonstrates the cultural continuity that ran throughout the history of the Mesopotamian world.

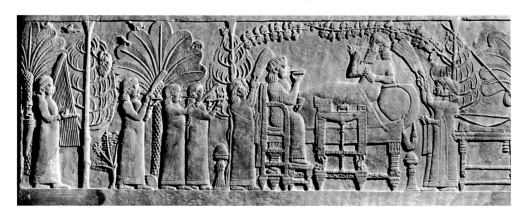

three millennia. The chronology of the region is known in considerable detail and is generally broken down into nine sections. The Early Dynastic (c. 3100–2755 BC) was followed by the Old Kingdom, the first major period of Egyptian history which lasted from around 2755 to 2255 BC. After the First Intermediate Period (c. 2255–2035 BC) came the Middle Kingdom (c. 2134–1786 BC). A Second Intermediate Period (c. 1786–1570 BC) led to the start of the New Kingdom (c. 1570–1070 BC), which included the rule of some of the best known Egyptian pharaohs, such as Ramesses II, Akhenaten and Tutankhamun. The Third Intermediate Period (c. 1070–656 BC) runs into the Saite Period (664–525 BC) with the Late Dynastic Period lasting until 343 BC before Egypt is taken over first by the Persian kings, and then, in 332 BC, by the Macedonians.

Unlike for Mesopotamia, no notation or discussion of tuning systems has been discovered, but a wealth of iconographic sources and many ancient Egyptian instruments have been found. In addition, deciphered hieroglyphics make numerous references to musicians, in relation to the gods and through descriptions of festivals, ritual and music-making in everyday life. A large corpus of hymn texts and both secular and ritual song lyrics also exists. Egypt's prestigious reputation for learning attracted a number of Greek and Hellenistic writers. The writings of Plutarch (fl. c. 50 AD–120 AD), among others, mention the sistrum, many examples of which still exist, and of music associated with the worship of Egyptian deities. Both Plato and Pythagoras are thought to have studied aspects of music in Egypt, but nothing suggests that their subsequent writings on music owe anything to this. Indeed little can be said with any certainty of the influence of Egyptian traditions on Greek and Hellenistic music, despite close contact between the two areas, and especially with the Hellenized city of Alexandria.

Aside from the sistrum, long associated with Egypt, other artifacts that have survived include clappers—often in the form of a human hand and perhaps associated with the practice of cheironomy—and drums of various kinds (one cylindrical example dates back as far as the Middle Kingdom or 12th dynasty). Idiophones and membranophones often seemed to be associated with a particular deity. For instance, Osiris was known as "Lord of the sistrum", an instrument with close links also to Hathor, and later Isis, whose head appears as a carving on the handle of many surviving examples. The god Bes was associated with a round frame drum, and he is often also shown with either a harp or lyre. The three Egyptian chordophones (harps, lyres and lutes of various types) seem to have arrived from Mesopotamia

to the west during the New Kingdom, although a notable exception is the arched harp, known from at least the fourth dynasty (Old Kingdom) onward. Although there have been attempts to reconstruct the tuning systems of existing instruments none of these have produced conclusive results. One instrument for which the sound is known is the Egyptian long, straight trumpet; two examples, one in bronze and the other silver, were found in the tomb of Tutankhamun and have been played, giving a bright and clear sound. Other aerophones included end-blown flutes, oboes and clarinets, although there are no surviving reeds, making the distinction between the two difficult.

Cheironomy—the use of hand gestures to prescribe melodic patterns—is one intriguing cultural survival from ancient times. The closest

it is possible to get to a notation of ancient Egyptian music may lie in the interpretation of hand movements depicted on tomb wall paintings. These bear considerable relation to gestures still used by cantors in the Egyptian Coptic Church, and incorporate both rhythmic and melodic symbolic movements. A number of instructions in the paintings have been identified, but there is also the possibility that the ancient practice could have been used to prescribe a type of polyphony (most likely a melody and drone accompaniment) given that on a series of paintings from Saqqara two sets of instructions seem to be conveyed to a harpist at the same time.

Greece
Of all the musical cultures of the ancient world, it is perhaps that of the Greeks which has been most studied. The Greek sources have been accessible for longer (hieroglyphics were only deciphered in

Ancient Egyptian sistrum, Ancient Egypt; 18th dynasty/1352–36 BC

The sistrum is a rattle with wires passing across a hoop against which they clash. Often discs, of metal or other materials, are strung on the wires to provide extra sound. The instrument was particularly associated with temple worship by the ancient Egyptians, and later the worship of the goddess Isis. Egyptian sistra had two main forms, one in the shape of an arch, the other which imitated the shape of a shrine. Both were generally decorated with the head of the goddess Hathor and may also have a representation of a cat, sacred to the goddess Bastet. In this fragment of a relief, a figure in a procession can be seen playing the sistrum.

the early 19th century and cuneiform shortly after) and although the written sources for the history of ancient Greece do not extend anywhere near as far back as those for either Mesopotamia or Egypt, for a long time it was felt that western Europe was the heir to the Greek musical tradition. There is a little truth in this, despite the influence of the theoretical works of writers such as Boethius, and it is impossible to point to any direct musical inheritance in the West. Such claims are based more on wishful thinking than hard evidence.

To the ancient Greeks music was a matter of practice and philosophy. Although the two intersect, many of the writings on music theory that are extant are as much about the Greek conception of the universe as about the actual performance and repertory of musical traditions. This is amply demonstrated by the place of the theory of the harmony of the spheres in Greek musical thought, an idea associated with the Pythagoreans and hugely influential on Plato. It attempted to describe the structure and workings of the universe through the mathematical principles demonstrated by Pythagoras's division of a monochord (a single, stretched string) by ratios. This initially seems a little complex, but the underlying principle is simple. A stretched string will sound a particular pitch: when the string is divided in half, then the sound is an octave that of the whole string: an octave above any given note is double the frequency of that note. Thus, Pythagoras said, the ratio of an octave is 2:1. If the equal subdivisions are continued it follows that two octaves are 4:1,

Harmony of the spheres

The ratios that Pythagoras considered the basis for musical tuning were also thought to be the relative sizes of the planets, posited by Pythagoras as perfect spheres. These were said to move in relation to each other at the ratios of 4:1, 3:1, 3:2 etc., and the vibrations that these movements gave rise to was said to be the "harmony of the spheres". Aside from the truth of this theory, which was finally dismissed by the Copernican Revolution of the 16th century, because of the "Pythagorean comma" these celestial ratios did not produce a perfect system. That this did not deter a whole school of Pythagorean scholars from continuing to build on these observations shows how the search for a mathematical basis to the workings of the universe—at least for these philosophers—took precedence over the establishment of a practical theoretical basis for music.

an octave plus a fifth 3:1 and the fifth and fourth 3:2 and 4:3 respectively. The whole tone is then expressed as the difference between the fourth and fifth, which comes out at 9:8.

However, when this strictly proportional system was put into practice it created a practical problem. In the Pythagorean system the fourth was divided into two whole tones, plus the remainder (known as the *limma* and which has a ratio of 256:253, somewhat akin to the later semitone).

Theoretically, if a fourth plus a fifth equals an octave, there are six whole tones to the octave. However, if the ratio of 9:8 is used to determine a whole tone then the sum of six of these whole tones comes out at slightly more than an octave (the so-called "Pythagorean comma", with its rather daunting ratio of 531,441:524,288).

The opposing view was given by the most highly regarded musical thinker of Greek antiquity, Aristoxenus (368 BC–?). Although he allowed that the philosophical study of music was still a science as opposed to a craft or skill, he dismissed the suggestion that music was a branch of mathematics and argued that it should be approached entirely on its own terms, the logical consideration of musical sound as perceived through hearing. He dismissed the "pure" ratios of Pythagorean thought and instead worked on Aristotle's principles of scientific investigation. He adopted as his basic material that which the trained ear could define precisely as a consonance, the fourth, fifth and octave. Other intervals were variable and adjusted according to context. This was of great importance, notably in that he placed emphasis on the training of the ear, the first instance of this being central to the study of musical phenomena. It also means that once the tetrachord (the interval of a fourth) has been laid out then the notes in between can be placed as the ear deems appropriate. This led Aristoxenus to propose the splitting of the whole tone into two equal semitones (as opposed to the *limma* of Pythagoras), which brought the distribution of notes closer to the musical system in use today.

Although Aristoxenus also wrote on rhythm, another first for Greek antiquity, proposing that rhythm should be considered aside from meter (the overall structure of the piece), and laid out a system for determining the *tonoi* (modes) of Greek music, it was a later writer Ptolemy (c. 83 AD–161 AD) who brought the two schools of thought together and laid out the practice of music theory in a clear and precise manner in his work *Harmonika*. Both Pythagoras and Aristoxenus are criticized, the former for arriving at conclusions that bear no relation to observable phenomena, and the latter for loosely defining intervals instead of using precise mathematical ratios to describe them. Ptolemy also proposed a system of seven *tonoi* or seven notes within an octave that with the later addition of the Hypomixolydian became, via Boethius, the eight principal modes of medieval music.

Sources for the actual practice of music in ancient Greece tend to lie outside of theoretical treatises. There are numerous references to song and musical performance in literature. Notably, Greek drama had a substantial musical element as a surviving fragment of musical notation from, among others, Euripides' *Iphigenia at Aulis* shows. There also exist many examples of iconography, surviving instruments and even a sizable body of musical notations including hymns and fragments of dramas. There are very early examples of musical iconography from the Cyclades (including the sculpture of a harpist from Keros, 3rd–2nd millennium BC) and finds from Minoan Crete and the Mycenean mainland, but the principal earliest references to music-making probably come from the *Iliad* and *Odyssey* (c. 800 BC) where epic singers are mentioned (although it is not sure if these epics were themselves sung). As well as epic song, references are made from Homer onward to a wide range of vocal genres, performed in almost every sphere of life. These include work songs, love lyrics and drinking songs, and the texts themselves for a great number of these have survived. Hymns were sung to the gods or for rites of passage ceremonies such as weddings: certain vocal repertories were reserved for either the gods or humans, or were considered suitable for both groups. Instrumental music was also highly prized, literally so in musical contests that were part of the many games and festivals. Highly virtuosic performances took place on the lyre, a plucked chordophone similar to a harp, an instrument that was played by both professionals and amateurs, and which was used in many contexts from accompanying singing and dance to solo performance. As well as clappers and cymbals of various kinds there were a number of aerophones including the *aulos*, thought to be a double oboe which had a similar virtuosic status to the lyre, and the *syrinx*, either a single or grouped set of panpipes.

Rome

The Greek world had a huge influence on that of the later Roman Republic and Empire, particularly after the Roman subjugation of the Greek mainland after 168 BC. In musical terms this meant not only the adoption almost wholesale of Greek musical theory but that Rome saw a huge influx of musicians from Greece, many of them highly accomplished. With them came more than theory—Greek drama became very popular and the immigrant musicians also brought their musical instruments to augment those adopted from the Etruscans. However, one of the most remarkable instruments of antiquity, the hydraulis, is said to have been invented in Alexandria by an engineer called Ctesibus during the 3rd century BC. Similar in structure to later organs—a keyboard, cylindrical bellows and pipes that produce the sound—its uniquely clever feature was the use of water pressure to ensure that the air flow remained constant. The air was pumped into a chamber with a one-way valve and water pressure expelled this air into the pipes while the bellows

were prepared to pump more air into the chamber. When the keys were depressed they slid open caps at the bottom of the pipes which allowed the air to flow through them. Although a considerable amount is known about the construction of the instrument there is little agreement as to how it was tuned, or whether the pipes were flues (as on the flute) or incorporated reeds (like a clarinet or oboe).

By the 1st century AD, given the expanding empire to the east, Rome also saw the arrival of musicians and instruments from west Asia and north Africa and the exoticism, to Roman eyes, of many of their songs and dances gave impetus to the further development of the existing pantomime dramas. These were based largely on Greek tragedies, as was the very popular mime theater. A further import, after Egypt was invaded in 30 BC, was the cult of Isis that brought with it the Egyptian sistrum, harp and long flute. The musical immigrants did not only bring their own traditions and preserve them intact, for the genius of the Roman melting pot was to adopt and adapt these influences and from them to produce a distinctly Roman musical identity. It was from the assimilation in Rome of these disparate strands that later developments in European music, including the music of the early Christian church and the instruments, and to a certain extent vocal forms, of itinerant secular musicians, took their cue.

Etruscan flute player, fresco at the Tomb of the Leopards; Tarquinia, Italy; c. 480–450 BC

Rome retained its musical legacy from the Etruscans, including the straight and curved trumpets, the tuba and cornu used by the Romans as military and processional instruments, and the tibia (similar to the Greek *aulos*) used widely in religious contexts.

MEDIEVAL MUSIC

SERVING THE CHURCH (800—1400 AD)

THE MEDIEVAL MUSICAL WORLD

The Middle Ages in Europe cover roughly the period between the collapse of the Roman Empire and the Renaissance, a huge span of time. In musical terms they not only saw the emergence of the Christian church as a major force and influence on musical styles and traditions, but also a diverse range of non-liturgical musics, especially love and epic songs. The political landscape of medieval Europe was complex and in flux, with many competing kingdoms, city states and centers of ecclesiastical power. Contact between these was extensive, through trade, inter-dynastic marriages and wars, but the overall picture remained one of a mosaic of centers of regional power, even if they did fall under the purview of a supra-national authority such as the Holy Roman Emperor or the Pope. Consequently the musical reality was similarly complex, although the influence of the church, especially that of Rome, did have some unifying effect on liturgical music.

There is some evidence for extant song traditions during the early Middle Ages, for instance the existence of Germanic and Scandinavian epics such as the *Nibelungenlied* and sagas. Although it is presumed that these were sung, the earliest actual evidence for this comes from a fragment of the German *Petruslied* which dates to around 850. Until the 12th century there are various sources indicating that composed song traditions, both religious and secular, did exist even if our knowledge of them is patchy. It is with the onset of the 12th century, however, that the secular lyric song blossoms in the poetry of the *troubadours* (in Provence), *trouvères* (in northern France) and *Minnesinger* (in Germany and Austria). These singers of courtly love poems were highly accomplished and trained musicians, working in a largely oral tradition. A related group were the *jongleurs*—a term often taken to mean an itinerant freelance minstrel or entertainer—who were performers of secular music such as *chanson de geste*, an epic poem form, a famous example of which is *Le jeu de Robin et Marion* by Adam de la Halle. In Germany, one of the most important sources of the time is the *Carmina burana*—a collection of secular Latin poetry, sacred Latin texts, German poetry and liturgical plays, dated early 13th century.

For the earlier part of the medieval period, from around 400 AD up to the ninth or tenth century, there are relatively few surviving sources, and the transition between the music of late antiquity and that of the newly emerging power structures that began to fill the gap left by the Roman Empire can only be surmised in

Group of troubadours, illustration from *Cantigas de Santa Maria* (made under the direction of Alfonso X and Leon); Manuscript; Biblioteca Monasterio del Escorial, Madrid, Spain

313: The Edict of Milan ensures religious freedom for Christians.

391: Christianity becomes the official religion of the Roman Empire; all other religions are outlawed.

476: The end of direct Roman imperial rule in western Europe.

500: Boethius writes *De institutione musica*.

540–604: The reign of Pope Gregory I.

751: Pippin the Short succeeds the Merovingian Childeric III as the first Carolingian king of the Franks and begins the institution of a single ecclesiastical Office based on the Gregorian Roman style.

800: Charlemagne is crowned emperor by Pope Leo III.

1010: Guido of Arezzo writes the *Prologus in antiphonarium*, laying the foundations of modern musical notation.

1096: The first crusade and conquest of Jerusalem.

1100: Johannes Cotto writes *De Musica* outlining the rules for composing organum.

1100–1300: *Troubadours, trouvères* and *Minnesinger* are active in the Provençal, French and German courts.

1100–1150: The abbey of St Martial de Limoges provides the earliest plainchant with melismatic upper lines and contrary motion.

1119: The foundation of the first European university in Bologna.

1150–1200: The establishment of rhythmic modes. Leonius of the Notre Dame School compiles the *Magnus liber*, subsequently revised by Perotinus.

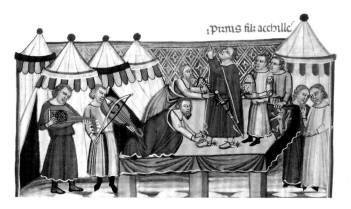

1300–1377: Guillaume de Machaut is the first composer to whom works can be ascribed with certainty.

1309: Pope Clemens V transfers the Papal See to Avignon.

1320: Philippe de Vitry writes *Ars nova* after which the dominant musical style of the century is named.

Troubadours playing the lute and vielle (right) during a knighting ceremony

1339–1453: The Hundred Years' War between France and England.

1378–1417: The Great Schism of the West with opposing Popes in Avignon and Rome.

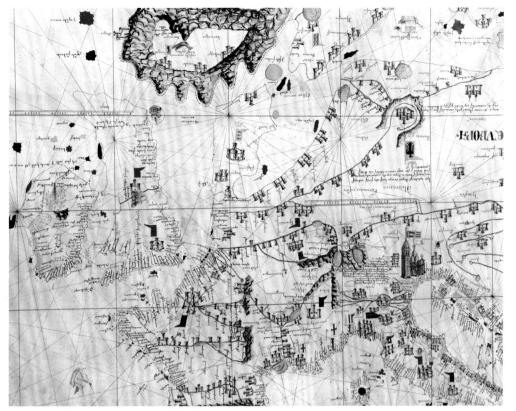

Monasteries and centers of population in western Europe,
Royal Geographical Society; London, UK; Created 1367 AD; Portolan (nautical chart) with inscriptions readable from all sides

In an attempt to impose some sort of order on the medieval world, musicologists have posited three main geographical musical regions. One takes in the southern portion of the continent, from northern Spain via Languedoc and Provence down into Italy and Sicily. This area was especially rich in courtly song traditions in the local Romance languages. The northern part of Europe, that of the British Isles, Scandinavia and the shores of the Baltic, comprises the second region. Much less is known about song traditions from this area; there are no written sources indicating a courtly tradition similar to that of the south. The exception appears to have been the British Isles, which were also home to a rich tradition of liturgical polyphony. The third of these divisions, the center of Western Europe, takes in most of modern France and German and runs down into northern Italy. This was the most urbanized region of medieval Europe, powerful in both the temporal and spiritual world. In particular, the musical influence of the polyphonic art song of the French court was to become ever more important as the Middle Ages progressed.

part. What is known largely concerns the music of the early Christian church. Of prime importance for liturgical music was the strong injunction by the vast majority of early Christian writers against the use of musical instruments, perhaps in part due to their association with the pagan temple, where their role was to a certain extent apotropaic, but also because instrumentalists performed, in the eyes of the church fathers, in immoral contexts such as feasts and the theater. This condemnation was vitriolic; it has been noted that instrumental music was described by John Chrysostom as "the devil's heap of garbage" and that Arnobius of Sicca claimed that it caused men to become "male prostitutes" and women "harlots". Not surprising, then, that it was not until the somewhat more liberal ninth century that instruments, in particular the organ, made their appearance in churches. By this time there was, however, a firmly established tradition of vocal liturgical music which has continued to dominate Christian worship ever since.

MUSIC OF THE MEDIEVAL CHURCH

By the mid-fifth century AD the roots of early Christian liturgical music had been well established. It is now thought that there were few initial musical adoptions from Jewish practice and the tradition of a sung Eucharist, established around the second century AD, was a Christian innovation. The very earliest hymns were monodic, solo lines probably performed by solo singers, which may have been punctuated by short responses from the congregation. These earlier hymns were often composed on Biblical material by contemporary church fathers, but during the fourth century there was a significant increase in the singing of psalm material from the Old Testament.

This increase in psalmody coincides with the rise of desert monasticism in Egypt, the movement to which all subsequent Christian monasticism owes its origins. The establishing of these austere institutions, where the intent of the monks and nuns was to dedicate literally all of their time to the worshipping of God, was exceptionally influential, especially on Church music-making. One important aspect of monastic life was, taking its cue from Biblical injunction, to ensure an almost continuous recitation of the Psalter, and within the monasteries this recitation of the psalms took a musical form. A parallel development, at least after Constantine's Edict of Milan of 313 which guaranteed the right of Christian worship, was the establishment of a twice daily office (that is, collective public act of worship) in large centers of population. Taking place in the morning and evening, the psalms and hymns chosen to accompany the two acts of worship, in contrast to endless recitation of the psalms of the monasteries, picked individual passages that were appropriate to the time of day.

Music example showing the eight principal modes

To simplify what must have been a myriad of differing practices, there seem to have been three types of psalmodic recitation and three forms of performance. These early forms of plainchant either set each syllable to a separate note (syllabic chant, the first type), or from two to four notes to each syllable (neumatic chant, the second type), or the texts were sung in a highly melismatic way (melismatic chant), with many notes per syllable, or in some cases with no text at all. This latter type is particularly associated with the *Jubilus* of the *Alleluia* section of the Mass. Although chant forms developed, for example from the ninth century onward some regional schools added melismatic sections, known as tropes, to certain parts of the Mass, and there was crossover between the three types, this tripartite classification can be used throughout the subsequent history of plainchant. The forms of performance also seem to have differed, from the straightforward end-to-end singing of a psalm, to a responsorial verse interspersed with choral refrains, to the antiphonal singing of alternate verses by two separate choirs. It is likely that the musical content of the chants had a great deal in common with earlier Greek monodic forms.

Gregorian Chant

There continued to be a great diversity in Christian worship until the eighth century, although the Roman form of chant did dominate to a certain extent, largely due to the influence of the Rome-based popes, in particular Gregory I (c. 540–604). However, it was not until the establishment of the Carolingian monarchy under Pippin the Short (751–68) that the Roman "Gregorian" chant,

so-called as Gregory was considered to have been the originator of the Roman style of plainchant, supplanted the others. Pippin and his descendants, including the emperor Charlemagne (768–814), were determined to impose a single ecclesiastical office over all the peoples they ruled. In order to achieve this, copies of manuscripts, derived from the writings of Gregory supplied by the Pope in Rome, were deposited in cathedral archives; also, perhaps even more importantly, *scholae cantorum,* schools to train cantors, were also established at important places of worship.

It was also around this time that notation of the chants became possible through the use of neumes. These were a system of signs that outlined the shape of a melody, though they did not give exact pitches or intervals; therefore, a certain degree of oral instruction was still a necessary part of learning the repertory. However, this invention did enable the recording of a large body of chants and was an important first step in the overall development of Western musical notation. The later use of neumes which indicated a degree of pitch, notably in the highly influential annonymous ninth-century treatises, the *Musica enchiriadis* and *Scolica enchiriadis,* were influential on the ideas of Guido of Arezzo, writer of the *Micrologus* and *Prologus in antiphonarium,* during the 11th century.

The pitches of the chants are derived from the system of the eight mode system, and Gregorian chant constitutes the largest repertory of modal music within the Western canon. From these eight principal modes (scales of seven notes known as the dorian, hypodorian, phrygian,

| Dorian |
| Hypodorian |
| Phrygian |
| Hypophrygian |
| Lydian |
| Hypolydian |
| Mixolydian |
| Hypomixolydian |

hypophrygian, lydian, hypolydian, mixolydian and hypomixolydian) derives the later diatonic tonal system. Hence their importance in Western music history; they themselves derive both from the *oktoechos* ("eight modes") of the Byzantine eastern church—itself heir to elements of Greek practice—and the theoretical writings of Greeks, largely as transmitted by writers such as Boethius. The eight modes are theoretically arranged in pairs, each pair consisting of an "authentic" mode, where the final note of the chant is the lowest of the scale, and its "plagal" companion, where the final note would be a fifth below the lowest note in the scale. For example, the dorian mode runs from d–d1, and its final note is d, whereas the hypodorian runs from a–a1 but its final is also d (and so on, the phrygians' final notes are e, the lydians' f and the mixolydians' g). It was also possible to "modulate" between the modes, particularly from a plagal mode which was, in this case, generally considered a transposition of the mode the piece ends in.

The Birth of Polyphony

Plainchant did not necessarily comprise just a single line of music, and from at least the ninth century onward simple polyphony (literally "many voices") in the form of organum was present. Organum refers to the addition of another voice to an existing chant (known as the *vox principalis*), generally either a fourth or a fifth below the melody. These were considered "concordant" intervals, following the theories of Pythagoras, as opposed to thirds and sixths which were heard as slightly dissonant, although these were used with increasing frequence as approach intervals to consonances as the Middle Ages progressed, or the tritone (the interval between f and b) which was considered not only dissonant but also associated with the devil. Since the tritone could crop up easily if the melody was followed a fifth or fourth below, to avoid this the lower voice (the *vox organalis*) would often hold as a drone. This characteristic texture has led a few scholars to surmise that the development of organum was influenced by instrumental music, in particular the organ itself, although there is some dispute about this.

At first the organum matched each voice note for note, either in parallel motion (that is, each voice traveling in the same direction) or as "free organum" where the *vox principalis* and *vox organalis* moved in both parallel and contrary (that is, away from each other) motion. The latter form became increasingly dominant, laying the foundations for later polyphony with its implication of independent but simultaneously sounding lines, until at the beginning of the 12th century Johannes Cotto—a German or Swiss monk, possibly of the Flemish monastery of Afflighem, and author of *De Musica*, the most widely copied treatise of his time—was writing that the *vox organalis* should move contrary to the *vox principalis*. By this time it was also common for the two lines to cross, and when the *vox organalis* set several notes to one of the *principalis*, it was placed above chant as a melismatic upper part. The earliest sources available for this, from the first half of the 12th century, are from the abbey of St Martial de Limoges in Aquitaine, where the repertory of pieces in two parts includes both upper melismatic lines and upper lines that move rhythmically with the chant but in contrary motion.

The setting of an upper decorated *organalis* against the held notes of the *vox principalis* gave rise to the "tenor" (from the Latin *tenere*, "to hold"). This became the voice that carried the *cantus firmus*, the melody against which the other voices in the polyphony are set. This more complex temporal organization of the music required a system whereby notes could simultaneously be ascribed precise rhythmic durations, and this was provided by the composers of the Notre Dame school, who were working in and around Paris during the mid-12th to mid-13th century. The great achievement of the Notre Dame composers was to add a metrical and rhythmic structure to the music, which they realized through a system of six "rhythmic modes". These were essentially two or three note rhythmic patterns, based on the poetic meters of the Greeks, assigned a symbol and a duration against which could be set the tenor. The works of the Notre Dame school are largely known through the *Magnus liber*, a huge collection of liturgical polyphony ascribed to Leoninus (*fl.* 1150–c. 1200) and revised by Perotinus (*fl. c.* 1200).

Boethius, Museo Civico Cristiano, Brescia, Italy; Fifth century; Ivory

Of great importance to the future history of Western music was the early church's attitude to the legacy of pagan Greek and Roman musical theorists. Music was considered one of the great liberal arts, with strong affinities to mathematics, and many of the most influential writers of the time, such as Augustine (354–430) and Boethius (c. 480–524), whose work *De institutione musica* assumed great importance during the reforms of the Carolingian monarchy, dealt with the Classical tonal system of antiquity in their writings.

As well as composing organum, musicians from both the St Martial and Notre Dame schools produced *discantus* (also known as *clausulae*, particularly by the Notre Dame composers) sections. These were, at least in the Notre Dame compositions, places where both the tenor and the upper part, now generally called the *duplum*, were written in modal rhythm, usually with simultaneously sounding but contrary motion. The *discantus* grew in length to better balance the organum and also provided a contrast as the tenor moved considerably faster in the *discantus*. Not only did the music now have a structure that fell into clearly definable sections, but around 1200 it became increasingly common to add a third voice (the *triplum*) to the other two. This did raise some problems as it was hard to add notes that were consonant—the fourth, fifth and unison or octave were still favored, though there is evidence to suggest that thirds and sixths, and even on occasion the tritone, were used—while still maintaining interesting lines.

SECULAR MUSIC TRADITIONS

In the work of the Notre Dame composers lies the roots of the dominant form of the later Middle Ages, the motet. By the early 13th century the *clausula* had become a separate piece in its own right, with all the techniques of modal rhythm associated with it, and composers, in particular Perotinus, began to set new texts to this evolving

form. Initially these were in two parts only—the addition of a *triplum* within the strictures of modal rhythm, which included overlapping phrases between the parts, was difficult—but as musicians became more familiar with shaping the material in new ways, up to three parts were added to the tenor. Perhaps the greatest shift came with the importance ascribed to the rhythm of the text itself, where the metrical layout of the poetry was taken account of in the musical setting, with a subsequent flexibility in the setting of the tenor line. French texts also began to be used and this use of the vernacular introduced secular themes, mostly love poems, to the motet form.

Although there were traditions of polyphony elsewhere in Europe, particularly in Britain where there exists a large corpus of 13th century liturgical music, it was in France that the motet was to receive the most attention, and the two composers most associated with it, Philippe de Vitry (1291–1361) and Guillaume de Machaut (*c.* 1300–1377), not only raised it to new levels but set the musical scene for the onset of the Renaissance. The 14th century was one of upheaval, not only politically and musically but also for the church with schisms and warring factions. This breakdown in papal authority meant that there was now less control over musical practice by the clergy and composers had a new-found freedom to develop their art, however much this was decried by those who wanted a return to the older and less rhythmically complex forms of organum.

Aside from his compositions, of which we know little for certain, one of Philippe de Vitry's greatest contributions to music history was the writing of the treatise *Ars nova*, from which the term describing much 14th-century music is taken. In it he builds on the ideas of an earlier theorist and composer, Franco of Cologne (*fl.* second half of the 13th century), who proposed in his *Ars cantus mensurabilis* that rhythmic durations of notes should be shown by a hierarchy of different-shaped note heads. De Vitry's achievement was to clarify and simplify the system by removing the hierarchy (that is, giving all the rhythmic values equal weight) so that the notation of more varied rhythmic structures was possible.

The first composer to whom it is possible to ascribe works with absolute certainty is Guillaume de Machaut, who in his grasp and exploration of the complex possibilities of the motet form, and for his secular interests (even though he was at the end of his life employed by the church) bridges the gap between the Medieval era and the Renaissance. Only a handful of Machaut's works are liturgical, most of his large musical output comprises settings of his own secular poems, many of them following the forms of *ballade*,

Philippe de Vitry, *The Book of Fauvel;* 14th century; Manuscript

Philippe de Vitry was a prolific poet, for which he was famed, and was in contact with the great Italian poet Petrarch. No motets can be directly ascribed to de Vitry but those regarded by scholars as being his through textual allusion and references in other treatises, display a great variety of musical, specifically rhythmic, techniques, including the widespread use of isorhythm as the underlying structural framework to the pieces. This technique, the repetition of rhythmic patterns in the tenor, provided the organizational basis of the vast majority of 14th century motets.

rondeaux and *virelais*. These build on earlier song forms associated with the *troubadours* but acquire a new character in Machaut's hands with their impressive rhythmic manipulation, greater expression in musical terms of the poetic content and by, at times, the incorporation of extra voices. He was the first composer to write a complete, through-composed Mass (*c.* 1360). Written largely in motet form, it is perhaps his most celebrated work and brings together many of his technical achievements in isorhythm and the handling of consonance and dissonance; he is also noted for a greater use of chromaticism (notes from outside the mode), a tendency of all Ars Nova composers. So much is known about Machaut's music in large part because he prepared his own collections of complete works, both purely poetic and musical. In these collections he divides the pieces by form and the subtle technical differences which separate the genres point to his intense awareness of the problems of large-scale musical form (of which he was a master in his handling of complex isorhythmic structures) as well as the intricacies of polyphonic voicing.

Courtly Poetry

Machaut's settings of courtly poems owe a great deal to the earlier traditions of the *troubadours*, *trouvères* and *Minnesinger*, French and German court poets and singers of the 12th–13th century. Many, but by no means all, of the poets were of high social standing and birth but the picture we have of them is clouded to a certain extent by their contemporary (and later) romanticized biographies which have noblemen pining away in castle towers for distant loves, and were based more on their poetry than any historical reality. What we do know is that the body of work that survives comprises some of the most accomplished and complex poetic forms of the Middle Ages. For these works there are melodies extant for around 10 percent of the poems. The tradition of courtly

love poetry, while it is thought to have initially developed around Poitiers and from there found its main centers in Provence, northern France and the German-speaking lands, had an influence in Italy, the British Isles, Spain and Scandinavia.

The poems are, for the most part, given strophic settings (that is, the same music is repeated for each verse) and rhythmically the musical lines of earlier examples tend to follow the text ascribing a note to each syllable, as in early Gregorian chant. Melismatic settings were at first in rhythmically free form but as the influence grew of the modal rhythm of church music then these too acquired a greater formal control over the rhythmic setting of the words. Although a large proportion of the songs owe something to ecclesiastical chant, not least the modes they tend to be set in, the three most popular and lasting forms, which became the *ballade*, *virelai* and *rondeaux* of Machaut's time, are likely to have developed from earlier dance and song forms, as the name *ballade* (from the Latin *ballare*, "to dance") makes clear. The three forms follow patterns that are familiar from later song forms (although there is no clear connection between them): the first has an AAB structure (this became the basic structure of the *ballade*); the second ABBAA (where the structure returns to back to the beginning phrase, hence the name *virelai*, possibly from the French *virer*, "to turn"); and the third follows a roughly ABABAB form, with varying patterns of return to the A section, which became the *rondeaux* (with has a formal similarity to the later rondo form of ABACAD etc.). Aside from the melodic material, the A and B sections tended to differ in the endings they employed, A sections used "closed" endings that landed on the final of the mode while B section endings were generally "open" and landed on any note other than the final, in a similar fashion to later cadences.

The *jongleurs* (known in Provençal as *joglar*) have a great deal poetically and musically in common with the *troubadours*, *trouvères* and *Minnesinger* of the courts (indeed a few well-known *troubadours* and *trouvères* rose to the position from being *jongleurs* or *joglars*), but they operated outside the courts and were generally itinerant. As well as being accomplished secular poets and musicians they were also known as instrumentalists and performed in a wide variety of contexts. There was not necessarily any social stigma attached to the profession, especially by the 14th century when they were organized into guilds, and there are cases of the court poets fulfilling both roles. However, during their early history they acquired a slightly scandalous reputation, perhaps due to a confusion with the so-called *goliards*, itinerant Latin poets and scholars who used earthy verse as a rhetorical device.

Guillaume de Machaut

One of the greatest medieval composers, Machaut (1300–77) is thought to have been educated in Rheims but other than that very little is known about his early life until he enters the service of John of Luxembourg in 1323. He traveled widely with the court between Luxembourg, Bohemia, Paris and Lithuania, and also spent a good deal of time at Durbuy near Liège. As court poet he composed many *dits* (poems) on the life and people at court, setting some of them to music. From 1340 he became a canon at Rheims cathedral but this did not prevent him from continuing his association with aristocratic patrons, for whom he composed poetry. The last years of his life were taken up with preparing a complete edition of his works.

The Middle High German Minnesänger Kanzler, flanked by two musicians, Codex Manesse, Zurich; *c.* 1340

It is these poet-musicians that perhaps best sum up the idea of an age of chivalry in the popular imagination with their lyrics of courtly love (also known by the contemporary term *fin' amors*, "pure love"). The height of the Minnesinger's art was reached by the great singer and poet Walther von der Vogelweide (*c.* 1200), praised in Gottfried von Strassburg's *Tristan* (*fl.* 1200–20), the source for Wagner's opera *Tristan und Isolde*. Wolfram von Eschenbach (*fl. c.* 1170–1220) is often considered the greatest medieval poet. His poems *Parzifâl* and *Titurel* were the basis for another of Wagner's works, *Parsifal*.

THE RENAISSANCE

The Renaissance lute, from the panel *The Presentation of Jesus in the Temple*, 1510; Galleria dell' Accademia; Venice, Italy

Shown here in the panel by Vittore Carpaccio (*c.* 1460–1525/6), the lute was one of the most important instruments of the Renaissance. Taken to a high degree of virtuosity by composers and players such as John Dowland, it became a ubiquitous presence at courts across Europe. With the rise of more reliable keyboard instruments during the Baroque it gradually fell out of favor.

THE PROTO-RENAISSANCE

The Ars Nova of the late-14th century, while still dominated by French composers, also flourished in Italy through the music of Matteo da Perugia (*fl.* 1400–16) and Johannes Ciconia (*c.* 1370–1412). Their work—sometimes termed *trecento*—was stylistically quite different from that of the French, concentrating on a greater simplicity but more equal treatment of individual parts than in the extremely florid French style, which revelled in rhythmic complexity and dissonance. The use of imitation as a device was more widespread in Italian music, and this and the striving for balance are some of the techniques that look forward to the musical preoccupations of the coming century. These developments coincided with extra-musical ideas being explored in the works of 14th-century Italian, and especially Tuscan, poets, writers and artists. In the works of Petrarch (1304–74), and also to a certain extent those of Dante (1265–1321) and Boccaccio (1313–75), these ideas promulgated the rise of Humanism, that is a revived interest in Greek and Roman art and philosophy allied to a human-based, rather than supernatural, system of rational thought.

In the visual arts, the first glimmerings of Humanistic concern are seen in the works of Cimabue (*c.* 1240–1302) where, for the first time since antiquity, the images are recognizably those of real people. The main exemplar of the new style, however, was Cimabue's pupil Giotto (1276–1336), whose naturalistic treatment of the human form has led to him being hailed as the first painter of the Italian proto-Renaissance. Renaissance literally means "rebirth", referring to the "rediscovery" of Greek and Roman texts and a "rebirth" of culture, harking back to a golden age after an imagined period of decline. In many ways, these developments in art and literature were only possible because of the newly emerging Italian middle class. As merchants and industrialists, especially in the city of Florence, began to acquire great wealth, their confidence also grew to intervene in the running of the city, to engage in scholarship and education and to commission works of art. Having less to gain from the status quo than hereditary rulers or the Church, this rising class was more open to new ideas and reflected these in their choices as patrons.

At the same time as Italy was forging the Renaissance in painting, sculpture and architecture, the first decades of the 15th century saw the work of the English composer John Dunstable (*c.* 1390–1453) achieve international recognition. Although Dunstable seems to have worked for a number of English royal patrons, he almost certainly spent time abroad, possibly in France, and many of the sources for his works come from either German or Italian archives. The overwhelming majority of his surviving pieces are for liturgical use, including Masses and a number of isorhythmic motets. The latter are interesting because by the end of the 14th century the motet had become a largely secular form. Dunstable

1401: Brunelleschi submits *The Sacrifice of Isaac* in the competition for the Florence Baptistery doors, marking the start of the Renaissance.

1421: Giovanni de Medici is elected head of Florence, beginning the rule of the Medici dynasty over the city.

1430: Donatello creates the first large-scale male nude bronze, *David*.

1501: The birth of music printing with Ottaviano Petrucci's *Harmonice musices odhecaton.*

1517: Martin Luther nails his 95 Theses to a church door in Wittenberg, starting the Reformation in Germany.

1519–22: Magellan circumnavigates the globe.

1545: Pope Paul III convenes the Council of Trent, which runs until 1563, marking the Catholic Counter Reformation.

1555: The "religious peace" of Augsburg regulates faith in Germany and confirms the schism between the Catholic and Protestant churches.

1556: Lassus becomes court composer to Albrecht V of Bavaria in Munich.

1558–1603: The rule of Elizabeth I of England.

1561: Palestrina takes up the position of a chorus master at Santa Maria Maggiore.

1571: Palestrina moves to St Peter's.

1590: St Peter's in Rome is finished to plans by Michelangelo. William Shakespeare writes his first plays.

The Council of Trent, 1588-89 (Fresco; Santa Maria in Trastevere, Rome, Italy)

and his English contemporaries, such as Leonel Power (*d.* 1445), not only revived the motet as a religious work but were the first to compose all elements of the music, instead of basing the piece on an existing chant.

However, English music of this time is of even greater importance to future developments (the so-called *contenance anglois*) in its widespread use of thirds and sixths, melodically and vertically, and triadic melodic movement. These elements bring the music much closer to a modern sound world, one to which it is almost possible to ascribe a sense of key or tonality. As well as these innovations in part writing, Dunstable and the Italian *trecento* composers are noted for their writing of freely composed top lines supported by, generally, two simpler lower parts—another element of their work that was to prove influential.

The Old Hall Manuscript, comprising sections of the Mass, antiphons and isorhythmic motets, is the most important source for late-14th and early-15th century English music. Although, surprisingly, it shows only one work by Dunstable it contains many valuable pieces by his contemporaries, including Leonel Power, Thomas Damett and Nicholas Sturgeon, and shows admirably the *contenance angloise* that was so influential on later French composers. It was with the identification of the importance of Dunstable and an English school that the Flemish composer and theorist Johannes Tinctoris (*c.* 1435–before 1511) outlined the first distinct period of the Renaissance in music. He is equally important for, through the discussion and championing of the music of his contemporaries Jean de Ockeghem and Antoine Busnoys (*c.* 1430–before 1492), establishing the basis of the discipline of musicology itself.

DU FAY TO JOSQUIN

These developments were taken on and refined by the French musician Guillaume Du Fay (1397–1474), regarded at the time as the finest composer and theorist of his generation, and his near-contemporary Binchois (Gilles de Bin, *c.* 1400–60). Du Fay's works, many of them liturgical, including isorhythmic motets and masses (although there is a considerable body of secular songs, generally *rondeaux* and some *ballades*), display a masterful treatment of the motifs that make up his melodic lines, they are tightly constructed and often rhythmically complex. At first his writing tends, as in earlier practice, to contrast a florid upper part against simpler lower voices, but toward the end of his life there is much more uniformity across the parts. Of more importance is Du Fay's use of *fauxbourdon*, a common 15th-century technique whereby two upper voices move together, generally in thirds, and a third voice parallels the *cantus firmus* a fourth below, effectively creating a string of first inversion triads. This had the effect of establishing a sense of tonality, which Du Fay strengthened by the use of cadences to reinforce the tonic chord (these both moved from chord V to I, a perfect cadence, and, during the second half of the century, IV–I, a plagal cadence). The placing of the *cantus firmus* higher up in the texture, as became common during the 15th century, gave Du Fay more leeway in his treatment of the lowest voice, enabling him to make a wider choice of harmonic movement and so a greater ability to establish a sense of tonality.

Similar concerns are addressed in the works of Ockeghem, who was as fêted during his time as was Du Fay. While undoubtedly a formidable intellect, writing a mass that could be performed in any one

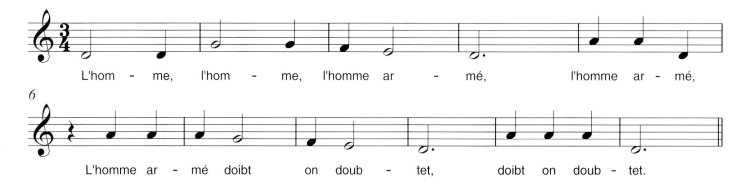

L'hom - me, l'hom - me, l'homme ar - mé, l'homme ar - mé,

L'homme ar - mé doibt on doub - tet, doibt on doub - tet.

of four modes and another that consisted almost entirely of double canons, it is his finely judged melismatic writing across all voices and his use of imitation as a structural device that sets him apart. His subsequent influence on later liturgical writing can be seen in the number of works that quote directly from his works, or use melodies from his *chansons* as a *cantus firmus*. That he was so admired is a tribute to his musical skills, but perhaps as interesting is that, not only was he active in other spheres such as mathematics and astrology, but he was regarded as having "reawoken" the art of music-making, making him an embodiment of the Renaissance man and placing him as perhaps the first true composer of the Renaissance.

If Ockeghem was the first true Renaissance composer, then the younger composer Josquin des Prez (whom it was rumored studied with Ockeghem, although there is no firm evidence to support this) was the finest exponent of the new musical style, and one of the most outstanding figures in the history of European music. Josquin's motets are perhaps the crowning glory of his output and these became models on which subsequent composers based their works; indeed, Josquin's music was cited in numerous treatises following his death, confirming his position at the center of the musical canon. His genius lay in gathering within the motet the rigorous structural and melodic devices of liturgical music alongside the expressive writing that dominated secular forms such as *chanson*. Particularly noted for his use of canon as a structural device, including at times reinforcing the *cantus firmus* by the use of a doubled tenor in canon, and for the almost constant presence of imitation between voices, his more homogenous textures not only lay the ground for later polyphony but prefigure some of the basic techniques of fugue. This is especially true of the counterposing of "real" entries, that is in exact imitation but transposed by a fifth, with "tonal" entries, where one phrase is answered with a version that reinforces the underlying tonality (usually by changing an opening rising fifth to a rising fourth, for example in a tonality centered on C, the movement C–G would become G–C). The handling of the *cantus firmus* in this way ensured that the basic material for a composition permeated all its voices and, to reinforce the sense of tonality, his writing is punctuated by numerous perfect cadences, often contrasting these homophonic sections with the surrounding polyphony.

Josquin's secular compositions are no less important, especially his *chansons*. In these his approach to the material is more free and expressive than in his liturgical motets and masses, constructing the pieces up from a series of motifs that build into phrases, each phrase consisting of a variation on a motif. This was radical in so far as it dispensed with the medieval practice of building a piece on an existing framework. In addition, by around 1500, Josquin and his contemporaries, including Jacob Obrecht (1457/8–1505), had reached the point where all voices in a composition were of equal weight, abandoning the earlier hierarchical structures that governed the function of each line. Nor were these compositions necessarily only sung, many would also have been performed by instrumentalists, and from now on there began to emerge a purely instrumental repertory.

PRINTING AND PROTESTANTISM

The beginning of the 16th century saw two events of overwhelming importance to the future direction of Europe, in the political, religious and musical worlds. The first was the birth of music printing from type in Venice in 1501 by Ottaviano Petrucci who produced the *Harmonice musices odhecaton* in this way. While plainchant had been printed using woodblocks before this date, the use of letterpress type was much more successful, allowing the setting and clear printing of complex scores, and enabling quicker and larger print-runs. The effect of this invention on the dissemination of music is hard to overestimate, and was particularly influential in building Josquin's Europe-wide reputation. The year 1501 also marks the beginning of music publishing, making music not only available to professional musicians in the courts or church but also to educated non-specialists, ensuring a wider transmission of musical texts and ideas, the latest of which would reach composers quickly and spread over a large geographical area.

The second revolution of the early-16th century began in Germany, sparked by the ideas of Martin Luther (1483–1546). As a young man, having been ordained as a priest, he was sent to Rome and had been shocked at the behavior of the Italian clergy, in particular the practice of selling indulgences. On returning to Germany he took up a post as a professor at the University of Wittenberg and became convinced that individual faith and adherence to the scriptures should form the basis of Christian belief, not the teachings of the church, leading him into conflict with the religious authorities. He was excommunicated in 1521 and went into hiding, a necessary precaution after the execution of the similarly dissident Jan Huss in 1415. He retreated to the castle of the Wartburg where he finished his translation of the New Testament into German, one of his greatest achievements.

On his return to Wittenberg in 1522 Luther began to organize the church there along new lines, issuing a new hymnal (much of which consisted of Luther's own compositions, largely chorales, or congregational hymns, which assumed great importance in Protestant music during the following centuries) and establishing Reformation doctrine through the Large and Small Catechisms (1529) and the Augsburg Confession (1530). Once

Palestrina

Giovanni Pierluigi da Palestrina (1525/6–94) was born in Palestrina in the Sabine Hills near Rome and almost his entire life and career was associated with the city, its patrons and the music of its churches. Noted for turning the developments of earlier French polyphony to the service of the Counter Reformation, and so hailed as the "savior of Catholic music", he forged a style that is still considered the model for strict diatonic counterpoint—it was Palestrina's music that inspired Johanne Fux's seminal treatise, *Gradus ad Parnassum*, published in 1725.

It is impossible to date with certainty events from Palestrina's early life, but it is known that he trained, in music and as a chorister, at the church of Santa Maria Maggiore in Rome, after which he became an organist at San Agapito in his home town of Palestrina. In 1551 he moved back to Rome, becoming a choir master at the Cappella Guilia in St Peter's. With the dedication of his first book of Masses to Pope Julius III in 1554 he seems to have gained papal favor as he was appointed to the Sistine Chapel in 1555. However, the death of Julius in the same year, and the short-lived (three-week) reign of Marcellus II, led to the appointment of Pope Paul IV whose strict views on celibacy—Palestrina was married by this time—meant that the composer had to resign his position. He then took up a post at the prestigious church of San Giovanni Laterano, where, although this seems to have been an unproductive period, he remained until 1560. He spent the next 14 or so years at Santa Maria Maggiore, during which time his fame began to spread throughout Europe, and then some time in the service of Cardinal Ippolito II d'Este, son of Lucrezia Borgia, on the outskirts of the city. In 1571 he returned to the Cappella Guila, where he remained until his death in 1594.

Palestrina's engagement with the Counter Reformation and the rulings of the Council of Trent begins in earnest with his appointment to Santa Maria Maggiore, where the presiding priest was Cardinal Carlo Borromeo, one of the leading members of the council. It is thought that it was during the first couple of years of his appointment that Palestrina wrote the *Missa Papae Marcelli*, notable for its largely homophonic style in which the text is clearly heard and which may have been instrumental in persuading the council that text-setting in the modern Mass could be intelligible—a "test" for these was made in the form of a concert of different Masses for Cardinal Vitellozzi in 1565. The *Marcelli* Mass was a free Mass (based on freely composed musical elements), although these form the smallest group of Palestrina's known works. The largest number of his Masses are imitation Masses, a common 16th-century device whereby the composition is based in its entirety (including form and motifs) on the work of another musician or of an earlier work by the present composer. A similar form is the paraphrase Mass which is based on the major theme, often an existing chant, of another work.

Although the Counter Reformation began with the intelligibility of the religious text as its central concern, the music that grew out of this was soon used for propaganda purposes and Masses, that were impressive and showed off the skills of the composers in the employ of the Church, were demanded, particularly with the accession of Pope Gregory XIII in 1572. Palestrina's later Masses and motets retain a clarity of text despite being larger and containing more complex writing for two or more choirs, known as polychoral Masses. Nor was Palestrina's writing wholly restricted to liturgical music—he composed a number of secular madrigals, in a lighter vein to that employed in his motet writing, although compared to madrigals written by his contemporaries they have more in common with earlier styles.

Adrian Willaert

The achievements of Palestrina owe much to the slightly earlier composers Adrian Willaert (c. 1490–1562) and Cristóbal de Morales (c. 1500–53). Willaert, a Netherlandish composer who worked at San Marco in Venice, was highly influential on younger Italian composers. He worked in almost all genres, from the madrigal (which he played a key role in developing) and *canzona* (a light, popular vocal style) to the motet and polyphonic Mass. His greatest works are his inventive motets, which combine the imitative polyphony of northern Europe with the more homophonic style of Italy, paving the way for the clear polyphonic text setting of Palestrina. Just as interesting is Willaert's composition of instrumental ricercare, short prelude-like pieces for lute or keyboard, which are similar in style to the polyphonic writing of his motets. Morales was born in Seville but also spent a considerable portion of his life working in Italy, some of it at the papal court. Considered to be the first great Spanish composer of sacred music, only surpassed by the great Tomás Luis de Victoria (1548–1611), his ability to set words clearly within polyphonic structures was second to none. His works, especially his *Magnificats*, were influential on Palestrina.

Luther had established the Reformation (as this "protesting" movement against the power and corruption of the Catholic Church would become known), the religious, and musical, map of Europe would never look the same. Thus was born the Protestant tradition that would henceforth divide Europe between, broadly, the Catholic south, with its Latin liturgy, and a Protestant north with a liturgy largely based in the vernacular.

THE COUNCIL OF TRENT

The Catholic Church found itself in a dire situation, with large swathes of Europe turning to the teachings of the Reformation. This led Pope Paul III to call the first meeting of the Council of Trent, which was to spearhead the Catholic revival of the Counter Reformation, in 1545. The

Orlando de Lassus playing spinet in Bavarian Court, illustration from choir book of Lassus' *Penitential Psalms;* Miniature by Hans Mielich (Codex)

Lassus traveled widely, especially in Italy during his youth, but spent most of his life, from 1556 onward, at the court of Bavaria in Munich. His output was huge, spanning Masses, Passions and *Magnificats*, motets with religious and Humanist texts, madrigals, French *chansons* and, later in his life, German *Lieder* (polyphonic song using similar techniques to the motet or madrigal). If Palestrina was the epitome of considered and controlled liturgical writing, Lassus was, to a certain extent, his opposite, setting texts from many sources, both secular and religious, and imbuing all his writing with a strong emotional content. This he achieved through a judicious use of chromaticism allied to a fine sense of vocal line that embellished the meanings of the text but never overwhelmed it. This freedom of expression is best exemplified in his numerous motets and madrigals. He exploited almost all techniques available to him, including canon and *cantus firmus*, but his motet writing is dominated by imitation.

Catholic meetings continued until 1563 during which a number of reforms were agreed upon, including on music in the Catholic liturgy. These largely concerned the Mass, for it was the core of the liturgy, and in particular the intelligibility of its texts, as well as a desire to banish secular influence from the music. The ways in which these measures were to be achieved involved reaffirming the position of Gregorian chant within the liturgy and allowing for polyphony, but one based on counterpoint (which at this point meant the pinning down of stricter rules for the treatment of polyphonic voices, especially dissonance) and clear annunciation of the text. The composer whose works embody the spirit of the Counter Reformation most clearly, and which is still held by some to be the "purest" example of Catholic musical sentiment, is Palestrina.

THE MADRIGAL

The other great composer of the mid- to late-16th century was Orlande de Lassus (1530/2–94), almost a direct contemporary of Palestrina. Lassus's motet writing bears a great deal of similarity to that of his madrigals. The madrigal, a form of secular polyphony, was to become the dominant secular vocal form of the second half of the 16th century, and lasted well into the following decades. As a setting of verse, its origins lie in the poems of Petrarch whose works were phenomenally popular during the 16th century.

Madrigals displaced an earlier form, the *frottola*, a secular song, generally accompanied by instruments, that also set poetic texts, whose main exponents were Bartolomeo Tromboncino (d. c. 1534) and Marco Cara (d. 1525). Emerging during the 15th century at the court of Mantua under the patronage of Isabella d'Este (1474–1539), the form soon spread throughout Italy. The love poetry that was set was lighthearted and by mostly anonymous writers, with the overall form consisting of stanzas followed by a refrain. However, once the cult of Petrarch had taken hold, with its all together more serious lyrics and freer verse, a new form was needed, one that was perceived as more weighty and which did not follow a fixed pattern of repetition.

The solution emerged in the form of vocal polyphony, for three to six voices, derived from the secular compositions of Josquin. By the time the new madrigal form had been established during the 1520s and 1530s by Phillipe Verdelot (c. 1480–1532) and Sebastiano Festa (c. 1490–1524) it was being taken up by composers such as Jacques Arcadelt (c. 1507–68), Adrian Willaert (c. 1490–1562) and Cipriano de Rore (1515/16–65). These composers not only expanded the choice of texts but experimented with the form, particularly the increasing use of chromaticism for expressive effect, the most extreme exponent of which was Carlo Gesualdo (c. 1561–1613).

The form grew in popularity, and toward the end of the century, it not only dominated the secular output of Italianate composers such as Lassus and Andrea Gabrieli (1532/3–1585), but had found a home outside of Italy in the works of English composers Thomas Morley (1557/8–1602), Thomas Weelkes (1576–1623) and John Wilbye (1574–1638). The circulation of printed volumes of Italian madrigals, and the presence at the court of Elizabeth I of Alfonso Ferrabosco (1543–88), prompted English poets such as Philip Sydney and Edmund Spenser to emulate Petrarch. This move prompted a similar effort from composers, based on the lighter *canzona* style of Italian composers such as Giovanni Ferretti (c. 1540–1609).

PARTHENIA
or
THE MAYDENHEAD
of the first musicke that
euer was printed for the VIRGINALLS
COMPOSED
By thre famous Masters William Byrd, Dr. John Bull & Orlando Gibbons.
Gentilmen of his Ma.tie most Illustrous Chappell.

ENGLISH POLYPHONY: TALLIS AND BYRD

Morley had been taught by William Byrd (c. 1540–1623) who in turn had been taught by Thomas Tallis (c. 1505–85). These two figures dominated English church music during the 16th century—the two men were close friends and colleagues at the Chapel Royal—as the country passed through one of its most turbulent periods, as successive monarchs from Henry VIII and Edward VI, to Mary I, to Elizabeth I embraced the Reformation, returned England to the Catholic Church and then rejoined the Protestant fold. To have survived these changes and to have retained his place at court, Tallis must have been a supreme pragmatist—indeed, debate still continues as to whether he was Protestant or Catholic. Byrd, however, was a staunch Catholic, a stance that at times made his life difficult. It is a tribute to the high esteem his music was held in, and especially his motets, a form associated with Catholic worship, that he continued to enjoy the patronage of the monarch.

In terms of his music, Tallis's work displays a great intellectual grasp of form, not least in the awe-inspiring 40-voice *Spem in Alium*. His changing style mirrors contemporary developments on the continent, from early melismatic works to his later tightly constructed imitative pieces. Byrd, whose wide-ranging work is notoriously difficult to sum up, occupies a similar place in English music to that of Palestrina in Italy, with a similarly lasting influence on the following composers. He retained elements of earlier styles, not least in the chromaticism of his false relations (semitonal chromatic contradictions between different voices), while these were set in new contexts, and he had an extraordinary grasp of form. Aside from his achievements in other genres, it is Byrd's motets that represent the pinnacle of English High Renaissance polyphony.

Parthenia or The Maydenhead,
Titlepage of the first collection of virginal music written in English by William Byrd, John Bull and Orlando Gibbons; London; 1612–13; publisher G. Lowe

If the Old Hall Manuscript is the greatest collection of early English liturgical writing, then the *Fitzwilliam Virginal Book* (compiled *c*. 1606–19 from works in print, as depicted here, or from manuscripts) is one of the finest sources of 16th-century English keyboard music, and also the largest, comprising some 300 works. The virginal, a smaller instrument than the similar harpsichord, consisted of a rectangular box, strung lengthways with a single set of keys, with a keyboard. When the keys were depressed, a quill plucked the appropriate string. The book contains works by England's greatest keyboard composers of the time: John Bull (1562/3–1628) and William Byrd.

JOHN DOWLAND

The Renaissance begins to see composers turning their attention to the writing of works for solo instruments or instrumental ensembles. Both Tallis and Byrd wrote instrumental music, most notably Byrd's masterly consort and virginal compositions, however the finest English composer of lute music was John Dowland (1563–1626). The greatest lutenist of his time, Dowland spent a great deal of his early career abroad, particularly at the court of Christian IV of Denmark. Dowland, however, hankered after a position at the English court, and although he was one of the most famous musicians in Europe he was not to be offered this until 1612. He is noted for creating the English lute song and his exquisite settings are deeply expressive, ranging from the carefree *Clear or cloudy* or *Shepherd in a shade* (both 1600) to the careworn *Lasso vita mia* (1612) or *Flow my tears* (1600). Dowland's virtuoso and highly contrapuntal solo lute music is some of the finest ever written, presenting considerable challenges to the player, while his consort music for viols or mixed consort, notably the *Lachrimae pavans* (1604) and various galliards, bring to ensemble music the

Dowland's *The First Booke of Songes*, title page, 1597

same degree of sophistication previously restricted to vocal polyphony. For this alone he is of utmost importance, as he paves the way for the development of an independent instrumental tradition.

BAROQUE MUSIC
THE AGE OF BASSO CONTINUO (1600–1750)

Henry Purcell's *The Fairy Queen*, 1946

An adaptation of Shakespeare's *A Midsummer Night's Dream*, *The Fairy Queen* is a semi-opera, first performed in 1692. Although the music does not link to drama particularly closely, nonetheless the work contains some of Purcell's most inventive writing.

As with all attempts to partition history, there is inevitably some overlap between the concepts and music that are considered to belong to the Baroque (roughly the period between 1600 and 1750) and the preceding and following eras. The term, adopted from art history, refers to a highly decorative and dramatic form of painting, sculpture and architecture that emerged during the Counter Reformation. Although the style retained a taste for the Classical in its themes and decoration, it is distinguished from the Renaissance by moving from a strongly linear technique to a more "painterly" one with greater theatricality in both architecture and painting. There is less idealism and more sense of humanity in its portraiture, and more use of emotional potential. These concerns were not totally unworldly—the newly-formed Jesuit order was quick to seize upon the potential of the new style an as evangelical tool. Highly decorated churches, that owned not a little to theatrical set design (and vice versa), were seen as a way of promoting a spectacular vision of Catholic ideology. The Protestant world too was establishing a clearer sense of its own cultural identity. While elements of the southern Baroque were influential in the north, in architecture and painting, the separate development of the Protestant liturgy was gathering pace, not least through the efforts of composers such as Michael Praetorius (1551–1621), who wrote a considerable number of Protestant hymns.

How far the concerns of art and architecture can be said to be those of the music of the same period is controversial; claims have varied from a parallel between the move away from linear design with the rise of Italian monody (as opposed to the "linear" form of polyphony), to a delight in decoration and the expression of emotion in highly ornamented solo vocal and instrumental parts. The use of theatricality that was evident in architecture has also been said to find a counterpart in the rise of opera as a dramatic form. However, the true parallels are likely to be found in more abstract concepts, such as the greater importance of the individual (as an artistic subject or soloist) or the exploitation of an emotional response to a work as the key to its comprehension (the idea that certain techniques are affecting in specific ways).

More generally, the period is distinguished by the adoption of the tonal system, where a strong central tonality with a clear diatonic identity is set against modulation to related keys, *concertato*, where contrasting musical ideas or groups of singers or instrumentalists are set against each other, as well as new forms, such as opera and the solo cantata and concerto, that would continue to have an impact long after the middle of the 18th century. Allied to these are two seemingly opposed ideas, the use of figured bass in the *continuo* to support a solo line and the use of counterpoint, although now as a technique in which the lines are harmonically functional rather than as a style.

1600: The East India Company is founded and given a monopoly on all trade with the East Indies.

1601: Peri's *Euridice*, the earliest surviving opera. The publication of Caccini's monodic song collection *Le nuove musiche*.

1605: The publication of *Don Quixote* by Cervantes.

1607: The first performance of Monteverdi's *Orfeo*.

1622: Richelieu is appointed as a Cardinal and becomes a powerful influence in France.

1633: Galileo is forced to retract his support of Copernican theory.

1643–1715: The reign of Louis XIV in France.

1644: René Descartes publishes his *Principia philosophiae*.

1648: The Peace of Westphalia ends the Thirty Years War.

1649: End of the English Civil War and declaration of the Commonwealth.

1664: Molière writes his play *Tartuffe*.

1666: The Académie des Sciences is founded in Paris.

1685: Louis XIV retracts the Edict of Nantes and the Protestant Huguenots leave France.

1686: Isaac Newton publishes *Philosophiae naturalis principia mathematica*.

1689: Constitutional monarchy in England under the Bill of Rights.

Lully's "Armide" (Biblioteca Reale, Turin, 1770; Drawing by Leonardo Marini, engraving by Angelo Gizzardi)

1701: Prince Frederick III of Brandenburg crowns himself King Frederick I of Prussia.

1703: Peter the Great orders the building of St Petersburg.

1714: Corelli's op.6 collection of *concerto grossi* is published.

1723: J.S. Bach moves to Leipzig and begins his immense cycle of cantatas and passions.

1733: The first performance of Pergolesi's *La serva padrona*.

1735: Linneaus develops a new system of classification for plants.

1740: Frederick II of Prussia abolishes torture and founds the Order of Merit.

1750: The death of J.S. Bach.

Indeed, contrast as a general principle was an important element of the Baroque with composers increasingly exploiting differences in dynamic (loud against soft), texture (homophonic against contrapuntal) and ensemble (solo against group). Composers were more mobile, taking advantage of greater formality in training and more detailed classification of musical developments, with D. Scarlatti, Lully and Handel all achieving fame outside the country of their birth. Developments in instrument building also contributed to the changes that took place, with the viol gradually giving way to the violin and cello, and, especially, the great German organ building of the 17th and 18th century that directly influenced the works of J.S. Bach.

The organ, Neue Kirche, Arnstadt

The magnificent organ here, a fine example of the German organ-builders' art, was built by Johann Friedrich Wender in 1702–3. It was played while new by J.S. Bach during his time in the city during 1703–7.

MONODY

The clearest break in musical practice was, ironically given the place the Classical world had played in the Renaissance, inspired by antiquity. Toward the end of the 16th century, a number of Italian academies (salons where intellectual discussions took place), especially in Florence, became interested in the performance of the dramas and music of ancient Greece. It was thought that the dramas were sung in a declamatory style that aided the comprehension of the texts and this idea was exploited in particular by Vincenzo Galilei (c. 1520–91), Jacopo Peri (1561–1633) and Giulio Caccini (1551–1618). Galilei was a lutenist as well as an important theorist who was one of the first composers to experiment with equal temperament. However, he is chiefly famous for his *Dialogo* (1581) in which he attacks polyphony as inferior to what was imagined to have been Greek musical practice and being incapable of clearly presenting a text and of exploiting its emotional potential in full. Unfortunately there are no surviving examples of Galilei's answer to this: monody, a single melodic line that clearly annunciates the text set against a homophonic accompaniment. However, the idea was quickly taken up by other composers including Peri, whose *Euridice* (1601) is the earliest surviving complete opera (his earlier work, *Dafne*, 1597–98, now lost, is thought to have been the first opera written). This newly emerged dramatic genre stemmed from a variety of earlier genres, including medieval religious dramas, the Italian *Commedia dell'arte* and *intermedi* (musical interludes of song, most often madrigals, or to accompany dance that came at the end of the acts of staged comedies). In *Euridice* it is possible to see Peri's use of the new technique of monody, most notably in the monodic dramatic recitation that links the sections, the first example of *recitative*, and in strophic songs with expressive vocal lines that repeat the musical material for each stanza and which are interspersed with refrains.

The expressive potential of monody was exploited more fully by Caccini in his groundbreaking collection of songs, *Le nuove musiche* (1601). In this he explains, in the preface, the manner in which the monodies should be performed and embellished, through the use of ornamentation, in order to heighten the emotional experience, a vocal practice that was to dominate the Baroque. Just as importantly, he is the first composer to notate the accompaniment to the melodies using figured bass (or *basso continuo*). This form of accompaniment, which was to remain throughout the Baroque, consists of a written bass line below which are series of numbers that indicate the harmony to be played at that point, for example, 5-3 would require the player to play the third and fifth above the bass note, a root position triad, while 6-3 indicates the third and sixth above the bass note which results in a first inversion; in time the system was abbreviated, 5-3 chords were no longer indicated, it was assumed the *continuo* players would add these as a matter of course, and 6-3 became simply 6. (Figured bass is still used as a teaching aid and a shorthand for musicians in referring to types of chords.) The *continuo* could be played on a variety of instruments capable of providing harmony—the organ or harpsichord, lute or chitarrone (a bass lute, also called the theorbo), viol or the cello. Both of these developments, decoration of the vocal line and figured bass, introduce an element of improvisation into the music and give the musicians the freedom to react to the emotional possibilities latent within it.

Claudio Monteverdi

The figure who dominates the early Baroque more than any other, and demonstrates through his own work the transition between earlier Renaissance practice and the newly emerging genres of the new style, is Claudio Monteverdi (1567–1643). He was born in Cremona and it seems, from dedications, as though he received his musical training from the choir master of the cathedral there, Marc'Antonio Ingegneri. This training was thorough, in singing, theory and in playing stringed instruments, and Monteverdi was sufficiently ambitious to publish his first works, the motets *Sacrae cantiunculae*, at the age of 15.

Claudio Monteverdi (1567–1643), by Bernardo Strozzi; 1630

After searching for employment for a number of years, and after he had completed his first two books of madrigals, he entered the service of Duke Vincenzo Gonzaga in Mantua during 1590–91. As well as giving him security, the court at Mantua with its active cultural life proved a lively training ground for the young composer. Exposed to music from composers already working in Mantua, and from neighboring courts, Monteverdi soon produced a third book of madrigals which displayed a more daring use of chromaticism, possibly influenced by the Flemish composer Giaches de Wert (1535–96), head of music at the Mantuan court.

Travels as a member of the court, notably to Hungary and Flanders, also broadened his horizons and it is likely that he attended the first performance of Peri's *Euridice* in Florence in 1600. That his music was considered modern is demonstrated by the attacks of the critic Giovanni Maria Artusi who objected to the widespread use of dissonance in the works. Monteverdi's fourth book of madrigals appeared in 1603, with a fifth two years later, the

latter tending to a greater theatricality in the vocal settings and also notable for containing the first set of madrigals to call for an obligatory *basso continuo*. These works foreshadow perhaps Monteverdi's greatest achievement of this period, his first opera *Orfeo*, performed in 1607.

Orfeo was followed in 1608 by another opera *Arianna*, much of which is now lost although it seems that it was equally successful and to have built upon the innovations of the previous work; famously the lament *Lasciatemi morire*, which still survives and was influential on later composers, was said to have made the audience break down in tears. A different work that also followed on from *Orfeo*, indeed using the same instrumental forces and reworking some of the material, although in a very different sphere, was the *Vespro della Beata Vergine* of 1610. This collection of liturgical works spans a variety of styles, from the strict imitation of the austere *Missa a 6 voci da cappella* based on a motet by Nicolas Gombert (*c.* 1495–1560) to the influence of his madrigals with highly expressive and chromatic writing. That this was a sacred work is surprising, considering he was not attached to a church patron and he had not produced any liturgical pieces since his very early compositions. Nevertheless, the *Vespers* remain one of his most spectacular creations with underlying structures based on variations that in their invention and organization surpass those of *Orfeo*.

It may have been fortuitous that Monteverdi had produced such a great piece of religious music as he was becoming increasingly unhappy with his position at Mantua and began to look for other

Monteverdi's *L'incoronazione di Poppea,* Bavarian State Opera and Welsh National Opera co-production, 1998; Catrin Wyn Davies as Poppea; Directed by David Alden

In this scene from Monteverdi's *The Coronation of Poppea*, Arnalta sings a lullaby to her mistress, Poppea (act 2, scene 11).

Orfeo **by Monteverdi,** by the English National Opera (ENO), with Jeremy White (Pluto) and Stephanie Marshall (Proserpina); Coliseum Theatre, London; April 2006

employment. When the head of music at San Marco in Venice, Giulio Cesare Martinengo (1564/8–1613) died, Monteverdi auditioned for the post and was accepted. He immediately took up the position and set to work on publishing his sixth book of madrigals, most of which had been composed in Mantua. The collection is notable for its version of the lament from *Arianna* extended as a composition for five voices.

As well as his duties connected with the basilica (which involved composing music for special celebrations and Masses) Monteverdi continued to produce commissioned secular works, including some for the court at Mantua and his seventh book of madrigals (1619) was dedicated to the Duchess Caterina there. This set differs somewhat from the volumes that preceded it, with little strict monody and a large number of highly embellished duets. They are notable also for their clear sense of tonality; by this time the modern tonal system of keys and tonic-dominant relationships was almost completely established and displaced the old modal style. The eighth book of madrigals did not appear until 1638 but it does contain one of Monteverdi's most striking works, the *Combattimento di Tancredi et Clorinda* originally written in 1624–25. This overtly dramatic setting of a poem by Torquato Tasso for two singers and a narrator is important for its use of the orchestra to depict the excitement of the battle scene through repeated semiquaver patterns (the so-called *genere concitato*, or "agitated style"). This purely instrumental word painting, which includes the first use of *pizzicato* (seemingly invented by Monteverdi), was a new departure in orchestration, as was the make-up of the orchestra itself, consisting only of *continuo* and strings, thus establishing the primacy of the strings within the modern orchestra.

Between the *Combattimento* and publishing of the eighth book of madrigals, Monteverdi composed the *Scherzi musicali* of 1632, a set of songs, some with a simple strophic structure with *continuo* accompaniment, others being sets of variations over a repeated bass pattern (known as *ciaccona*). This form, also known as *chaconne* or *passacaglia*, gained considerable popularity over the next three centuries and was revived by some 20th century composers as a deliberate archaising of their works. After publication of the eighth book Monteverdi again turned his attention to opera, with *Il ritorno d'Ulisse in patria* (1640, only surviving in an incomplete version) and *Le nozze d'Enea in Lavina* (1641, now lost). These were followed a year later by Monteverdi's crowning work, the opera *L'incoronazione di Poppea* (1642–43). This builds upon some of the ideas explored in *Ulisse* and, presumably, *Le nozze d'Enea*, moving away from the primacy of *recitative* in pushing the plot forward instead using a greater number of *aria* forms with their greater melodic interest. The orchestral writing also picks up on earlier ideas, with the use of *genere concitato* to heighten the excitement and emotional effect at appropriate moments in the score.

The theoretician Giovanni Maria Artusi (1540–1613) was a staunch defender of traditional compositional practice in the style of Palestrina. His coining of the term *seconda pratica* in 1603 in criticizing Monteverdi's free use of dissonance sparked off a controversy that highlighted the difference between earlier practice, said to be *prima pratica*, in which the beauty of polyphonic part-writing was the aim, against the new use of dissonance as ornamentation to highlight the text. This *seconda pratica* was said to have stemmed from the ancient Greeks, chiming in with the claims that monody was the revival of the drama of antiquity.

OPERA AND BALLET

The first truly satisfactory opera is Monteverdi's *Orfeo*; an astounding work for its time. Earlier operas, with their almost constant use of monodic

Il pomo d'oro, Slumber of Ennone scene (act IV, scene 2); Engraving by L. Burnacini after M Küsel, 1668

Cesti's first opera, *Alessandro vincitor di se stesso*, was performed in Venice in 1651. However, the following year he was appointed director of the Kammermusiker at the court of Innsbruck. Here he produced his opera *Cleopatra* to general acclaim and, after a quarrel that cut his links to Venice, remained in Innsbruck until 1659, producing his most famous work, *Orontea*, there in 1656. Cesti then spent two years in Rome in the service of the pope, by which time he was one of the most famous musicians in Europe, before—risking excommunication—he returned to Innsbruck in 1661. In 1666 he was summoned by the emperor to Vienna to take up an important position at the court, and it was in Vienna that Cesti had one of his greatest successes, the performance of *Il pomo d'oro* in 1668, composed for the wedding of Kaiser Leopold I and Margarete Therese of Spain.

declamation, lacked variation in the musical settings and had little overall structure. Monteverdi brought all the expressive skill from his madrigal settings to bear on the *recitatives*, that serve to move the plot on, making them satisfying and musically dramatic. To bring relief to the texture he intersperses the *recitatives* with choruses, duets, songs (two of which are in the ABA form that was to dominate songs of the next two centuries) and instrumental passages. The orchestra that accompanies the singers is on a bigger scale than anything that had preceded it, consisting of harpsichords, organs, violins, violas, cellos, viols, recorders, trombones, cornettes (wooden trumpets with fingerholes) and trumpets. The orchestration was, in part, tied to the structure of the work, so that, for instance, the trombones are associated with Hades and the recorders with pastoral moments. Of particular interest is the solo *arioso* for *Orfeo* "*Possente spirito e formidabil nume*".

Here the music is notated in two ways, one a plain vocal line alongside which is a highly ornamented version showing the expressive possibilities which are to be realized in performance.

By the time of Monteverdi's death in 1643, even though Venice was to remain the center of opera in Italy until around 1680 (largely due to efforts of composers such as Francesco Cavalli, 1602–76, and Carlo Pallavicino, c. 1640–88), developments had started to take place elsewhere in Europe, even if they were greatly influenced by an Italian composer working largely in a Venetian style, Antonio Cesti (1623–69). Cesti and his near contemporary Cavalli dominated the opera world after the death of Monteverdi and they are chiefly known for their lyrical vocal writing (sometimes termed *bel canto*) that replaced the earlier more declamatory style. Their works might also be seen as the point at which the tonal system makes its dominance complete, Cesti in particular favoring straightforward harmonic progressions. This was partly a result of a much more homophonic structure (where the melody and accompaniment are clearly separated) to support the "tuneful" vocal melodies, but also a concern to reinforce a central tonality. These progressions included frequent cadences, particularly the II/IV–V–I perfect cadence with a preceding supertonic or subdominant chord that was to run through all subsequent tonal compositions.

The effect of Cesti's work, and that of other Italian composers, on Central and Northern Europe was strong, and the repertory of opera houses in Munich, Hamburg, Vienna and Dresden was dominated by their works, sometimes in translation. However, the first German opera, *Dafne*, was written as far back 1627 by the country's first great international musical figure, Heinrich Schütz (1585–1672). The music for this work is now lost but it, and subsequent German operas—in particular the earliest surviving work in German, *Seelewig* of 1644 by Sigmund Staden (1607–55)—might be best described as *Singspieler*, musical dramatic works broken up by sections of spoken dialogue, a characteristically German form that continued up to Mozart's *Die Zauberflöte* and Weber's *Der Freischütz*. Opera in the north did face a degree of opposition from the more extreme proponents of the Reformation, with its general suspicion of the secular world and entertainment, and it took longer to become established in part because of the disruption caused by the Thirty Years' War (1618–48). However, with the Treaty of Westphalia that brought an end to the conflict there was a rise in general prosperity, particularly for the great trading port of Hamburg. Here the first public opera house in Germany opened in 1678 with an opera by Schütz's pupil Johann

Theile (1646–1724), better known as one of the greatest composers of 17th-century contrapuntal church music.

Germany's main opponent in the Thirty Years' War was France and, perhaps surprisingly given the country's Catholic traditions, opera did not gain a following there until the 1670s. The ending of the war was followed in France by a further five years of internal conflict and this coupled with differing musical preferences, particularly the French taste for ballet, meant that it was not until the public staging of Robert Cambert's (c. 1628–77) *Pomone* to a libretto by Pierre Perrin (c. 1620–75) in 1671 that French opera truly arrived. Cambert and Perrin had collaborated on a number of stage works before the composition of this opera, largely under the patronage of Cardinal Mazarin, but it was only with *Pomone*, thought to have been completed by 1661 but the first performance of which was delayed due to the death of Mazarin the same year, that their work becomes through-composed.

The success of *Pomone* inspired France's greatest 17th-century composer, Jean-Baptiste Lully (1632–87), to write his first opera *Les fêtes de l'Amour et du Bacchus* in 1672. Lully's opera, however, had not appeared as if from nowhere and as composer and dancer to the royal court he had composed numerous ballets and *comédies-ballets*, a genre established by Molière, whose mixture of song, *recitative*, choruses and dance as well as spoken dialogue was already moving toward full-blown opera. Lully, originally Italian who was born as Giovanni Battista Lulli in Florence, received his musical and dance training in Paris and entered the service of Louis XIV in 1651 as a dancer and in 1653 became court composer of instrumental music. As such he was expected to not only perform but also write new dances for

the entertainment of the court. These were usually part of a larger work with contributions, including songs, from other composers but the first that he wrote in its entirety was *La galanterie du temps* in 1656. Soon he was writing the vocal parts as well and this led, in time, to his producing sacred works for the royal chapel (in particular the *Miserere* of 1663).

In 1661 Lully was made the master of music of the king's chamber, the highest appointment in France, and from this point on his fame was assured. Perhaps his greatest opportunity came in 1664 when he began his collaboration with Molière on his *comedies-ballets*, among them *Le bourgeois gentilhomme* (1670) and *George Dandin* (1668). The performance of *Les fêtes de l'Amour et du Bacchus* (based on *comédies-ballets*) was followed by his first operatic tragedy, *Cadmus et Hermione* (1673), by which time Lully had become director of the Académie Royale de Musique. This position gave him great power and the ability to restrict access for performances of his rivals' music meant that he could dominate the musical scene in and around Paris. Several operas followed *Cadmus*, predominantly on classical themes, such as *Thésée* (1675), *Isis* (1677) and *Psyché* (1678). Lully's operatic dominance not only had the effect of warding off an influx of Italian works, and thus establishing a strong indigenous tradition, but also meant that his style was stamped on the French operatic repertory.

Lully's legacy was taken forward by Jean-Philippe Rameau (1683–1764). Rameau was much influenced by the Enlightenment and the work of figures such as Newton, Descartes and Kepler, and the spirit of its scientific revolutions is evident in his theoretical writings. Convinced of the scientific basis of music, Rameau set out to establish the fundamental principles that govern harmony and melody. These were set out in his ground-breaking *Traité de l'harmonie* (1722) in which he makes several important observations and classifies certain harmonic elements for the first time. Perhaps his most relevant statement to contemporary

Jean Baptiste Lully

Perhaps Lully's chief contributions to operatic developments in France were his concern over the clarity of the sung text, especially in his *airs*, and his carefully considered orchestration. The first meant that French vocal writing was less florid than the style predominating in Italy, harking back in some ways to the earlier monodists, while the second grew out of the strong ballet tradition, where the instrumental passages were more prominent in their role as an accompaniment to the voice; the inclusion of numerous dances was an essential part of the French operatic style. This concern with orchestral writing also extended to Lully's overtures, and he was almost single-handedly responsible for establishing the two-part form consisting of a slow introduction followed by an *allegro* section that was taken up across Europe and was so popular that it achieved independence as an instrumental form. Particularly characteristic of his orchestral writing, for ballets and operatic overtures, was the use of sharply dotted rhythms.

Jean-Philippe Rameau

As important for his theoretical writings as his operatic works, Rameau, the successor of Lully, was the most impressive French composer of the early 18th century, his influence lasting long after his death.

practice was that all melody should imply the accompanying harmony, a concern that ran throughout Baroque counterpoint. He also was the first to classify 6-3 and 6-4 chords as inversions of the root position 5-3 triad (and so show the implied bass to any harmonic progression), and

to point out that the tonic, sub-dominant and dominant triads of a key are its most important (as well as representing the nearest tonalities to the tonic apart from the tonic minor). His ideas were refined throughout his lifetime and he left a body of theoretical work that has remained the basis for teaching the fundamentals of harmony.

The succession was not, however, smooth, and supporters of Lully were resistant to the innovations made by Rameau. Rameau's early motets and cantatas do show a flair for dramatic forms but the performance of his first opera _Hippolyte et Aricie_ (1733) late in his career was a sensation. Aside from Rameau's extremely fertile musical imagination in which the skill of his characterization exceeds that of almost any other composer of the time, _Hippolyte_ and subsequent operas, including _Castor et Pollux_ (1737) and _Dardanus_ (1739), were notable for tackling French _tragédies_ when such serious subjects were becoming unfashionable. Perhaps the most shocking element of Rameau's operas to his contemporary audience was his rich harmonic language, full of chromaticisms from

added 7ths and 9ths, augmented and diminished chords, and modulations to distant keys. This expressive use of an extended tonal musical language undoubtedly stems in part from his theoretical concerns, and also passed over into his melodic style, with unusual leaps and intervals and an ability to extract the most from an emotional situation through a judicious use of appoggiaturas and suspensions.

Rameau's stage works have been criticized for their libretti and plots, and compared unfavorably to the taut dramatic structures of Lully's operas. While it is true that some of Rameau's works can appear to be disjointed with sudden shifts of scene and plot twists, the composer was quick to capitalize on this apparent flaw by exploiting the musical potential of the spectacle, especially in his lighter _opéra-ballets_. For example, in _Les fêtes de l'Hymen_ (1748) or _Les Indes galantes_ (1735), the audience is transported to such exotic locations as Egypt, Turkey, Peru, Iran and North America. Given the strong element of dance in these works it is not surprising that Rameau also paid great attention to his highly virtuosic orchestral writing, experimenting with adding instruments such as horns and clarinets and new string techniques such as glissando and pizzicato. He was also responsible for turning the overture from a piece that had little to do musically with the drama to follow, to one that either comprises themes from the subsequent music or evokes a sense of what is to come.

At the same time that Lully was dominating the opera world in France, the main center for opera in Italy had passed from Venice to Naples. However, what has become known as the Neapolitan style in reality derives from the reforms of composers and librettists from, or working in, Venice, Rome

and Vienna. The two most influential librettists were Apostolo Zeno (1668–1750) and Pietro Metastasio (1698–1782). Both men attempted to remove much of the extraneous spectacle and numerous side plots of the prevailing style and to give a greater dramatic focus to the works. Hand in hand with this went a greater simplification of the musical structure that alternated *recitativo secco* ("dry" *recitative*) with arias, the former with little musical interest but which served to move the plot on contrasting with the latter that were often highly virtuosic, musically interesting and which sought to affect an emotional response to that particular stage of the plot. Both Zeno and Metastasio worked for the imperial court in Vienna (Metastasio replacing Zeno as court poet in 1729), but many of their libretti were set by composers working in Italy and the same libretto might be set many times by many different composers.

The major composer working in the Neapolitan style, and who is often credited with forming it, was Alessandro Scarlatti (1660–1725). Initially from Naples where he was greatly influenced by Venetian opera, Scarlatti moved to Rome to take advantage of the greater opportunities the city offered, Rome being dominated by the church which, officially at least, frowned on opera as a public entertainment. His later Neapolitan works differ from his earlier operas in their streamlined, though often convoluted, plots and a simplification of the orchestral writing. The Neapolitan style came to be largely dependent on continuo plus a melodic line, often provided on violin or trumpet, whereas Venetian and Roman works had tended to display a greater complexity and contrapuntal texture to the instrumental accompaniments. Scarlatti's later orchestral writing did become more imaginative toward the end of his life, writing for larger ensembles including flutes, oboes, bassoons and horns, but a clear, largely homophonic style remained that was to set the scene for composers of the early Classical period. However, it was in the writing of *da capo* arias (literally "to the head") with their simple ABA structure, that he excelled. The clear texture left him free to concentrate on the melodic lines, which with their florid ornamentation and technical challenges, were more than enough to satisfy the demands of the virtuoso singers and their adoring public. Scarlatti's simple direct style also extended to his overtures, which in contrast to the French contrapuntal compositions, were homophonic and had a quick–slow–quick structure. These *sinfonias* were, like their French counterparts, to become an independent form and were important for the later development of the symphony.

Another composer working in Naples at the same time as Scarlatti was Giovanni Battista

A factor that had a great influence on the musical content of Neapolitan opera was the popularity of *castrati*, male singers who had been castrated before puberty to maintain their high voices. Such was the popularity of these virtuosi that there were relatively few major roles for women's voices in the Neapolitan repertory. The most famous of the *castrati* was Carlo Broschi, better known as Farinelli (1705–82). Brought up in Naples he made his first appearance there in Porpora's *Angelica et Medoro* in 1720. This opera had a libretto by Metastasio and through this performance both men became life-long friends. His fame soon grew and Farinelli toured throughout Italy, appearing in operas in Rome, Venice, Florence and Milan, though he eventually settled in Bologna. He also appeared in London, prompting ecstatic reviews, and famously was retained by King Philip V of Spain to sing the same three *arias* each night to help cure the king of depression.

Pergolesi (1710–36), one of the most successful composers of the new *opera buffa* (comic opera), as opposed to the *opera seria* on heroic themes that had predominated so far. *Opera buffa* had first been performed in Naples as a local dialect drama but by the time of Pergolesi its stock plot concerned two pairs of lovers whose lives become entangled but by the end of the work are reunited with their true partner; the most famous of these being Pergolesi's *La serva padrona* (1733). This basic pattern, along with a stock cast of minor characters, remained constant and it can be seen in later works such as Mozart's *Le nozze di Figaro*. While there were composers working elsewhere in Italy, notably the predominantly *opera seria* works of Baldassare Galuppi (1706–85), Vivaldi and Tomaso Albinoni (1671–*c.* 1750) in Venice, the influence of Naples spread far beyond Italy and before long quite a number of composers working in Austria and Germany were producing what were essentially Neapolitan operas.

This was not, however, the full story. Particularly in the north a German-language opera style, centered on Hamburg, was flourishing through the works of Reinhard Keiser (1674–1739) and, later, Georg Philipp Telemann (1681–1767). The libretti for their operas were extremely diverse, from heroic classical subjects to, especially in the works of Telemann, comedies. As in the vocal duets and operas of Agostino Steffani (1654–1728), an Italian composer who spent almost all his life in Germany, Keiser's and Telemann's operas show the influence of French works although Italian opera was undoubtedly dominant, especially on their later works. Steffani was also notable for the interest he maintained in his orchestral accompaniments, especially in his instrumental duet writing, and

As in Germany, the Puritan revolution
that culminated in the English
Commonwealth (1649–60) and especially
the destruction of musical institutions,
education and texts by the winning side,
meant that opera was slower to establish
itself in England than elsewhere. It
really only began to spread under the
Restoration of Charles II (1660–85),
though it was in England that the
influence of Lully was most strongly felt,
especially on the work of the greatest
English composer of the time, Henry
Purcell (1659–95). The majority of
Purcell's stage works are not operas in
the strictest sense of the word as they
are not through-composed, the exception
being *Dido and Aeneas* (1689), and
contain passages of spoken dialogue. This
was the favored style in England and
through-composed operatic works did
not begin to dominate until into the 18th
century. Aside from *Dido and Aeneas*, the
two best-loved of Purcell's many stage
works, *King Arthur* (1691) and *The Fairy
Queen* (1693), amply demonstrate to the
world what the English masques most
often sought to portray: the first full of
legendary kings and knights, nymphs
and shepherds, the second a reworking
of Shakespeare's *A Midsummer Night's
Dream*, all with a good measure of
pantomime added.

the use of imitation between the orchestra and
voice. Similar concerns can be seen in the operas
of Johann Fux (1660–1741), one of the greatest
Austrian Baroque composers who worked at the
court in Vienna, though generally better known
for his sacred works and the didactic *Gradus ad
Parnassum* based on the polyphony of Palestrina.

Many Italian composers came north to work at
the Austrian and German courts, but the traffic
was not all one way. One of the most successful
composers in the Neapolitan *opera seria* style was
Johann Hasse (1699–1783). Born near Hamburg

he trained with Scarlatti and subsequently worked
in Naples and Venice before returning to the
German-speaking world where he moved between
Dresden and Vienna. While in Vienna he came into
contact with Metastasio with whom he maintained
a long and fruitful partnership. As well as having a
fine touch for melody, Hasse, in common with other
German composers, ensured that his orchestral
writing matched the interest of the vocal line.
The German opera composer, however, who was
to excel in the Italian style above all others was
George Frederick Handel (1685–1759).

Born in Halle, Saxony, where he attended the
university, Handel's first significant move was to
Hamburg to try his luck as an opera composer.
There he wrote several German-language works—
the first *Almira* in 1704—that were heavily
inspired by Italian models albeit with French
influence in the treatment of the overture. The
success he achieved in Hamburg, coupled with his
respect for the Italian tradition, seems to have
persuaded him that a spell in Italy would polish his
style. Leaving in 1706 he traveled to Florence and
Rome, producing his first Italian opera, *Rodrigo*,

in Florence in 1707. A later opera, this time the
comic *Agrippina*, was produced in Venice in 1709
and both operas plus a number of dramatic cantatas
in the Italian style were highly successful. In 1710
he took up a position at the court of Hanover, at
that time the seat of the future King George I of
England, and paying a visit to London, where
Italian opera was becoming more popular, the
same year he arranged a performance of his new
opera Rinaldo for 1711. In 1712 Handel revisited
London, and the city was to be his home for the
rest of his life. Further operas, the form to which
he had by now largely dedicated himself, were
produced in the following years to considerable
acclaim, including *Giulio Cesare* (1724), *Admeto*
(1727) and *Alcina* (1735). Although Handel
did not significantly contribute any changes to
the operatic form, adhering in general to the *da
capo aria* and reserving ensembles of the soloists
for the final scene, he not only was responsible
for radically increasing the popularity of opera
in London, but his works rank among the finest
examples of late-Baroque Italian opera and the
earliest in today's active repertory.

SACRED MUSIC AND ORATORIO

If Italian opera dominated almost all of Europe
bar France, the difference between north and south
was more pronounced in the sphere of sacred music,
although opera was influential, particularly as
composers often worked in both areas. The history
of sacred music of the Baroque is delineated by
the great achievements of Monteverdi in Venice
and Bach in Leipzig, although Monteverdi's sacred
music, especially that for San Marco, owes much
to that of a predecessor at the basilica: Giovanni

Gabrieli (c. 1554–1612), noted for his religious settings for voice and instrumental ensemble of brass and strings. In general, however, much Catholic liturgical music of the 17th and 18th centuries adhered to the precepts of the *stile antico*, essentially a reworking of the musical ideas of Palestrina, hence Fux's *Gradus ad Parnassum* which codified the five species of counterpoint that Palestrina was imagined to have worked to (the first species refers to note against note counterpoint, the second to two notes against one of the *cantus firmus*, the third to four notes against one of the *cantus firmus*, and so on). This technique was augmented by the Baroque practice of adding *continuo* and by arranging the choirs and instrumentalists in *concertato* fashion to add interest.

Outside of the liturgy it was from the vocal works of composers such as Luigi Rossi (1597/8–1653) and Giacomo Carissimi (1605–74) that a new concert setting of Biblical texts was to emerge, the oratorio. Rossi and Carissimi, both working in Rome, were together the chief composers writing solo cantatas, a form that grew out of the fusing of madrigals and monody. Owing a great deal to the *bel canto* writing of early opera, the cantata was a poetic setting for solo voice and modest instrumental resources that alternated *arias* and *recitatives*. As a form it was hugely popular, not least as it could be performed in the home, and went on to become one of the dominant genres of the Baroque, generally falling into the pattern of two *arias* separated by a *recitative*.

The cantatas were not restricted to secular themes and soon were adopted for use in setting sacred texts and entered the liturgy, especially in the *Concerti Sacri* of Alessandro Scarlatti (although in this case they were referred to as motets, which by this time were essentially any religious setting of a Latin text). The popularity of the form spread throughout Europe, finding its greatest exponent in the Protestant world in J.S. Bach.

When the cantata was adapted and expanded, with contrapuntal choruses, homophonic chorales and greater instrumental forces, to set extended sections of the Bible (often self-contained stories) it became a form of semi-staged sacred opera known as the oratorio. Performed both in and out of church, the oratorio was notable for being in the vernacular, in Italian, German, English and French (the *oratorio latino* favored by Carissimi and his contemporaries being the exception), and also by the beginning of the 18th century for the large part played by the chorus in the overall scheme, often in impressively large contrapuntal set pieces. Carissimi was the teacher of Marc-Antoine Charpentier (1643–1704), a great rival

Il Gesù, depicting *Triumph of the Name of Jesus* by Baciccia; Rome

This church in Rome by the architect Giacomo Barozzi da Vignola was built in 1568–75 and is considered the first example of the Baroque in architecture. Its powerful design became the template for churches built over the next two centuries and it expresses the confidence of the newly resurgent Catholic Church following the Counter Reformation.

of Lully and a composer heavily influenced by the Italian style. Although the sacred music of the French court was essentially backward looking, with polyphonic motets by composers such as Thomas Gobert (c. 1600–72) and Nicolas Formé (1567–1638) dominating the repertory. Charpentier, like Lully, not only composed a wide range of Italian influenced Masses and motets including magnificent settings of the *Te Deum*, but also introduced the oratorio to France and wrote a number of fine cantatas which combine a *bel canto* style with the heavy ornamentation beloved of French composers of the time.

The development of sacred music in the Protestant north followed a slightly different path. Crucial to the Lutheran concept of worship was collective and participatory music-making that found its expression in the homophonic chorale, or congregational hymn, which had the added benefit that it could be easily performed for domestic worship. As well as Michael Praetorius, the most important exponents of the style before J.S. Bach were Johannes Crüger (1598–1662), whose works most often set the texts of Paul Gerhardt

Handel's *Messiah* frontispiece

Since the first performance of Handel's *Messiah* in Dublin in 1742 it has become one of his most famous works, along with the orchestral suites *Water Music* (1717) and *Music for the Royal Fireworks* (1748), dominating the repertory of English choral societies. Such is its unassailable position that two notable scholars have written that, "its popularity is probably the greatest single obstacle to the revival of Handel's oratorios today." This can be ascribed in part to the power of the large choruses that pepper the work, and also to a cult-like worship of the composer that grew up after his death, persisting into the 19th century. There is, however, no evidence to support the anecdote that the tradition of standing during the chorus *Hallelujah* was first started by King George II who rose to his feet during one if its first performances.

(1607–76), Johann Schein (1586–1630) and Samuel Scheidt (1587–1654). The chorales were initially accompanied by organ with the later addition of larger instrumental forces, and these accompaniments and vocal settings began to show the influence of Italian concerto style where smaller groups, often more virtuosic, are pitted against a larger ensemble. The surviving works of Praetorius, aside from a set of instrumental dances *Terpsichore* (1612), are almost all sacred and comprise an astonishing collection and development of the chorale form. His inclusion of earlier techniques akin to those employed by the madrigalists, including polyphonic imitation, the treatment of the chorale theme as a type of *cantus firmus* from which all the other material derives and antiphony lays the ground for later developments in the Protestant cantata.

The chorale was almost completely shunned, however, by Heinrich Schütz who having trained in Italy was at home in both *stile antico* and the *concertato stile moderno*, often juxtaposing them to great dramatic effect. Working in the German-language Protestant tradition, he brought to his large-scale settings the discipline of the contrapuntal *stile antico* as well as richly decorated solo vocal lines but set within far more complex orchestral settings than were the norm in Italy. This was achieved without obscuring the harmonic flow of the work, and this perfect marrying of counterpoint with harmonic progression was the hallmark of his style; one that was to profoundly influence the music of J.S. Bach who claimed that all harmony was the outcome of counterpoint. These developments were taken up by Dieterich Buxtehude (1637–1707), another composer who greatly influenced Bach, and Johann Pachelbel (1653–1706) who marrying them with the chorale types explored by Praetorius formed the first true Protestant church cantatas. Schütz was also important in bringing to fruition the German oratorio which, growing in part out of the tradition of Passion chants punctuated by polyphonic choruses, tended to be more austere in style to its Italian equivalent, including chorales and a less florid and operatic approach to solo vocal writing.

This austerity was not so evident in later opera-Passions, a much more Italianate form of the oratorio that flourished in Hamburg—a great operatic center—and set poetic versions of the Biblical story rather than the Gospel texts. Telemann was prolific in producing these, as was Handel for whom it was an important grounding for his later English oratorios. On his move to England in 1712 Handel was keen to establish an English choral tradition within the oratorio which was to present a tightly constructed story, for the praise of God, while presenting the dramatic action and characterization as much through the music as the text. These were to take place within public concerts and his first work for this context was *Esther* (1732). Numerous works followed in the same vein, including a *sinfonia* or overture, choruses, *recitatives* and solo *arias*, such as *Saul* (1738–9), *Israel in Egypt* (1739) and *Jeptha* (1752), but perhaps reaching the apotheosis of popularity with the first performance of *Messiah* in Dublin during 1742. Having in the later part of his life abandoned opera, he could turn all the experience of working in dramatic forms to the musical characterization of the oratorios, and was lucky in having a middle-class audience with a suspicion of opera as somehow decadent but nonetheless craving dramatic musical entertainment that could be sated by the respectability of the ostensibly religious oratorio.

INSTRUMENTAL MUSIC

The arrival of the Baroque sees for the first time the emergence of a truly independent instrumental repertory, one that did not have its roots in vocal practice. Due in part to the development of a strongly tonal basis for musical organization, and so not dependent on a text for its structure, the

establishing of a purely instrumental tradition was to have a considerable impact on the music of the next three-and-a-half centuries. The new instrumental repertories were to take their cues from three sources—collections of music for dance, which became the suite; earlier instrumental works, especially that for the virginal by English and Italian composers; and monody with a *continuo* accompaniment. The task of creating a purely instrumental form not based on vocal models was first taken on by the Italian keyboard composer Girolamo Frescobaldi (1583–1643). Largely active in Rome, Frescobaldi spans the divide between the Renaissance and Baroque in his music, from his early training in polyphony and madrigals to his later works based on functional harmonies and key. His music is characterized by sudden changes of tempo, long and highly ornate cadential passages and the manipulation of parcels of melodic material through counterpoint and variation, the overall unity of a piece coming from an initial musical idea that is developed, or from structures such as a ground bass, and musical variety coming through the violent juxtapositions. This juxtaposition of tempo changes and variations of themes was taken up by Italian

composers such as Biagio Marini (1594–1663) and Giovanni Fontana (?1589–?1630) who adopted the monodic form of a solo line or duet supported by *continuo* in pieces with several distinct sections, often based on counterpoint, dance rhythms or a variation form such as the ground bass; often these were arrangements of vocal pieces and were known as *canzonas*. These grouped pieces also became known variously as sonatas or *sinfonia*, generally either solo sonatas for instruments such as the violin, which were virtuosic, or after the works of Salamone Rossi (1570–1630), the trio sonata for two violins and continuo. The continuo was provided by an instrument such as the harpsichord and generally supported by a cello or viol in the bass. In time the forces used for the performances expanded and the movements of the sonatas began to settle into accepted patterns.

Of great importance to the development of the sonata was a group of composers around the northern Italian city of Bologna, many of them taught by the *maestro di cappella* at San Petronio, Maurizio Cazzati (1616–78). Cazzati only left a small number of instrumental works but they began to codify elements of the Bolognese sonata, writing a body of works for trumpet and strings, in idiomatic styles, that moves toward the solo concerto and adopts a strong sense of functional harmony. It was around this time that a distinction began to be made, especially by Cazzati's pupil Giovanni Vitali (1632–92), between different types of trio sonata, the so-called *sonata da chiesa* and the *sonata da camera*. The former being contrapuntal in style and generally in four sections arranged in a slow–quick–slow–quick pattern, the latter being essentially a set of three or four dance movements suitable for either entertainment or for performance in a domestic setting. The distinction was not always clearly made between the two differing types and by

Thomas Arne, by W. Humphrey

Following on from Purcell, Thomas Arne (1710–78) was, along with Handel, the most important composer in England during the first half of the 18th century. He was particularly noted for his Italianate works for stage, although few of his manuscripts survive, and his orchestration was acclaimed for its invention and innovation, being the first English composer to include clarinets in the orchestra.

Bach's *St John Passion* score, harpsichord part in Bach's handwriting

J.S. Bach's choral works, cantatas and passions (works recounting the passion of Christ according to the New Testament), composed in Leipzig, are some of the most important of the Baroque. In the Leipzig order of service the cantata would follow the gospel reading and precede the Creed and sermon, and in general the cantata would last around 30 minutes and be scored for some 18 singers and an equal number of instrumentalists; the church organist would often perform the continuo part. In addition there were the large-scale oratorios and passions, such as Bach's *St John Passion* (1724) and *St Mathew Passion* (1727), that took the same part in the service as the cantatas but were scored for much greater forces and were considerably longer. His passions are notable for the great number of their chorales, which are interspersed liberally between the narrations, choruses and *arias* that set the gospel texts.

Arcangelo Corelli, holding score by John Smith after H. Howard

As well as being a composer, Corelli was a famous violinist. He exercised firm discipline over his students and musicians, being one of the first players to insist that all bowing should follow in the same direction (an instruction that players today take from their section leaders). He is almost as important for the legacy he left through his violin students who spread his methods across Europe, as for his works. His involvement in instrumental technique comes through in his compositions and he was the first composer to achieve fame through sole concentration on instrumental works.

Domenico Scarlatti

A similar position to that of Couperin in France can be ascribed in Italy to Domenico Scarlatti (1685–1757), son of Alessandro, even though he spent much of his working life in Portugal and at the Spanish court. A virtuoso harpsichordist, many of his works are for keyboard, comprising single movement sonatas (although there is evidence that many of them were meant to be paired), these were also, later, labeled *Essercizi* ("exercises") which gives a clue to their style. Often of astonishing virtuosity, the vast majority are either labeled *allegro* or *presto* and the fast tempo aids what is perhaps Scarlatti's overriding feature, the condensing of contrapuntal ideas through figuration into essentially a harmonic structure.

around 1700 they had to all intents and purposes merged. It was a composer based in nearby Ferrara and Venice, Giovanni Legrenzi (1626–90), who finally codified the style that was to be taken up by composers of the early 18th century. In his sonatas for up to six musicians, he wrote fluid idiomatic string parts over well conceived tonal structures that gave shape to the form, and, especially in his fugal writing, counterpoint that was dependent on its harmonic function.

The fugue, one of the most important contrapuntal devices of the Baroque, provides a means of overlaying thematic material by introducing a basic subject in each successive voice, alternating tonic and dominant entries (known as the subject and answer). Especially associated with German organ and harpsichord composers, particularly those who followed Jan Sweelinck (1562–1621) who occupies a similar position in German music to that held by Frescobaldi in Italy. Sweelinck taught Heinrich Scheidemann (1595–1663) who established the major forms of organ chorale, essentially a solo line akin to vocal compositions over *continuo*, and the chorale fantasia, a large-scale contrapuntal working out of a chorale melody. A slightly different lineage came from the composer Heinrich Schütz, who trained Matthias Weckman (?1616–74). Both Scheidemann and Weckmann influenced later German composers such as Bach, and Weckmann's compositions reflect Schütz's interest in Italian polyphony, especially in his chorale variations for organ. Weckmann also wrote a number of impressive freely-composed toccatas, works designed to show off technique with many ornaments and rhetorical flourishes.

The link between the Italian, French and German traditions was made in the works of Johann Froberger (1616–67). Born in Stuttgart, he trained with Frescobaldi in Italy and became the court organist in Vienna. His travels also took him to France and England, and the exposure to differing musical practices may account for his highly personal, and influential, syncretic style that included numerous programmatic pieces such as the *Allemande, faite en passant le Rhin dans une barque en grand péril* (n.d.). Influencing German composers such as

Weckmann and the later Buxtehude, and the wide-ranging keyboard styles of Bach and Handel, he also had a great effect on the music of his French contemporary Louis Couperin (1626–61), uncle of the later François Couperin. Froberger is known as one of the first composers of keyboard suites, a collection of works based on dance rhythms. These usually include an *allemande* in duple time that acts as an "introduction" to the suite in general; *courante* in triple time and either fast, in an Italian suite, or slow and stately in the French version; *sarabande* again in triple time and with a fast and slow version; and *gigue*, a fast lively movement often in duple compound time.

In Italy the developments in the sonata of the Bologna school were being taken up by a new generation of composers, in particular Arcangelo Corelli (1653–1713). While influential through his trio sonatas, his op.6 collection of 12 works (published 1714) in particular remains the exemplar of the *concerto grosso*, although it is possible that the *concerti* of Guiseppe Torelli (1658–1709) slightly predate these. The *concerto grosso* was one of the most important large-scale orchestral form of the late Baroque, finding its ultimate expression in the Brandenburg concertos of J.S. Bach. In these later works the concept had been expanded to include a wider instrumentation but the earlier version consisted of two bodies of string players, supported by a *continuo* generally on harpsichord, these two groups were divided into soloists, the *concertino* (usually two violins and a cello), and a larger body of musicians, the *ripieno*. During the performance the music passes back and forth between these two groups, in a similar fashion to the solo concerto, the most popular instrumental form of the late Baroque, where a single instrument, such as a trumpet, violin or flute, was pitted against a larger body of string players.

The general pattern of movements in both types of concerto was fast–slow–fast, adopted wholesale after the innovative *concerti* of the Venetian Tomaso Albinoni (1671–1750/1). The Venetian master of the form, however, was Antonio Vivaldi (1678–1741). Vivaldi was responsible for the refining of the *ritornello* form, by which large-scale structures could be maintained. In this the *ritornello* is the central musical idea that acts as a refrain, played at significant points during the movement to reinforce the tonality reached at that point after having established the tonic at the beginning. Between these *ritornelli,* the solo instrument, or group, plays contrasting music that often carries the modulations that occur throughout the movement. Vivaldi was also adept at bringing in programmatic elements to the music, by this time a technique highly developed by opera composers, as in, for example, his *Le quattro stagioni*. Vivaldi's innovations were not only taken up by fellow Italian composers, in particular Pietro Locatelli (1695–1764) and Giuseppe Tartini (1692–1770), but had an effect on musicians across Europe. This was especially true of Germany, where *concerti* of the prolific and endlessly inventive Georg Telemann clearly displayed Vivaldian elements, as well as influencing the works of J.S. Bach and Handel.

Composers writing for keyboard adopted a good many of the formal devices of the concerto and this is seen to good effect in the works of François Couperin (1668–1733). The most important French composer between Lully and Rameau, his early training as an organist gave him a strong sense of line and counterpoint, while his admiration of Italian music led him to adopt many of its formal principles. Although Couperin wrote fine sacred and secular vocal works and pieces for the organ, it is his works for harpsichord and chamber music, including the first French trio sonatas, that are most important. His early keyboard works consolidate the French dance suite, though later works considerably reduce the reliance on dance forms, and his adoption of other formal schemes, such as the AB binary form, *chaconne* (ground bass or *passacaglia*) and the *rondeau* (similar to the *ritornello* of Italian music) is of considerable importance to the genre. Couperin's trio sonatas are among the first to import into French music the four-movement pattern and contrapuntal style of the works of Corelli, although, as in his keyboard music, the melodic treatment is unmistakably French with intense ornamentation and a widespread use of dotted rhythms. Toward the end of his life he composed an extraordinary set of pieces that consolidate many of these elements into works for continuo and solo viol, which bear

much in common with the music of the virtuoso viol player Marin Marais (1656–1728).

If France was to follow, to a certain extent, Italian patterns in its keyboard music, the concerns of composers in Germany were a little different. (Austrian composers tended to follow Italian models.) Although J.S. Bach and Handel drew on a range of eclectic sources in their ensemble music, particularly that of the Italians, Bach's keyboard works in particular take much from a specifically German preoccupation with counterpoint. With both a strong tradition of polyphony and organ performance, the keyboard became the instrument on which counterpoint was most strongly explored. The two most important figures for this before Bach, on whom they had a strong influence, were Johann

Marin Marais playing the viol,
by André Bouys; Musée de l'Opéra de Paris, France

The viol is a bowed stringed instrument which, depending on the size, is either played balanced on the knee or held between the legs. It differs from the cello that replaced it by having a greater number of strings and a fretted fingerboard. Very popular during the Renaissance and Baroque eras, it had ceased to be written for by around 1750 with Marais being one its last great champions.

Pachelbel and Dieterich Buxtehude. Both men were famous organists and both showed a predilection for polyphonic writing and for improvisatory structures and melodic development that stemmed from the expectation that north German organists would be able to improvise preludes to sections of the liturgy. As well as fugues, both composers used ground bass patterns as structures, for their long contrapuntal workings-out of a theme and its variations.

Johann Sebastian Bach

Johann Sebastian Bach (1685–1750)

Johann Sebastian Bach (1685–1750) was the most outstanding German musician and composer of the late Baroque. Not necessarily as innovative as earlier figures of the period, he nonetheless towers above almost all his contemporaries in his ability to draw together and achieve a synthesis of many different styles—although not opera—and techniques and to then forge a musical language and identity that was to remain influential for well over a century and a half. Known chiefly as a keyboard virtuoso during his lifetime, his compositions excel in their handling of all aspects of technique, from melody to harmony to counterpoint. Coming at the end of a long period of musical change, Bach's music sums up the Baroque aesthetic through a logical and elegant musical language that has remained the basis of all subsequent tonal harmony.

Leipzig at the time of Bach, 1725

Born into a family of musicians in Eisenach, central Germany, Bach was brought up as a Lutheran, a religious identity that was to color most of his work, and one that goes some way toward explaining why he did not write for the operatic stage. It is thought his earliest music education came from his father, a string player, and then from his elder brother, Johann Christoph, an organist in Ohrdruf. In 1700 he was sent to study in the Michaelisschule in Lüneburg where he sang in the Mettenchor until his voice broke. While at the school he made a number of trips to Hamburg to see the famous organist at the St Katharinen church, J.A. Reincken

(?1623–1722). Reincken, a pupil of Sweelinck, made a great impression on the young Bach and both his playing and compositions seem to have influenced him greatly. Aside from its proximity to Hamburg, Lüneburg also had the advantage of a fine orchestra belonging to the local duke.

It is thought Bach left Lüneburg in 1702 and in 1703 he was employed briefly as a musician at the court of Weimar before taking up the position of organist at the Neue Kirche in Arnstadt the same year. His duties at the church were light, and hence he could dedicate himself to composition, but even so he was not happy in the post, famously taking leave in 1705 to travel to Lübeck to hear Buxtehude play (although the dates make it unlikely that this actually happened). In any event, on his return in 1706 he fell out with the church authorities and began to look for other work. In 1707 he gained a new position as organist at St Blasius in Mühlhausen where he received a larger salary, thus enabling him to marry Maria Barbara, his first wife, and where his music, especially his cantatas, were well received. By 1708 he had not only gained a following of students, but had attracted the attention of the Duke of Weimar who was eager to employ Bach.

With a prestigious position and a larger salary, Bach remained at the court for nine years, becoming the Konzertmeister as well as organist in 1714. Here he wrote most of his organ works as well as, toward the end of his time, a good number of cantatas. However, squabbles in the ruling family of the court began to make Bach's life difficult and when he was offered the post of Kapellmeister at Köthen (a promotion) he asked for permission to leave. The duke was unwilling to let him go and it was not until the end of 1717 that Bach was finally dismissed. Duke Leopold of Köthen was a much more suitable patron for Bach, being both a keen musician and having a Lutheran mother and Calvinist father. Bach was at Köthen until 1723, and during this short but extraordinarily productive period he wrote cantatas, the Brandenburg Concertos (1721), his unaccompanied sonatas and partitas for violin and the solo cello suites (both 1720), as well as book 1 of *Das wohltemperirte Clavier* (the "48", 1722; book 2 followed much later in around 1740) and the Anna Magdalena *Clavierbüchlein* (1722–5). Anna Magdalena was his second wife, a court singer or musician whom he married in 1722, Maria Barbara having died in 1720.

Das wohltemperirte Clavier is one of J.S. Bach's most important works, a series of keyboard freely-composed preludes with a partnering fugue (in strict counterpoint) in each of the major and minor keys. It was, and remains, the greatest example of a systematic exploration of the entire tempered diatonic system whereby modulation to any key is possible without encountering problems of intonation. This was the supreme demonstration of the advantages of equal temperament. A number of systems were developed by the early-18th century whereby each of the 12 semitones of the octave were equally, or almost equally, spaced. Previous tuning systems had unequal spacing to provide a more perfect tuning, based on the 4th and 5th, in relation to the tonic (generally held to be C, and so the predominance of works in C or closely related keys such as a G, D and F major and A minor). The trouble with this being that as modulation occurred to ever more remote keys the distribution of the unequally spaced pitches bore no relation to the new tonic and made these distant tonalities sound out of tune.

Bach's move to Leipzig in 1723, the city in which he was to spend the rest of his life, was not a promotion and his willingness in accepting the post was due in part to troubles at the Köthen court. Ideally the city authorities wanted a general teacher, one who could teach Latin as well as music, but in the end they compromised and grudgingly took on Bach (the post had initially been offered to Telemann but he had opted to stay in Hamburg). The actual position was of Kantor at the Thomasschule, a very prestigious post, controlling the music for the four most important churches in the city as well as teaching at the school. Once established in Leipzig Bach set about composing one of his greatest series of works, five different sets of cantatas for the entire year (each set consisting of around 60 cantatas). It had been customary for the Kantor to perform a cantata for each different gospel reading for the appropriate day in the church calendar but Bach's volume of work was exceptional.

In 1729 Bach also became director of the Leipzig collegium musicum, a voluntary orchestral group of students and professional musicians of a high standard. Under Bach's direction they gave a series of weekly concerts, giving him, after a period of concentrating on sacred works, the chance to once more concentrate on the instrumental repertory. Bach, however, did not neglect the sacred, and the dedication of the first sections of his monumental *Mass in B minor* in 1733 to the elector of Saxony in Dresden was made with the hope of gaining a court position, a move that eventually paid off in 1736 when he was granted the title of Hofkomponist. The Mass, intriguingly thought to be for the new Catholic church in Leipzig, was not complete until 1748–9, and is perhaps his greatest scared work and a fitting conclusion to his liturgical writings.

During the 1740s Bach traveled widely in Germany, including making a trip to one his many children, Carl Philipp Emanuel in Berlin, and one to Dresden in 1741 where it is possible he composed, or received the commission for, the *"Goldberg" Variations* for keyboard. In technical virtuosity these surpass any of his other keyboard works and show the unmistakable influence of Domenico Scarlatti. The crowning glory of Bach's travels was undoubtedly his trip to the court of Frederick the Great in Potsdam in 1747 where his virtuosic improvisations on the harpsichord on a theme supplied by the king himself met with great applause. On his return to Leipzig he worked the theme into his *Musikalisches Opfer* ("musical offering") which included keyboard works, a trio sonata and instrumental canons. One of the last of his works to appear was *Die Kunst der Fuge* ("the art of fugue", 1749) a didactic contrapuntal work for keyboard. By now he was in poor health with deteriorating eyesight and after a period of suffering he died on July 28, 1750 and was buried in the graveyard of the Johanneskirche in Leipzig.

Das wohltemperirte Clavier score page, Book One, C Minor with 3 voices, first page of 2nd fugue

CLASSICISM

SIMPLIFICATION OF MUSIC (1750–1800)

The years between 1750 and 1800 are most often described as the Classical period, a confusing label as a classical influence had been predominant since the early Renaissance. It is not only the label that is problematic, much of the music itself can be seen as either an extension of Baroque practice or as a form of proto-Romanticism. There are even greater problems in identifying (following the scheme of art history) an intermediate Rococo period, a term now rejected by most musical scholars, although 18th century French works that display a Classical lightness of style are sometimes referred to, using a contemporary description, as *galant*. In general, however, musicologists tend to discuss an emerging proto-Classicism or the sentimentality of *Empfindsamkeit* when dealing with earlier works of the style. There is a further difficulty in ascribing these 50 years a clearly identifiable pan-European musical movement as many of the major developments of the time were concentrated to a narrow geographical area. Given these observations, it is perhaps better to consider the period as one of transition with rapid change and development, during which the musical innovations were largely confined to the court of the Elector Palatine at Mannheim, through the works of musicians such as Stamitz, and through composers working in and around the Habsburg imperial capital Vienna. The composers who exemplify what is thought of as the Classical era are those of the so-called *Wiener Klassik*; Viennese classicism as seen in the works of Christoph Willibald von Gluck (1714–87), Joseph Haydn (1732–1809), Wolfgang Amadeus Mozart (1756–91) and Ludwig van Beethoven (1770–1827).

In general the period sees musical dominance move from Italy in the south to the German-speaking world north of the Alps, where it remained for much of the next century-and-a-half. This was coupled with a gradual change in the sources of patronage for composers, and by the first decades of the 19th century the system that had predominated throughout the Renaissance and Baroque, whereby composers were retained by either the church or court, had by and large disappeared in favor of a dependence on wider public performance for income; the already sizable audiences for public concerts, principally of works by Handel, in London during the late Baroque can be seen as a precursor of this trend. By the second half of the 18th century the move toward making melody a functional component of harmony had been fully realized, with melody of the Classical period largely comprising straightforward scales and arpeggios with unmistakable harmonic implications. Under the influence of operatic writing, phrase length and structure also underwent a change: phrases became longer, and so the underlying harmonic rhythm became slower with the meter marked in the bass rather than by strong accents in the melodic line. It has been pointed out that Baroque ornamentation was to please either the performer or a small group of listeners; once the performance becomes public, ornamentation is a hindrance to a wider comprehension of the music. This may account for the simplification of melodic lines and, with the additional homophonic conception of music that tends to fall into eight-bar antecedent and consequent phrases, underlies much of the Classical aesthetic. By the end of the

The Classical orchestra

It was with developments in instrument design and technique that the Classical orchestra developed in this period, comprising string instruments played even today: violins, viola, cello and double bass.

1759: British Museum opens to public.

1761: Haydn begins working for the Esterházy family.

1762: The first performance of Gluck's *Orfeo ed Eurydice*.

1765: Joseph II becomes Habsburg Emperor and begins a series of social and political reforms.

1781: Mozart moves to Vienna.

1789: The French Revolution begins with the storming of the Bastille.

1790: Joseph II dies and is succeeded first by Leopold II and then the more authoritarian Franz II.

1791: The death of Mozart.

1798: Haydn's *Die Schöpfung* is first performed.

1799–1814: The rule of Napoleon Bonaparte in France.

1803: Beethoven's Third "Eroica" Symphony is first performed.

1809: The death of Haydn.

1815: The Napoleonic Wars end with the Treaty of Vienna.

1827: The death of Beethoven.

King Frederick is playing the flute (by Adolph von Menzel, 1852)

18th century, instrumental music had assumed its central position in the European canon and new forms too emerged that were to remain dominant until the present day: the symphony, string quartet and piano sonata.

During the first half of the 18th century Europe began to undergo profound philosophical and political change. This was due in part to the growth of an educated and moneyed middle class who were demanding a greater say in the running of their lives as well as a growing suspicion of the part played by the church, particularly the Catholic church in central and southern Europe, in the governance of the state. The ideas of the Enlightenment (*Aufklärung* in German) were gaining support and movements in literature, especially in northern Europe, proving influential beyond the sphere of writers. Following the writings by Descartes and *Encyclopédistes*, such as Diderot in France as well as Locke and Hume in Britain and Kant in Germany, artists, writers and musicians were inspired by the call to dispel superstition and embrace a rational view of the universe. Rationalism found a corollary in the desire for social reform, and this was aided by the accession to important European thrones of relatively enlightened rulers such as Catherine the Great in Russia, Frederick II of Prussia and, especially, Joseph II of Austria. In France, where the call for reform went largely unheeded, the Enlightenment found its ultimate expression in the series of revolutions that began in 1789.

The call for rationality was not necessarily anti-emotional and, seeking to incorporate the apparently anti-rational ideas of Jean-Jacques Rousseau of the mid-century within the Enlightenment aesthetic, it was argued that sentiment and emotion were heightened by rational thought and so were interdependent rather than independent spheres of human activity. (This complimentary duality of reason and emotion was to remain influential in France long after the end of the 18th century.) The arts did not, however, escape a certain degree of anti-rationalism, particularly during the mid-century when the movements of musical *Empfindsamkeit* ("sentiment") and literary *Sturm und Drang* ("storm and stress") sought to heighten an emotional response, in the former by a concentration on the human elements of a story, in the latter through the invocation of terror, awe and, in a nod to Rousseau, savagery. If this appeal to pure emotion did not last, at least in music, much beyond 1770, the work of *Sturm und Drang* writers such as Goethe and the anti-rational aesthetic was influential on the emergence of Romanticism at the beginning of the 19th century.

THE ORCHESTRA AND PIANO

Many of the changes in composition that occurred between the Baroque and Classical eras were helped by developments in instrumental playing, and the evolution of the Classical orchestra had much to do with innovations in instrument design and technique. By 1750 the main string body was well established, generally consisting of divided violins, viola, cello and double bass, while earlier instruments such as the viol had largely died out. The greatest innovations, however, came in the scoring for wind and brass instruments. Flutes gained movable head joints, facilitating tuning, and keys that took the pitch down to middle C, oboes had narrower bore, facilitating a softer tone in the

Schiller and Goethe, memorial in front of National Theater, Weimar, Thuringia, Germany

The influence of poets such as Goethe and Schiller on composers of the time is perhaps most famously seen in Beethoven's Ninth Symphony, "the Choral". In this the scale and sense of striving of his earlier "Eroica" (the Third) are augmented by a choral setting of Schiller's *An die Freude* that forms the last movement, a masterly dramatic touch and revolutionary addition to the form that would be taken up much later by composers such as Gustav Mahler.

upper register, and more reliable tuning, while the clarinet began to enter the orchestra around the mid-century in the works of Rameau and, famously, Mozart, who wrote a concerto for the instrument. All of these instruments were helped by a greater use of keys rather than finger holes which made tuning and fast passages a lot easier, and this development was particularly welcome on the bassoon helping to extend its range greatly. Pairs of trumpets and horns became standard additions to the orchestra and the potential for the horn was extended with the invention of hand-stopping (inserting the hand into the bell of the instrument to modify the pitch). From around 1750, the orchestra tended to grow, earlier scorings varied greatly, sometimes only including a pair of oboes and horns, but by the end of the 18th century a standard layout was emerging of double woodwind (two of each instrument), two trumpets, four horns, timpani and strings. A further addition was made later by both Mozart (in his liturgical works and *Die Zauberflöte*) and Beethoven (in Symphony 5) of three trombones, an alto, tenor and bass.

The late 18th century saw the demise of the harpsichord in favor of the piano. Instead of plucking the strings with a quill, the piano used rebounding hammers to strike the strings with a subtler attack, more uniform sound and greater range of dynamics; the rebound of the hammers also ensured the note could be sustained. The first instrument is thought to have been made by the Florentine Bartolomeo Cristofori around 1700, although it was not until the mid-century when it caught the attention of makers in Austria and Germany that it began its ascendancy. The instrument was favored by Mozart among others—J.C. Bach is credited with introducing the piano to London—and it soon began to acquire a large repertory with many 18th century musicians

MOZART, AGÉ DE DOUZE ANS
Dirigeant l'exécution d'une messe qu'il avait composée

composing piano concertos and sonatas, brought to the height of their potential by Beethoven whose monumental works ensured the instrument's central place in the repertory of the 19th century. By 1800 the piano, suitable for solo as well as chamber performance, was well on the way to becoming the most common domestic instrument, a role that it fulfilled for all of the 19th and most of the 20th century.

THE SYMPHONY AND SONATA

If there was one development that truly distinguished the period between 1750 and 1800 from the Baroque, and one that transformed composers' conceptions of large-scale works well

into the 20th century, it was the emergence of sonata form. This system of musical organization depends upon the juxtaposition of two main blocks of music of contrasting material and key that are "developed" and then restated at the end in a way that reinforces the tonic. The first section of a sonata form movement is the exposition—sometimes preceded by a slow introduction—in which the first subject group (of one or more ideas, the most of important of which is called the first subject) in the tonic key is set against the contrasting second subject group in a different key, most usually the dominant. The development section follows in which the musical ideas of the exposition are explored and taken through a series of more distant modulations, before returning to the material of the exposition for the recapitulation. This brings the music back to both the first subject group and the tonic, and the restatement of the second subject group is this time also in the tonic. The piece either ends with a tonic cadence at the end of the exposition material or a short coda, also in the tonic.

This form was almost always used for the first movement of a symphony, concerto, string quartet or piano sonata (and hence the other, if misleading, name of "first movement form"), and often for other movements as well. Sonata form gave rise to the sense of a large-scale work being "in" a particular key (for instance Mozart's Symphony in G minor K 550) and the overwhelming importance of the tonic (the process could be seen as a statement of the tonic from which the music sets off to different tonal centers and to which the music returns at the end). Although movements of the Baroque tended to revolve around a single musical idea or affection, the origins of sonata form lie in a number of Baroque forms, especially the AB binary form common in dance suite movements with its two contrasting sections. The idea of a return to the initial material stems from the *da capo aria* (ABA form) and the opera overture, the latter being particularly important as a forerunner of the symphony. The contrasts that were made between first and second subject groups, as well as between the exposition, development and recapitulation enabled composers to hold the audience's attention for a much longer span within a single movement than had previously been possible. It was in the symphony that sonata form first emerged, although it was not finally codified until the early works of Haydn, the earliest examples of symphonic first movements being more a variant of returning binary form with its simpler ABA structure.

The symphony grew out of a number of sources, including trio sonatas, the *concerto ripieno* of Torelli and Vivaldi (essentially a *concerto grosso* without a soloist) and the Italian opera *sinfonia*

Grand piano forte, Repository of Fine Arts; July 1826; illustration, hand colored Ackerman

The rise of the popularity of the piano as both an instrument for public recital and domestic use prompted composers to produce more works for it. In part this led to an explosion in the writing of keyboard sonatas, notable examples of which were composed by Haydn, Mozart and Beethoven.

as developed by Alessandro Scarlatti, with its tripartite fast–slow–fast structure. At first the name itself, *sinfonia*, was only one of many applied to a broadly similar group of works, including sonata, *pastorale*, overture, concerto, divertimento and serenade, and the clear identification of the symphony as a distinct genre only become possible toward the mid-18th century. While the symphony emerged as a distinct form, many of these other terms continued to be used, in particular the divertimento, serenade and *notturno*, to denote multi-movement solo or chamber works that were frequently performed as table music (music played at banquets) or outdoors. Owing something to the dance suite and the sonata, the individual movements were often in a type of binary form and the instrumentation varied from a solo keyboard to, particularly in works by Haydn and Mozart, a chamber orchestra, although the orchestration was sometimes tailored to the circumstances of the performance. While the function of works such as the divertimento was to provide background music, the compositional skill and inventiveness on display places them alongside the symphony, solo sonata and concerto as one of the exemplars of the Classical instrumental style.

The emergence of the symphonic form was gradual, and it is impossible to say with certainty exactly when the overture became the symphony. However, some of the earliest examples of three-movement symphonies are found in the works of the composers Giovanni Sammartini (1700/1–75) and Antonio Brioschi (*fl. c.* 1725–50). Given that during the first half of the 18th century Italian opera was the dominant dramatic force in European music, it is unsurprising that it was in Italy that the *sinfonia* first made its move from the opera house to the concert hall, with considerable crossover between the music of the

sinfonia and the fledgling symphony. Similar to its role in opening the drama, once the move had been made to the domestic or wider public sphere the instrumental symphony seemed to have initially been an introductory piece within public and private concerts, where the focus was often on a solo vocal or instrumental work, before taking a more prominent role in programming later in the century. Both Sammartini and Brioschi were active in and around Milan in northern Italy and are thought to have been composing three-movement symphonies from the mid-1720s onward. Their early work still shows the characteristics of Baroque style in the melodic writing, although, as was current with much Italian operatic writing,

the music is largely homophonic, and by the 1730s both composers were writing in an identifiably Classical idiom.

There were later composers from Italy who produced symphonic works, notably Luigi

Sammartini

Giovanni Battista Sammartini (1700/1–75) was born in Milan, the city in which he spent all his life, and worked as *maestro di cappella* at the church of San Ambrogio. As well as producing liturgical works and symphonies, he wrote a number of operas, including *Memet* (1732) and *L'Agrippina* (1743) that were to have an influence on Gluck.

Stamitz, Czechoslovakian stamp

Born in Německý Brod in Bohemia, Stamitz's first musical education came from his father, although he studied at the University of Prague during 1734–5. It is thought that he was given an appointment at Mannheim in 1741 and before long he had become one of the most highly awarded violinists at the court. Once he had been granted full control over the instrumental music at the Mannheim court, he produced a string of influential works for orchestra. Aside from a successful trip to Paris in 1754–5, he spent the rest of his life at the German court, dying there at the young age of 39.

J.C. Bach, portrait in London, by Thomas Gainsborough; 1776

J.C. Bach, while coming from a strongly Lutheran family, was more attracted by the Italian tradition, going to study in Italy and converting to Catholicism there. His earlier works show the influence of his brother Carl Philipp with whom he trained, but on moving to Italy he embraced the Italian operatic style. Bach moved to London in 1762 where he continued to produce operas but also became active in other fields, including the symphony. His symphonic works are especially noted for their strongly contrasting first and second subjects and rich orchestration, best exemplified in his op.18 works of 1781. Perhaps Bach's most lasting contribution to music was the influence he had on Mozart when the family visited London in 1764–65.

Boccherini (1743–1805) who spent much of his working life in Spain, and Neapolitan opera composers who contributed greatly to the development of orchestral writing, including Giovanni Pergolesi (1710–36) who was largely responsible for the rise of *opera buffa*. However, it was north of the Alps, particularly in the Catholic courts of southern Germany and the Habsburg lands, that the symphony was to be adopted with particular enthusiasm. With the notable exception of the prolific Gottlob Harrer (1703–55) in Dresden, who was the first to use the designation *sinfonia* for his works, initially the Protestant north of Germany was slower to adopt the new form. It was at the regional Catholic court of Mannheim that the Bohemian composer Johann Stamitz (1717–57) was to further develop the symphony with the addition of an extra movement and through the sustained scoring of the wind and brass sections for harmonic support.

Innovations that are sometimes, wrongly, ascribed to the Mannheim composers, are the *crescendo* and *diminuendo*. These had, in fact, been in use for some time but their hairpin notation only came into use during the 18th century and it was the fine musicianship of the Mannheim performers that brought to the fore such expressive potential. Stamitz was the driving force behind the exceptional court orchestra of Mannheim, employing the best musicians he could

CESKOSLOVENSKO

60h

JAN·V·STAMIC·1717·1757

find to put together unquestionably the finest ensemble of its time. This, and Stamitz's own reputation, attracted other composers, many of whom played in the orchestra and wrote music that exploited the advanced instrumental technique of the Mannheim string and wind players. Chief among the composers was Stamitz himself and his surviving 58 symphonies are notable for the addition, after *c.* 1748, of a minuet and trio before the final *presto* or *prestissimo* movement. Up to this point the vast majority of symphonies followed the plan of a sonata form first movement, second slow movement and fast or *moderato* finale. After the innovations of Stamitz, the four-movement scheme became the standard symphonic form up until the early-20th century.

The pre-eminence of Catholic Mannheim and Vienna, discussed below, is perhaps due to their close links with Italy—regarded with more suspicion by the Protestant north—and in many ways the Classical idiom stems as much from the lyricism and homophony of Italian opera as from any home-grown innovation. However, Protestant Germany did not ignore the developments happening elsewhere and the works of two sons of J.S. Bach, Carl Philipp Emanuel (C.P.E. Bach, 1714–88) and Johann Christian (J.C. Bach, 1735–82), include a large output of symphonies. The symphonies of C.P.E. Bach, written for the court in Berlin and during the composer's later life in Hamburg, are hard to categorize, retaining elements of his father's Baroque style, particularly in motivic development, but with a Romantic sensibility that makes them some of the finest examples of musical *Empfindsamkeit*. This juxtaposition of Baroque counterpoint and variation with the storm and stress of rapid changes of dynamic, however, was highly individual and was less widely influential than the music of his brother.

The importance of Mannheim, London and even Italy during the latter 18th century pales next to that of Vienna. As a crossroad at the center of Europe and the capital of the immense Habsburg Empire, Vienna was one of the most cosmopolitan cities in Europe with a wide range of employment opportunities for musicians, not least the patronage of the court and the aristocracy who maintained palaces in the capital. As such, it attracted composers and performers from across Europe and gave them an environment in which to flourish. During the 18th century, Vienna was renowned as a center of opera (particularly Italian) and the influence of both Italian and French overtures can been seen on the early Viennese symphonists, such as Georg Wagenseil (1715–77), most of whose symphonic works are, following the overture model (he was a prolific opera composer), in three movements. Slightly later composers—especially the trio of Leopold Hofmann (1738–93), Carl von Dittersdorf (1739–99) and Johann Vanhal (1739–1814)—adopted the four-movement scheme of the Mannheim composers and wrote in a more clearly discernible Classical style. However, the two symphonists who defined and dominated Viennese classicism during the second half of the 18th century were Joseph Haydn and Wolfgang Amadeus Mozart.

Joseph Haydn

Haydn was born in Rohrau in Niederösterreich into a family of artisans and showed musical promise from an early age. He was educated as a choral scholar, first in Hainburg and then Vienna at the Stephansdom, after which he became a teacher and musician in the city. It was during this period (the early 1750s) that Haydn made the acquaintance of Metastasio and the Italian opera composer Nicola Porpora (1686–1768) from whom he took lessons. As he began to compose and receive some recognition for his works, especially the early string quartets and symphonies (of which he finally wrote 106), he attracted the attention of Prince Paul Anton of the Esterházy family. Haydn entered the employment of the family in 1761, first as Vice-Kapellmeister and then, from 1766, Kapellmeister, a role that he fulfilled until 1790. This move gave the composer access to a wide array of musicians and ensembles, from the court opera to the orchestra and chamber groups, and his workload to provide for them all must

have been exceptionally taxing. For his position of Kapellmeister he wrote symphonies, string quartets (of which he might fairly be considered the first great composer) and a wide range of concertos. In addition, particularly toward the end of his employment, Haydn produced a large number of operas, now rarely performed.

Aside from his oratorios such as *Die Schöpfung* (1798) and *Die Jahreszeiten* (1801) and his keyboard sonatas, the works for which Haydn is best remembered are his symphonies and string quartets that, in form, follow the symphonies but display wonderfully idiomatic writing. As well as refining the sonata principle into the ursatz scheme used by musicologists as a benchmark for the

Joseph Haydn, portrait at Rohrau in Niederösterreich (his birthplace)

As well as being a great composer in his own right, Haydn was friendly with, supported and taught a number of other important figures, including Mozart and Johann Albrechtsberger (1736–1809). The latter became Kapellmeister at the Stephansdom in Vienna and was, along with Haydn, one of the teachers of Beethoven.

form, Haydn was responsible for popularizing the quick sonata-rondo last movement (a scheme that continues to return to an original idea, ABACA etc.) and for the use of theme and variations in his slow movements. Perhaps even more importantly, he was a master at deriving more complex musical material from apparently simple phrases and motifs—foreshadowing Beethoven in this respect—and was daring in his use of key and modulation, composing in far flung tonalities such as f# minor, and modulating by thirds rather than the more common dominant or subdominant relationships.

Haydn was also inventive in his use of the orchestra, including challenging instrumental writing and in creating dramatic, often witty, musical effects, as in the "Surprise" Symphony (no. 94, 1791) with its loud and unexpected

Wolfgang Amadeus Mozart

One of the most famous composers of Western music history, Wolfgang Amadeus Mozart was born in Salzburg in 1756. Mozart was as successful in writing opera, symphonies and concertos as he was in producing string quartets, piano works and chamber music. The epitome of the Classical composer, he excelled consistently in his grasp of form, elegant melody and wide-ranging harmony; indeed the use of "classical" as applied to the works of Mozart and Haydn was initially as a sense of excellence, compared favorably to the works of antiquity. Like

Leopold Mozart with Wolfgang Amadeus and Nannerl, Austria; 1763; watercolor

Many of the courts of Europe were open to novelty and this was exploited by Leopold Mozart, Wolfgang Amadeus's father, who was keen to show off his children as exceptionally gifted young virtuosos. In 1762 the family visited both the court at Munich, where they played to Maximilian III, and Vienna, performing for Maria Theresia, to great acclaim. On their return to their home in Salzburg, a longer trip, of three-and-a-half years, was planned. This took them up through Germany and down to Paris, where they played for Louis XV, ending up in England where the children were received with great interest (reports of Wolfgang's ability to improvise glowed with praise, although the older Nannerl was acknowledged as a better player).

his great predecessor Bach, Mozart was eclectic in his influences—from Italian opera to German instrumental *concerti*—but succeeded in forging from them a consistent and individual style.

At the time of Wolfgang's birth, his father Leopold Mozart (1719–87) was already well known as a composer and violinist. Leopold took it upon himself to provide Wolfgang, and his sister Maria (better known as Nannerl), with a thorough education but one that inevitably concentrated on music. Wolfgang soon showed exceptional promise and, according to his father, had composed an *Andante* and *Allegro* (K 1a and b) by the time he was five. Not above exploiting the musical abilities of his children, Leopold soon had both Wolfgang and Nannerl playing the harpsichord and touring the courts of central Europe. The years up to 1772 were taken by almost constant travel, including long visits to Italy,

but throughout these years Wolfgang continued to compose. The exposure to different musics, and meetings with other composers, especially Johann Christian Bach, influenced his developing style. Notable works from this period include his first published pieces (sonatas for violin and keyboard, K 6–9), the *Singspiel Bastien und Bastienne* (?1768) and a number of symphonies (those up to K 112).

At the very end of 1771 the family returned to Salzburg, at the time an active musical center. However, the following year Hieronymous Colloredo became Archbishop (and so ruler) of Salzburg and set about reforming music-making in the city, the effect of which was to limit the opportunities for composition and performance, especially for German musicians who took second place to the highly regarded Italians. Even so, in 1772 Wolfgang was taken on as a Konzertmeister (violinist) by the court, for which he received a salary. During the next few years he did, as was expected, compose several Masses, but threw himself with greater enthusiasm into writing instrumental music, generally for private patrons. These works included string quartets, concertos for violin and keyboard as well as serenades and divertimenti, but he also achieved some success with an opera for the stage in Munich *La finta giardiniera* (1775). By 1777, however, life in Salzburg was beginning to pall and Wolfgang asked to be released from his duties at court. He then set out for the famous musical center of Mannheim, hoping, with no result, for an appointment at the court there. Although he wrote a number of works there, Leopold, back in Salzburg, was not happy with his son's progress and told him to leave for Paris. Paris seems not to have suited Wolfgang; he was forthright on his low opinion of French music, and he seems to have written little while in the French capital, although he did meet again with J.C. Bach who was visiting from London.

It was while in Paris that Wolfgang heard of his mother's death and, not long after, that a position was now available as court organist back in Salzburg. Arriving back in the city in 1779 he took up the new post, composing some fine liturgical music, including the "Coronation" Mass (K 317) during the same year. He did not, however, neglect instrumental composition and continued to produce works for private patrons in the city, including the symphonies 32–4 (K 318, 19 and 38) and the concerto for two pianos (K 365), that limited the time he spent on the post as organist which Wolfgang was finding increasingly irksome. His break with Salzburg, and Archbishop Colloredo with whom he had a difficult relationship, came after his first great operatic success *Idomeneo* (1781), again for the Munich stage. At this time the Archbishop was in Vienna and he ordered Mozart to join him, a command that the composer found demeaning. Although he did travel

to the city, his resentment grew until later the same year, following a row, he was literally kicked out of the Archbishop's service. Finding himself in an awkward position, he moved into the house of the Webers whom he had met in Mannheim. He married their daughter Constanze the following year.

The young composer made a great impact on musical society in the imperial capital and was soon in great demand as a performer on keyboard, on one occasion being asked by the emperor Joseph II to compete against the Italian keyboard player and composer Muzio Clementi (1752–1832). Around this time Mozart composed a number of works for keyboard, violin and piano sonatas as well as piano concertos, but his greatest triumph was the opera *Die Entführung aus dem Serail* (1782). The opera attracted the attention of Gluck, by this time pre-eminent in Vienna. The influence of the older composer was evident in the work—perhaps explaining the praise he lavished on it. After a trip to Salzburg to see his father in 1783, on the way back from which he wrote the "Linz" symphony (K 425) in the city of the same name, Mozart found himself at the center of musical life in Vienna. A string of compositions followed, some of his greatest works, including the piano concertos 14–19 (K 449–51, 53 and 56) and string quartets K 515–16, many of which were now being published and finding performances across Europe. However, the decision to open a new Italian opera house by Joseph II in 1782 was to lead to three of Mozart's greatest triumphs, his opera collaborations with the librettist Lorenzo da Ponte (1749–1838). The three comic operas they produced together—*Le nozze di Figaro* (1786), *Don Giovanni* (first performed in Prague in 1787 where he also wrote the "Prague" symphony K 504) and *Così fan tutte* (1790)—contain some of Mozart's finest music and demonstrate how much his style owes to the lyricism of Italian opera.

Leopold Mozart had died in 1787 and between this date and the completion of *Così fan tutte,* Wolfgang wrote comparatively little, though he supplemented his income from composing, performing and his published works with teaching at the court where had been appointed Kammermusicus. Joseph II was succeeded by Leopold II in 1791, and for the coronation in Prague Mozart produced another opera, this time the serious *La clemenza di Tito,* based on a text by Metastasio. However, it was in German that Mozart was to write his final opera for the impresario and actor Schikaneder in Vienna. This was *Die Zauberflöte*, a fairytale whose plot of enlightened knowledge triumphing over the darkness of ignorance betrays not only Mozart's Masonic allegiance but the currents of Enlightenment thought in general. It was first performed in 1791 and at the same time he was commissioned to write a requiem Mass—this was to remain unfinished by Mozart but it contains some of his most impressive choral and orchestral writing. By December of 1791 Mozart was seriously ill with rheumatic fever. He died on the 5th and was buried with a simple ceremony in Vienna's St Marxer Friedhof.

Michael Haydn

The younger brother of Joseph Haydn, Michael (1737–1806) was also a fine composer. After training in Vienna at the Stephansdom, he eventually ended up in Salzburg at the beginning of the 1760s, where he became court Konzertmeister to the Prince Archbishop, for whom he initally composed operas. When the more austere Count Colloredo was enthroned in 1772, he turned his attention to the liturgical works that comprise his finest compositions. He was for a time the teacher of Anton Diabelli (1781–1858) and Carl Maria von Weber.

Gluck's *Orfeo ed Eurydice*, Pauline Anna Milder-Hauptmann as Orpheus

The ancient Greek Orpheus myth has captured the imagination of a number of composers, including Monteverdi, Gluck, Stravinsky and, with his tongue firmly in his cheek, Offenbach. The myth follows the story of the musician and shepherd Orpheus who is grief-stricken at the death of his love Eurydice. He descends to the underworld to win her back, moving the gods through his musical skill. He is granted his wish on the proviso that he does not look back at Eurydice until they have left the underworld; this is thwarted by the Furies who make a huge noise causing him to glance back and so he loses Eurydice once again.

punctuation of the slow movement, or the "Farewell" Symphony (no. 45, 1772) where the players leave the stage one-by-one as they finish playing in the last movement (initially written as a protest). The composer's long career also maps out the changes in patronage that took place during the 18th century. Although he spent much of his life attached to the Esterházy court, working at the family palace in Eszterháza with only brief annual visits to the capital, by the 1790s, his music was being published and widely disseminated across Europe. In 1791 he effectively left his employment and, at the behest of the impresario Johann Salomon, arrived in London where he was commissioned to write a number of works for public concerts. This trip lasted until 1795, by which time his fame, and fortune, was assured, and on his return to Vienna, he was treated as a returning hero.

GLUCK AND THE REFORM OF OPERA

There was more overlap between the Baroque and subsequent Classical style in opera than in almost any other genre. Particularly around the mid-century, while musical language was gradually adapting to the new style, aesthetic changes in dramatic technique emerged gradually, with some composers continuing to work in the existing, particularly *opera seria*, style. Although the successful reforms of Zeno and Metastasio had sought to give opera a taut dramatic form, by the mid-18th century a different philosophical worldview meant that there were calls for an

even greater realism in plot and structure. In part this was politically motivated; the ideals of the Enlightenment demanded that the heroism of the people and the events they found themselves caught up in were to be celebrated, as opposed to plots involving mythological monarchs or deities. In this context, the text itself gained a greater importance and so the clarity of word setting became of paramount importance. If the symphony and sonata were to have been developed most fully in the German-speaking world, it was, at least initially, in Italy and, fittingly given the prominence of its Enlightenment philosophers, France that the greatest changes were to be seen in the field of opera.

It was in *opera buffa*, following the developments of Pergolesi, and its French equivalent *opéra comique*, that a shift of both emphasis and musical language can first be discerned. Chiming with the sentimentality of *Empfindsamkeit*, works by composers such as Niccòlo Piccinni (1728–1800), who worked in both Italy and France, and Domenico Cimarosa (1749–1801) transposed the stock comic devices of the earlier mythological operas to plots that involved human characters, often set in the contemporary world. The music was molded to the character and situation, often to intensify the sentimental impact of the moment. Plots might

Orpheus aus der Oper gleichen Namens

be derived from contemporary literature, as in one of Piccinni's most successful works *La buona figliuona* (1760) based on Richardson's *Pamela*, or from history, as in the French composer André-Ernest-Modeste Grétry's (1741–1813) *Richard Coeur-de-lion* (1784). Despite these changes, aided

Despite these changes, aided by a greater interest in orchestral color and taken to new heights by the collaboration of Mozart and da Ponte in Vienna, there still remained the problem of how to adapt *opera seria*, and its mythological concerns, to the new aesthetic. This was to be solved by a Bavarian composer who trained in Italy with Sammartini, worked in Vienna and spent the first half of his career writing Metastasian Italian *opera seria* and French *opéra comique*: Gluck.

As director of the Burgtheater in Vienna, Gluck was called on to provide operas and ballets of his own as well as oversee productions by other composers. As such he was well-acquainted with developments happening across Europe and in touch with numerous visiting artists. A decisive meeting with one of these, the poet Ranieri Calzabigi, in 1761 was to lead to a change in his musical and dramatic thought. Calzabigi was a critic of Italian *opera seria* and advocated the merging of it with contemporary developments in France. However, their first collaboration was a ballet, *Don Juan* (1761), and the dramatic skill of Gluck's fiery orchestral writing made an immediate impact. The return of ballet to a serious and sentimentally powerful theme was perceived as "reforming" in Vienna, though it built on the developments in dance under discussion in France. Of greater importance, however, was their first opera *Orfeo ed Eurydice* (1762), the first of Gluck's so-called "reforming" operas. In its plot and general scheme, *Orfeo ed Eurydice* is little different to contemporary Italian *opera seria* or the mythological operas of Rameau. However, the manner in which it was presented, plain melodic lines that dispensed with the vocal gymnastics of the *da capo aria* and the absence of *continuo* in the orchestra (making the *recitative* flow more smoothly into the subsequent *aria*), make it clear that this was a new direction. There was, also, an underlying moral cause: *opera seria* had become an end in itself, the moral and emotional lessons of the plot being lost in the vocal display and dramatic manipulation of music. In *Orfeo ed Eurydice* the clarity and simplicity of the well-proportioned melodic lines, and unencumbered directness of the plot, could be compared favorably to the Classical ideal of ancient Greek drama and sculpture, with the moral virtue of heroic truth it was supposed to embody.

Gluck and Calzabigi went on to produce further "reform" operas, including *Alceste* in 1767 (where Gluck went as far as to include a manifesto in the preface, outlining his aim to remove superficialities from the score and to make the music serve the text, not the other way around) and *Paride ed Elena* in 1770. The music in these became increasingly symphonic in conception, with instrumental development of themes and a musical argument taking place within the score to mirror the conflicts of the characters on stage.

Following these works, Gluck was to take his ideas to Paris, where he moved in 1774. Here he

adapted *Orfeo* for the French stage as *Orphée* and wrote an entirely new work to a libretto by du Roullet on Racine's *Iphigénie en Aulide* (1774). Although his reception was not always as positive as he may have hoped and he returned to Vienna in 1779, facing criticism in the press and from rivals such as Piccinni, he was strongly supported by figures such as Rousseau and greatly influenced subsequent generations of opera composers working in France. Notable among these was the Italian-born Luigi Cherubini (1760–1842), the most important opera composer in France during and after the French Revolution of 1789, who was to reform the Paris Conservatoire when he took over the post as director in 1822. Cherubini managed to form a synthesis of Viennese classicism and French and Italian opera styles that is hard to categorize. His early Italian works include settings of Metastasio and Zeno (including *Olimpiade* 1783) although later French librettos cover historical, contemporary and mythological themes (such as *Médée* in 1797 and *La prisonnière* in 1799). In many ways Cherubini, much like Beethoven, spans the gap between the Classicism of 18th century France and the new world of 19th century Romanticism.

Cherubini, drawing by Ingres; Rome; 1830

Originally from Florence, Cherubini moved to Paris in 1786. Once there, he produced a string of operas, including *Démophon* (1788) and *Médée* (1797), that proved popular throughout the Revolutionary period. In 1795 he became a teacher at the Conservatoire where he composed works for Revolutionary celebrations. As well as being later the superintendent of music at the royal chapel, he was appointed director of the Conservatoire in 1822. He was to be responsible for completely overhauling all aspects of the workings of the institution, introducing exams, awards and classes in instruments such as valved horn and trombone, as well as separate classes for different aspects of vocal performance.

Ludwig van Beethoven

The importance of the German composer Ludwig van Beethoven to the history of Western art music cannot be overstated. He produced works of such power, intensity and formidable musical logic that they have not been absent from the concert stage since they were first written. The musical embodiment of the political and philosophical upheavals of the turn of the 19th century as well as the archetypal musical genius, his work spans the end of the Classical period and launches music into the Romanticism of the 19th century. It is a testament to the force of his musical personality that after Beethoven music would never be the same. The only other individual figures in Western music history that have come close to making a similarly sustained and widespread impact have been Richard Wagner and Igor Stravinsky.

Born in the German city of Bonn in 1770 into a family of musicians—his father was a music teacher and his grandfather had been a singer and Kapellmeister—Beethoven was, like Mozart, given musical instruction from an early age. Little is known for certain about his early childhood but at around the age of 10 he was taking lessons from Christian Neefe, and contemporary reports show him to be a gifted pianist and starting to compose at that young age.

By the time he was 13 Beethoven was playing the keyboard in Neefe's orchestra at the court of the Elector Maximilian Friedrich, to whom he dedicated his three early piano sonatas, and where he was granted a post as organist in 1784 as well as playing viola in the court chapel and theater. Playing seems to have taken up much of his time for the next

German composer Ludwig van Beethoven (1770–1827)

Beethoven's Symphony No. 3, from his "Eroica" sketch book

few years, but in 1790 Beethoven began to compose in earnest, including ballet music for the *Ritterballett* of Count Ferdinand Waldstein, a friend of the composer who suggested that he go to study with Haydn in Vienna, to be paid for by his employer the Elector.

Beethoven had paid a visit to Vienna in 1787, where he met Mozart, but in 1792 he left Bonn for good to settle in the imperial capital. In the end the lessons with Haydn lasted no longer than a year and they do not seem to Beethoven's mind to have been entirely satisfactory. However, a far stricter regime, particularly in counterpoint, was to be found under Johann Albrechtsberger (1736–1809) to whom Haydn recommended his student when he left for London in 1794. Beethoven was aware that his salary from the Elector was finite and he turned his attention to the aristocratic society of Vienna, noted as the most enthusiastic patrons of music in Europe. His virtuosity on the piano soon attracted attention, as well as board and lodging, from a number of families including some (such as the Lichnowskys) who were to remain lifelong friends and supporters. Perhaps because of his burgeoning career as a concert pianist many of his works of this period are for the keyboard, including the first and second piano concertos (op.15 and 19, both 1795). By this time Beethoven was well-established in Viennese circles and in 1796 felt able to travel to Prague, Dresden and Berlin to play at their respective courts.

The two years after his return to Vienna saw the publication of some important early works, including the piano sonatas 4–7 (op.7 and 10), however, Beethoven now felt compelled to branch out and turn his attention to genres other than the chamber works for piano that had dominated his output so far. The results of this were his first set of string quartets (op.18, 1798–1800) and the First Symphony (op.21, 1799–1800). Both were well received and already it is possible to see essential elements of Beethoven's style, his careful working out of the themes and motifs in the sketchbooks for the quartets—Beethoven's endless inventive and logical exploitation of basic motifs is one of his greatest legacies to later composers—and in the symphony the much fuller scoring for the woodwind and brass than was common at the time. The years 1801–2, however, were to prove a turning point for the composer as he realized that a creeping deafness was to be total and incurable. This was a devastating blow and was to contribute to a feeling of isolation that was to dog the already shy and proud Beethoven.

Throughout this difficult period he continued to work and a second symphony (op.36) was completed in 1802 and the following year saw the Third Piano Concerto (op.37) and Kreutzer Violin Sonata (op.47). However, the bulk of 1803 was taken up with the composition of one of his greatest works, the third "Eroica" Symphony (op.55). The idea of a grand heroic work dedicated to Napoleon Bonaparte had been nagging at him ever since it had been suggested to him in 1798. The story of Beethoven's rage and removal of the dedication to Napoleon on hearing of the latter's proclaiming himself emperor is well known, and that passion is carried over into the work itself. Truly revolutionary, the work is conceived on a large scale and displays a coherence and daring use of motivic integration and key structure that no other composer of the time could have attempted. The heroic conception of the "Eroica" passes through all Beethoven's subsequent odd-numbered symphonies, culminating in the mighty ninth, but was also seen in smaller scale works that came in the following years, the "Waldstein" and "Apassionata" piano sonatas (op.53 and 7, 1803–4 and 4–5) and "Rasumovsky" string quartets (op.59, 1806).

After the poor reception of his only opera *Fidelio*, subsequent works, including the fifth and sixth symphonies (op.67 and 8, 1808)—the latter notable for its explicit pastoral program and inclusion of bird song—were a great success. The years between 1809 and 1812, while productive and including piano sonatas 24–6 (op.78–9, 81, all 1809) and the seventh and eighth symphonies (op.92 and 3, 1811–12), were difficult ones for Beethoven personally with a number of doomed romantic entanglements. They were enlivened, however, by a meeting with Goethe in 1811, although Beethoven was characteristically acerbic about the poet's bourgeois leanings.

The personal turmoil of these years seems to have sapped Beethoven's creative energies and between 1813 and 1821 he produced far less, only picking up

around 1818 to compose the huge "Hammerklavier" sonata (op.106) for a commission from London and then beginning work on the monumental Missa Solemnis (op.123) that took from 1819–23 to complete. This, however, Beethoven considered his finest work. Working on these two masterpieces saw him regain momentum in his composing and aside from the 33 "Diabelli" variations for piano (op.120, 1819–23) and the late piano sonatas (op.109–11, 1820–2), he began work on his last great orchestral work, the Ninth Symphony (op.125, 1822–4).

Beethoven suffered from bad health for much of the last 10 years of his life, and on the completion of the Ninth Symphony turned his attention to the project that was to dominate his final years. His late string quartets and Grosse Fuge (op.127, 30–3 and 5) are some of the most remarkable works ever produced, both lyrical and dissonant with dramatic

shifts in mood and texture and some ferociously complex contrapuntal writing. That they continue to fascinate audiences and scholars is a testament to their power and intensely intellectual working out of motifs and form.

The beginning of 1827 saw Beethoven's health deteriorate rapidly and he died in Vienna on March 26. Such was the high regard he was held in that over 10,000 people attended his public funeral held on the March 29, 1827.

ROMANTICISM

THE ARTIST AS HERO (1800—1900)

The dominant aesthetic of the 19th century is Romanticism, an overarching rubric of diverse approaches, styles and philosophical outlooks. It emerged at the end of the 18th century as the classicist tendencies of composers and musicians began to be discarded in favor of new directions that were being mapped out in literature and the visual arts. Common themes coalesced from the works of writers such as Goethe, Schiller, Hoffmann, Schlegel, Scott and Byron, and the painters Turner, Delacroix, Friedrich and Goya, all active during the later 18th and early 19th centuries and all contemporaries of Beethoven. In music, the role of the artist as the transcendent genius whose autobiography was inextricably linked to the emotional power of his or her works found its ideal in Beethoven. The sense of struggle that is evident in many of Beethoven's works and their at times overwhelming effect on the listener gave rise to a cult-like adulation of the composer and a sense that he perfectly embodied the ideal of the Romantic artist; indeed the writer E.T.A. Hoffmann (1776–1822) was one of the first to apply the term to music in his essays discussing Beethoven's Fifth Symphony. If, however, Beethoven was to represent the ideal against which subsequent composers must measure themselves in the symphonic realm, in opera the most influential figure was Carl Maria von Weber (1786–1826).

Weber's early life followed a similar pattern to that of Mozart, to whom he was distantly related by marriage. His father had been Kapellmeister at Eutin in Schleswig-Holstein, but had given this up to found a traveling theater company and Weber's childhood was spent moving between German cities before settling between Salzburg and Munich where he received training from, among others, Michael Haydn. It was his father's intention to set the young Weber up as a virtuoso, and his first compositions date from this time.

Weber's break with his father came on moving to Vienna in 1803, where he took instruction from Georg Vogler who obtained for him his first position as conductor to the German opera company in Breslau and from this point on Weber was to be professionally associated with German opera. He moved on to Stuttgart in 1807, from which he was banished after a scandal involving fraud and debt, and then passed through Mannheim and Munich before settling in Prague in 1813, where he became music director of the Estates Theatre. During this time Weber supported himself by composing pieces that either he could perform as a pianist, such as his C major Piano Concerto (1810) or for concerts in which he would be conducting. He had also by this time composed two operas, the early *Silvana* (1810) and the more successful one-act *Abu Hassan* (1811). However, it was not until he moved to Dresden in 1817 to found a new German opera company that he encountered *Der Freischütz*, a novella by Johann August Apel, that was to become Weber's greatest operatic success when first staged in Berlin in 1821. With its plot of a hunter who makes a pact with the

The Wolf's Glen from *Der Freischütz*, aqua tint set, by Holtermann and Lieber

The central scene of *Der Freischütz* is set in the Wolf's Glen. Its visitations from demonic apparitions and the Wild Hunt was to prove influential on many composers from Meyerbeer to Wagner, and the richness of Weber's orchestration and musical effects lays the ground for enduring musical tropes of the 19th century, from horn calls to the association of folksong with purity and simplicity (an idea already explored in Beethoven's Sixth Symphony).

1807: Abolition of slavery in Britain.

1821: The first performance of *Der Freischütz*. The start of the Biedermeier period under the regime of Chancellor Prince von Metternich in Austro-Hungary.

1827: Ottoman defeat at the Battle of Navarino leads to Greek independence a year later.

1828: The death of Schubert.

1829: The Catholic Relief Act is passed in Britain.

1830: Belgium becomes independent, Louis Philippe ascends to the throne of France. The first performance of Berlioz's *Symphonie fantastique*.

1848: Revolutions break out across Europe but are put down by troops.

Franz Joseph I becomes emperor of Austro-Hungary.

1851: The Great Exhibition takes place in London.

1853–70: The plans of French civic planner Baron Georges-Eugène Haussmann are used to redesign the center of Paris.

1857: The Indian uprising is defeated and India is absorbed into the vast British Empire.

1858: Tsar Alexander II begins the emancipation of the serfs.

1859: Darwin publishes *On the Origin of Species* laying out the theory of evolution.

1861: The unification of an independent Italy.

English poet Lord George Gordon Byron (1788-1824), painting by Thomas Phillips, 1813

1865: The first performance of Wagner's *Tristan und Isolde*.

1870: The Franco-Prussian war ends in defeat for the French and the collapse of the Second Empire.

1871: The unification of Germany under Otto von Bismarck. The Société Nationale de Musique is founded in France.

1875: Opening of the Palais Garnier as the Paris Opéra.

1876: Queen Victoria is proclaimed Empress of India, marking the start Britain's imperial domination. The first Bayreuth Festival in Germany and complete performance of *Der Ring des Nibelungen*.

1889: The Eiffel Tower is erected for the Exposition Universelle in Paris.

supernatural forces of the forest to obtain magic bullets this was to fully deserve Weber's subtitle of a *Romantische Oper*. The work does not, of course, appear from nowhere and it owes a great deal to the music of Mozart, Beethoven and contemporary musicians in France such as Cherubini. However, Weber's skill in associating motifs or sonorities with characters, particularly that of the diminished 7th chord and shifts of tonality by a tritone with Samiel the demonic "dark hunter", prefigures the innovations of Wagner in providing a parallel within the musical structure to the action on the stage. Although the rest of his career was overshadowed by the phenomenal success of *Der Freischütz*, Weber went on to compose two further operas, *Euryanthe* (1823) and *Oberon* (1826) in which he refines the musical ideas explored in the earlier groundbreaking work. It was on a trip to London in 1826 to promote the performance of this last work that he died.

Alongside *Der Freischütz*, the other opera that was to be influential on Romantic composers was Mozart's *Don Giovanni*. Its portrayal of Don Giovanni's descent into hell and the moment the statue comes to life to tell him of his fate chimed well with Romanticism's preoccupation with the supernatural. It was extremely popular during the first two decades of the 19th century and was seen by the Shelleys and Byron in London. On the continent it made an impact on the writer E.T.A. Hoffmann and was greatly admired, after his initial suspicion of its Italian libretto was overcome, by Wagner. Its influence can also be traced in the works of Hector Berlioz (1803–69) whom it greatly affected; Berlioz knew the opera by heart and even wrote new *recitatives* for the work for a performance at the Paris Opéra in 1841.

BERLIOZ AND THE SYMPHONY

If Weber represents the early Romantic in music, although in his case with an element of Biedermeier conformity and German cultural chauvinism, this was even more true of the greatest French composer of the first half of the 19th century, Hector Berlioz. Iconoclastic and revolutionary, his autobiography *Mémoires* (published in Paris in 1870) sets Berlioz up as the archetypal autodidact whose genius was misunderstood and whose personal life was a model of heroic striving and strong passion. This highly entertaining piece of writing is self-serving in its promotion of the Berlioz myth but does admirably demonstrate the ideal of the Romantic artist as an individual struggling against wider society to realize his personal vision of the sublime.

Berlioz was born in La Côte-Saint-André near Grenoble and his early education from his father, a doctor, was broad and eclectic, although his tastes tended to the more emotional passages of Virgil and accounts of travels in distant lands.

He soon, however, discovered music and began to learn the flute and at the same time began to study Rameau's *Traité de l'harmonie* on his own. Almost all of Berlioz's practical musical experience came from playing the flute and guitar and not through the keyboard—the usual tool of the 18th and 19th century composer—and this no doubt gave him a perspective from outside the accepted pattern of learning that aided his revolutionary insights into the problems of composition. He was sent to Paris to study medicine in 1821 but soon was spending more time at the Opéra and studying music with the composer Jean-François Le Sueur (1760–1837). Much against his family's will he abandoned medicine in 1824 resolving to become a great composer, but found himself cut off from funding and was forced to take work where he could find it, teaching or writing criticism for newspapers. He was by this time composing—the first successful performance of one of his works, the *Messe solenelle*, took place in 1825—and

The Wanderer Above a Sea of Fog,
by Caspar David Friedrich

Key to the Romantic imagination was a sense of the sublime; that which produces "an overwhelming sense of awe or other emotion through being vast or grand". This was evoked, through ideas growing out of Rousseau's espousal of the irrational, in the Gothic novel or through an interest in dreams, and also in the power of art to overwhelm the emotions. This idea of being overwhelmed was related to the rise of landscape painting with its awe at the transcendent beauty of the natural world, particularly landscapes regarded as wild and untamed such as in Scotland or the Alps. Set against this was the figure of the hero, stemming from Goethe's hugely influential works *Faust* and *Werther*, who—tragic or triumphant—stood against the world and, in the guise of the artist, assumed the role of the individual genius.

Marschner

Heinrich August Marschner (1795–1861), a composer of Romantic operas, was a near contemporary of Weber and his works provide a German-language link between those of the latter and Wagner. Marschner's early compositions were in the German *Singspiel* tradition of musical numbers interspersed with dialogue, as were Mozart's *Die Zauberflöte* and Weber's *Der Freischütz*, both of which were influential on the composer. He achieved considerable fame for his later operas *Der Vampyr* (1827), a racy adaptation of the Gothic vampire stories of the time, and *Der Templer und die Jüdin* (1829), derived from Walter Scott's *Ivanhoe*. His last successful work was *Hans Heiling* (1833), based on a Bohemian legend, after which he had little else of note performed during his lifetime.

in 1826 he entered the Conservatoire to study composition, counterpoint and fugue.

The following two years were momentous ones for Berlioz. In 1827 he encountered the works of Shakespeare for the first time. In addition, through attending a performance of *Hamlet*, he met the actress Harriet Smithson. She provoked an all-consuming passion in the young composer who saw in her his Romantic ideal woman, an unreasonable demand that could not be sustained and after their marriage in 1833 they drifted apart. A further literary discovery was that of Goethe's *Faust* but the most important musical event was his attending a performance of Beethoven's Third and Fifth Symphonies. These had an overwhelming affect on Berlioz and through them he was able to see the emotional power of purely instrumental forms.

He had already been introduced to the music of *Der Freischütz* through its French incarnation *Robin des bois* and this too had had an effect on his handling of orchestral forces, an area in which Berlioz was to be influential long after his death through his *Grand traité d'instrumentation et d'orchestration modernes* (1843). Along with Gluck, whose Classical simplicity Berlioz greatly admired, Beethoven and Weber were the greatest influence on his early work.

Berlioz was awarded the Prix de Rome in 1830, for which he had to spend time in Italy, but before his departure came the composition of one of

his most important and revolutionary works, the *Symphonie fantastique*. The explicit programme, an *Episode de la vie d'un artiste*, that Berlioz issued with his *Symphony fantastique*, with its unmistakable biographical overtones, lies at the heart of its radical conception. The opening movement, *Reverie–Passions*, presents the idée fixe, a musical theme that represents the artist's love for a woman (a not-very-well-disguised Harriet Smithson) and which runs throughout the entire symphony; a precursor of Wagner's *Leitmotifs*. A glimpse is caught of the belovéd at *Un bal* during the waltz of the second movement, but after a pastoral third movement the hero has taken opium and killed her, prompting the *Marche au supplice* (march to the scaffold) of the fourth movement. The last movement, depicting a witches' sabbath, owes something to *Der Freischütz* in its unearthly noises but also presents a highly individual twisting of a *Dies irae* theme and wild *fugato* in the witches' dance. As well as the innovative use of an *idée fixe* and a strong program, the orchestration of the work also breaks new ground, with two sets of timpani, valved cornets (the valve was a new invention making all brass instruments chromatic) and the introduction of the cor anglais into the symphony orchestra.

With this he was to show a future direction for the symphony and give the form a new lease of life. The shadow of Beethoven fell heavily on 19th-century composers of symphonies as it was widely accepted that the form had achieved perfection in his hands and therefore not capable of further development. It took the unorthodox genius of Berlioz to break this impasse, but earlier composers such as the Viennese Schubert were at first very much constrained by the influence of Beethoven's symphonic works. Berlioz was to follow the *Symphonie fantastique* with a number of other symphonic works: the Byron-inspired *Harold en Italie* (1834), practically a viola concerto written for, but never performed by, Paganini; the Shakespearean *Roméo et Juliette* (1839); and the *Grande symphonie funèbre et triomphale* (1840).

Berlioz only spent one year in Italy though he seems to have been greatly impressed by its landscapes, and returned to Paris, a city he professed to loathe but which remained his home for the rest of his life. Although his reputation was increasing and he received two government commissions, the monumental *Grande messe des morts* (1837) and the *Grande symphonie*, Berlioz struggled to make a living from his composition and was forced to fall back on criticism as a career. By the 1840s he began to travel widely, especially as his reputation spread and he continued to face opposition and incomprehension at home in Paris. By this time he had made the acquaintance of Franz Liszt

(1811–86) and Richard Wagner (1813–83) who were, initially, both very supportive of Berlioz's music. Indeed Berlioz dedicated his large choral work *La Damnation de Faust* (1845–6) to Liszt, who in return dedicated his *Faust Symphonie* (1854–61) to Berlioz. An opera by Berlioz had already been performed at the Paris Opéra in 1838, *Benvenuto Cellini* (1836–8), but it was not until 1858 that his monumental five-act *Les Troyens* was completed. Based on Virgil's *Aeneid* it was so large in conception that it was first performed in two parts, acts 1–2 entitled *La prise de Troie* and acts 3–5 *Les Troyens à Carthage*, and even then only the second part made it onto the Opéra stage in 1863. Although this was well received, Berlioz was embittered by the experience of trying to get his music accepted and played as he wished, and the final years of his life were solitary ones (Harriet Smithson had died in 1854, his second wife Marie Recio in 1862 and his son Louis in 1867). Berlioz died in 1869 without the recognition that would later be given to his works.

THE AUSTRO-GERMAN TRADITION

The programmatic symphonies of Berlioz were to prove influential on his near contemporary Liszt and later composers of tone poems such as Richard Strauss. However, during the first half of the 19th century Austrian and German composers were generally to remain closer to the Beethoven symphonic model. Schubert was only 31 years old when he died—astonishing considering how much he had written by that time—and only just starting to find an individual symphonic voice. His first six symphonies (written between 1813–18) are well crafted and pleasant but highly derivative works written for an amateur orchestra, of which the Fifth is most often performed. Interestingly his next two symphonic works both remain unfinished (the name by which his Eighth Symphony, 1822, is best known) and there are numerous surviving sketches demonstrating his dissatisfaction with the pieces but also showing a more radical exploration of symphonic form. The Eighth Symphony is considered one of his masterpieces, set in the then unusual key of B minor, its dramatic contrasts, modulations and play with rhythm setting it apart from his preceding works. This was followed by the completed Ninth Symphony in C major, a large-scale work replete with Romantic horn calls and lyrical melodic writing that marks his arrival as a fully-formed symphonic composer.

Schubert's early death combined with the limited dissemination and performance of his music at the time meant that the Austro-German symphonic tradition was to be taken forward by other composers, among them Felix Mendelssohn (1809–47) and Robert Schumann (1810–56); both of whom admired and promoted Schubert's work even if they were not greatly influenced by it. Mendelssohn and his sister Fanny (1805–47), a talented composer in her own right, were given musical instruction from an early age and like other brother-and-sister musical pairings promoted as child prodigies, although it was Felix who was expected to make music his profession.

Berlioz conducting, caricature

The innovations of Berlioz, and especially those of his orchestration, were too much for the more conservative elements of his audiences to bear. The extent to which he augmented the orchestra with trombones, trumpets, tubas and extra percussion led to the unjust accusation that he was merely interested in producing a cacophony of loud and violent sound; a charge that was taken up with some glee by contemporary cartoonists.

Neue Leipziger Zeitschrift für Musik

An important institution that supported a number of 19th century composers was the secret society, a gathering of like-minded people who discussed the arts, philosophy and politics with the aim of promoting the ideas and works of its members. Weber was a member of the musical Harmonischer Verein, established in 1810, that also included Meyerbeer among its members. Schumann was nominal head of the Davidsbündler (established around 1833), a group of musicians and writers, some of them imaginary, who were often included as characters in Schumann's compositions and writings. The Davidsbündler was based in Leipzig and established its own journal, the *Neue Leipziger Zeitschrift für Musik* to which Schumann contributed much of his musical criticism.

Borsdorf Horn, Royal Academy of Music

One of Schumann's boldest experiments was in the *Concertstück* of 1849. Written for four solo horns and orchestra, this was designed to exploit the full potential of the valved horn, by then starting to be widely used. Highly virtuosic, with extremes of register, this amply demonstrates the Romantic interest in horn writing, especially the use of horn calls to conjure up visions of the forest or as a representation of the Romantic hero. The sound of the horn became so ubiquitous through the use of a four-part horn section to carry the harmonic foundations of a piece that the characteristic 19th century orchestral texture became known as "blanket of horns writing".

Eduard Hanslick

With the rise of the public concert as the major form of patronage for composers there also arose the possibility of the specialist commentator as a mediator between often challenging new works and the public. With the huge increase in print journalism during the 19th century it was inevitable that this need was fulfilled by newspaper critics, writing in the feuilleton section. These arbiters of taste came to acquire considerable power and influence and one of the most influential was the Austrian critic Eduard Hanslick (1825–1904) whose defense of the Classical, and especially the works of Brahms, against the, in his view, modern depravities of the music of Wagner led to him being memorably parodied in *Die Meistersinger von Nürnberg* as the ineffectual Beckmesser. Hanslick's influence was so great in Vienna that his continued opposition was a source of great misery to Anton Bruckner.

He began to compose early on and wrote his First Symphony at the age of 15. Three years earlier he had attended a performance of *Der Freischütz* and the influence of Weber, as well as Mozart and Beethoven, is evident in this early work. Three other acknowledged symphonies were to follow, the "Italian" (published as the Fourth) was written by 1833 and recorded the composer's impressions of his trip to Italy in 1830. This was preceded, however, by the work in which he first presents a mature style, his incidental music for *A Midsummer Night's Dream* (1826). An extraordinary work for such a young musician in which all the themes depicting the various characters are derived from the chords heard in the woodwind at the beginning of the piece. Extracting themes from basic motif became one of Mendelssohn's most characteristic techniques and one which is heard to good effect in his concert overture *Die Hebriden* (1830). This was inspired by a visit he made to Scotland in 1829, and the same trip was the starting point for his last "Scottish" symphony (published as number Three). In this work too, he derives his material from a basic motif or set of notes. Unlike Berlioz, Mendelssohn did not issue explicit programs for his works but there is a nod toward Scottish traditional music in some of the pentatonic themes and treatment of rhythm.

Evocative titles were also given by Schumann to two of his symphonies, the First *Der Frühling* ('spring', 1841) and his Third, the *Rheinische* (1850). Schumann was deeply imbued with the spirit of Romanticism and his forward-looking works made him influential on many subsequent composers including figures as different as Gustav Mahler and Pierre Boulez. Born in Zwickau, Saxony, he initially studied law in Leipzig and did not take the decision to dedicate himself fully to music until moving to Heidelberg in 1829, although he had by this time been playing and composing from his childhood. Following this decision, the piece that was to launch his career and begin the spread of his reputation across Europe was the *Thème sur le nom Abegg varié* (1830) for piano. This set of variations took the letters of the name Abegg, the putative dedicatee, as the basis for the theme and its subsequent

transformation. Interestingly, Schumann had recently fallen under the spell of Schubert's music in which the development of themes from short motifs was a prominent feature.

While studying in Leipzig he had taken music lessons with Friedrich Wieck and he resolved to return to the city to continue his musical studies. Wieck's daughter, Clara, was to become a central figure in his life as first his lover and then wife. Like Fanny Mendelssohn, Clara Wieck (1819–96) was an exceptional pianist and a talented composer and she was to become Schumann's muse following their first declarations of love in 1835. Important figures in Schumann's life often form the basis of works, particularly those for piano. Besides Clara, two of the most common are Florestan, the heroic virtuoso, and Eusebius, a thoughtful and withdrawn figure, two sides of the composer's own character. Aside from the deeply personal approach to the character of his music, Schumann was greatly influenced by the fantastic writings of E.T.A. Hoffmann whose Romantic vision appealed to his own sensitive imagination. The music of Chopin had been a revelation to the composer and as a critic Schumann also set himself up as a champion of Berlioz, writing a long and detailed analysis in defence of the latter's *Symphonie fantastique* in 1835.

As well as his great output of *Lieder*, piano and chamber music—Schumann was keen to maintain a German tradition in which composers were active in all musical genres, as Beethoven had been —it was inevitable that he should also turn his attention to the symphony. This occurred relatively late in his career, the first numbered work dating from 1841. Even though by this point Schumann was a mature composer at the height of his powers, his symphonies show him constantly experimenting and revising his ideas of the form, from the full-blooded orchestration of the First Symphony, to the

LIEDER

Musical aesthetics in the early-19th century had in large part taken their cue from literature, inspired by the poetry of Goethe and Schiller. It is fitting, therefore, that one of the most representative genres of musical Romanticism, *Lieder*, were vocal settings of German poetry. *Lieder*, German art songs either through-composed or strophic, grew out of the German *Singspiel* operatic tradition and songs with keyboard accompaniment set by composers

such as Beethoven. The *Lied* stands apart due to its melding of the accompaniment to the sentiment or situation of the text. Thus, in what is considered the first example of the genre, Schubert's song *Gretchen am Spinnrade* (1814), the restless, revolving accompaniment is suggestive of the spinning that is the heroine's work. The music ceases to be a mere accompaniment to the lyrics but is integral to the telling of the story. It is Schubert's skill in exploiting musical resources to suit the poetry and his prolific melodic gifts that make his over 660 songs the core of the *Lieder* repertory. His vast output exploits countless musical devices as a unifying force, some surface effects such as the "leaping" runs of the accompaniment to *Die Forelle* (1817), others operating on a deeper level through rhythm, tonality or imitation. Perhaps his most famous song is that of the *Erlkönig* (1815), where the alternating voices of a father and son requires considerable vocal skill to maintain the differences in tone and register.

The poetic texts of *Lieder* often concentrate on the emotional struggles of the individual, be they of love, death, fear or happiness. The intensely personal nature of the settings was readily identified with by a newly-emerging educated middle-class and *Lieder* found a home in the burgeoning realm of domestic music-making. Some of Schubert's last songs were

settings of the poet Heinrich Heine (1797–1856), also set by Schumann, who took up Schubert's mantle as the leading composer of German song. Both Mendelssohn and Carl Loewe (1796–1869) produced a large number of *Lieder* but they did not, unlike Schubert and Schumann, produce a synthesis between the music of the keyboard and voice. Fanny Mendelssohn, who wrote over 300 *Lieder*, was much more successful in this respect than her brother. Almost half of Schumann's 260 or so *Lieder* were written in one year (1840–1), and his settings of Heine in *Dichterliebe* and *Liederkreis* are among his finest works. Schumann's later settings of Goethe and Friedrich Rückert (1788–1866) abandoned a purely diatonic language and in finding a new, motivic organizing principle paved the way for Wagner's development of the *Leitmotif*.

Both Wagner and Liszt wrote a number of *Lieder* but it was Brahms who produced a more sizable body of works. His songs owe a great deal to his instrumental duo writing, with long melodies that float over the accompaniment. The two last great composers of *Lieder*, Hugo Wolf (1860–1903) and Richard Strauss (1864–1949), were very different figures though united in their respect for the music of Wagner. Wolf's *Lieder* are notable for their involved piano writing which is set contrapuntally against the vocal line. Strauss by contrast set many of his songs for voice and orchestra, culminating in the sublime *Vier letzte Lieder* (1948), the last gasp of the German song tradition. Its end had come about through its removal from domestic sphere, where the emotional upheavals of the individual had a more immediate impact, and, by the end of the 19th century, the collapse of the German heroic poetic tradition.

Schubert, Gesellschaft der Musikfreunde; Vienna, Austria

Franz Schubert (1797–1828) was one of the few composers working in Vienna to have been born in the city. Although he composed nine symphonies, two of them unfinished, his real contributions to the history of music lie in piano works, chamber music and, especially, *Lieder*. His early musical experiences came through singing in the Hofkapelle under Antonio Salieri and through violin teaching from his father, with instruction in counterpoint and harmony from the local organist Michael Holzer. In such a musically active city the young composer was soon exposed to the orchestral works of Haydn, Mozart and Beethoven as well as the operas of Gluck. He began composing at around the age of 13 and even his early works display a revolutionary degree of modulation. He embarked on a wide range of compositions, from piano works, to operas, to Masses. In around 1814 Schubert began to compose *Lieder* and, from this point on, produced a vast body of work, much of which was performed during informal gatherings at friends' houses or domestic musical soirees.

Schubert's *Der Erlkönig,* based on the poem by Johann Wolfgang von Goethe; Illustration by E. Kutzer

Chopin Playing the Piano in Prince Radziwill's Salon, by Hendryk Siemiradzki, 1887; oil on canvas

Although there were considerable developments in musical instrument technique throughout the Romantic period, prompted to a great extent by the invention of the valve for brass instruments and the key work of Theobald Boehm for the flute, it was the piano that was the supreme domestic instrument of the 19th century. It was rare to find a household above a certain income without a piano, the invention of the iron frame making it a more powerful and expressive instrument that held its tuning longer and the development of the small upright piano around 1800 making it easier to house in a domestic setting. Not only was there a huge output of works for solo piano, the playing of which was considered a useful social accomplishment for young middle-class women, there were also numerous arrangements of popular and contemporary instrumental and operatic works arranged for four hands or piano duet. These were, up until the invention of recording and its mass dissemination during the 20th century, the chief way through which new works could be heard and evaluated by a wider public.

Nicolò Paganini, by Sir Edwin Landseer, c. 1831; Pen, sepia ink and wash

The Italian-born violinist Nicolò Paganini (1782–1840) was one of the most flamboyant virtuosos of the 19th century, with a life-history that involved numerous love affairs, great success and fame throughout Europe. His exceptional technique enabled him to play works of eye-watering difficulty, many of which he composed or arranged himself, and this ability to stretch the instrument to new limits was highly influential on Liszt who applied a similar talent to the piano. Among his numerous technical achievements he was particularly noted for his skill in double-stopping, playing on the very highest harmonics and, especially, the speed at which he could rattle off long passages of notes.

lighter sound of the symphonic Overture, Scherzo and Finale also composed in 1841. One technique that, literally, knits his symphonic works together is the idea of thematic return in his compositions, where motifs return in successive movements to give the work coherence and a feeling of being through-composed.

Schumann had suffered from bouts of depression for years before his final illness, marked by his attempted suicide by drowning in the Rhine, saw him confined in a liberal asylum during the years 1854–56. Like other artists of the time Schumann's life had been marked by all-consuming passions, especially for Clara, and intense struggles to present a personal musical vision that was often misunderstood by contemporary audiences and critics.

During the last few years of his life both Robert and Clara were in close contact with Johannes Brahms (1833–97), a German composer from Hamburg who spent much of his life in Vienna. Brahms was, above all, seen as the direct heir to Beethoven and was championed during his lifetime as bulwark against the modern excesses of composers such as Wagner and Liszt. The position of Brahms within the 19th century is somewhat paradoxical, his musical language is very much of its time with a finely judged use of far-flung harmonic shifts and treatment of tonal ambiguity, yet formally he is seen as a conservative, almost obsessively canonical in his awe of Beethoven's symphonic legacy. Perhaps his greatest legacy was his unparalleled technical skill in weaving complex harmonic and contrapuntal textures that moved forward through a processes of continuous variation, a technique mirrored in the complex textures of much of the 20th-century music.

Brahms struggled with his first symphony, taking over 15 years to complete it, perhaps feeling the weight of expectation that was on his shoulders; when it was finally performed in

1876 it was dubbed "Beethoven's Tenth", not altogether unfairly as Brahms had taken the Ninth as his model. The potential of his orchestral writing had already been heard through his First Piano Concerto (1859) and sets of variations and overtures for orchestra. However, the generally favorable reaction to his First Symphony seems to have given him confidence and the following three symphonies contain some of his most impressive working-out of form and melodic variation. The Second (1877) is often seen as the lighter half of a pairing with the First and it does not display the signs of struggle that are evident in the earlier work. The Third and Fourth symphonies followed a few years later (1883 and 1884–85 respectively) and in these more tautly-constructed works Brahms reaches the apotheosis in his understanding of sonata form and the knitting together of all the elements of the work across all its four movements. In the Third this is achieved through an equal balance of the separate sections and by an overall key structure that follows a tonic–dominant–tonic pattern. This is also used as a structural device in the Fourth Symphony but here Brahms manages also to relate the overall motivic development to the harmonic structure, with melodic major 3rds complementing a widespread use of augmented triads.

CHAMBER MUSIC

Berlioz produced very little solo piano or chamber music, preferring to work on a larger scale, however, Schubert, Mendelssohn, Schumann and Brahms all made great contributions to these genres and some of their greatest works are either for solo piano or written for smaller ensembles such as the string quartet and piano quintet. The

string quartet, following the example of Beethoven, continued to be the place where composers worked out some of their most serious and intimate essays on the problems of sonata form, the symphony also having to present a certain monumental quality achieved through orchestration. Schubert's most impressive achievements in this area are in a characteristically unfinished work, *Quartettsatz* (1820), but even more so in the late quartet in D minor known as *Tod und der Mädchen* ("Death and the Maiden") after the *Lied* from which it quotes. His later works are remarkable for their suspension of tonal certainty and the range of their instrumental gestures. His string quintet in C major (D956) is especially rich in its imaginative use of instrumentation (a string quartet with additional cello), and in its thematic use and formal construction ranks among the greatest works of the chamber repertory.

Both Schumann and Mendelssohn wrote string quartets, as did a host of other mid-century composers, though it has been argued that the proximity of the works of Beethoven, particularly his difficult late quartets that only gained a wider audience from the 1850s onward, was still a restraining influence on further innovation. Interestingly, it was not until 1873 that Brahm's produced his first two quartets and he was only to produce three, the final quartet arriving in 1876. These display the same concern with formal logic and intense working out of motivic development as his other works. Brahms reserved some of his greatest efforts for his chamber music and although he only produced three string quartets, his duos, trios, quintets and sextets, for varying forces, comprise the greatest corpus of chamber works since Beethoven. It is in these that the principle of continuous variation, and his skilful manipulation of tonal ambiguity, is most fully explored.

The string quartet was adopted more readily by composers in Bohemia, in particular by Antonín Dvořák (1841–1904) who wrote 14 quartets displaying the same formal skills that are evident in his symphonies and exploiting folk-like melodies that give them a nationalist flavor. Of the more unusual forces used by composers, both Schubert and Mendelssohn wrote octets that are masterpieces and still regularly performed, but by far the greatest number of 19th-century chamber compositions are for solo piano. These range from albums of impressionistic miniatures, such as Schumann's *Papillons* (1830–31), to collections of preludes and studies, often of considerable virtuosity. There was a huge demand for piano works of all kinds and degrees of technical difficulty, and the ethos of Romantic individualism was well suited to the idea of solo performance. The piano sonata continued to fascinate composers, including Schubert,

Schumann and Brahms, whose contribution to the form was as significant as for their other chamber works. However, its most radical treatment was seen in the hands of Fryderyk Chopin (1810–49) and Liszt, whose Sonata in B minor (1853) is one of the century's most individual reworkings of sonata form.

THE VIRTUOSO SOLOIST

As pianists Chopin and Liszt, along with the violinists Nicolò Paganini, Ole Bull (1810–80) and Joseph Joachim, embodied the ideal of the musical Romantic individual. Their unprecedented virtuosity made them internationally famous and through their playing and own compositions, or the works of composers with whom they closely collaborated, they were responsible for the central place of the instrumental concerto in the 19th-century canon. A large number of the concertos written during the 19th century are no longer part of the standard repertory, in part a reaction against Romantic ideals and taste during the 20th century, but also due to a generally unfounded idea that the form tends to favor virtuosity over serious musical content. This is not a criticism restricted to the 20th and 21st centuries, some contemporary commentators—among them Schumann, himself the composer of a number of concertos—unfavorably contrasted Beethoven's works with contemporary showy pieces that lacked, in their view, intellectual content and musical sophistication. Schumann held that it was in the solo piano repertory that subtle ideas and pianistic technique, although only in the service of the compositional idea, were best explored. This, however, was not the position taken by the middle-class concert-going public whose appetite for concertos grew rather than diminished. In turn, the larger sound needed to project the piano against the orchestra fed back techniques in piano writing, such as a widespread use of double octaves, into the solo repertory. The projection of the sound of the piano would have been impossible had it not been for the development of the iron frame, which not only allowed greater tension to be placed on the strings but also held its tuning longer against the more physical style of playing required to raise its dynamic level above that of an orchestra.

Cult-like status was afforded to a number of virtuosi but pre-eminent among them were Chopin and Liszt. Chopin was born near Warsaw and his talent for composition and keyboard performance was soon recognized, predictably leading to him being labeled as the next Mozart. He had a number of teachers but he soon outstripped them all and, after giving public concerts to great acclaim in Warsaw and Vienna, he resolved to leave Poland and traveled to Vienna in 1830, never to return. Political conditions in Austria

Liszt Academy, Budapest

Although at the time of his birth Hungary was part of the Austro-Hungarian Empire and the composer was German-speaking, Liszt has been co-opted into the building of a specifically Hungarian musical identity, and Budapest in particular has a plethora of monuments in his honor.

were not comfortable for Poles and he soon left and, traveling via Stuttgart, arrived in Paris in 1831. Chopin found the French capital a far more congenial place and he was to spend much of the rest of his life in the city. The following year he gave his first public concert in Paris to great acclaim and he soon made the acquaintance of Berlioz and Liszt. It was through Liszt that he met the early feminist and novelist George Sand, and in 1838 they became lovers. They moved to the Spanish island of Mallorca later the same year and it was there that Chopin became seriously ill. This was the tuberculosis that was eventually to kill him, and on moving back to France the two artists,

whose relationship became increasingly rocky, divided their time between Paris and a château at Nohant in central France until his death in 1849.

Chopin retired from full-time public performance relatively early in his career to concentrate on composition for the piano. His piano works are perhaps the finest of the 19th century in their exploitation of all aspects of technique and exploration of the instrument's timbre. Although Chopin wrote six works for piano and orchestra, including two concertos, he was not comfortable writing for orchestral forces and his greatest achievements are in his collections of solo works. Almost all of his works require a high degree of pianistic skill and they vary from virtuosic scherzos and études, to dance-like mazurkas and waltzes, as well as large-scale ballades and a cycle of preludes. The earlier nocturnes of the Irish composer John Field (1782–1837) were greatly influential on Chopin's meditative works of the same name. Chopin's early influences came from composers such as Weber and, especially in terms of melody, the *bel canto* of Bellini, but he soon developed an individual voice displaying a forward-thinking approach to harmony that pushed distant modulation and ambiguity to unthinkable degree.

Although Chopin was fêted during his lifetime, the adulation he received pales beside that heaped upon Liszt. Originally from Raiding (former Doborján) in Hungary, Liszt studied with the great piano teacher Carl Czerny (1791–1857) in Vienna and, by the time he had finished his studies, a great natural facility had turned into the most prodigious technique of any European musician. This natural ease also passed over into his ability to compose, which he did quickly and with a seemingly endless flow of invention. Based in Paris from 1823 on, it was here he met the married Countess Marie d'Agoult who became his lover and bore him three children, one of whom, Cosima, was to marry Wagner. As the scandal grew, they fled and began the so-called "years of pilgrimage" passing through Switzerland and Italy, although Marie was to return to her other family in 1839.

In 1847 Liszt both gave his last professional concert and met Princess Carolyne von Sayn-Wittgenstein, who, although married, was to be his partner until 1861 when, in a drama worthy of a novel, as they were on the point of having her marriage annulled and were to be married themselves her family intervened and Liszt was left, almost literally, at the altar. It was possibly this emotional upheaval that prompted him during the last period of his life to take holy orders as an abbé. Liszt's decision to stop performing in public was to enable him to spend more time on composition and to this end he took the post of Kapellmeister at the court of Weimar. During his time there Liszt became a great champion of the "progressive" composers Berlioz and Wagner against the "conservatives", Mendelssohn, Schumann and Brahms, whose support came in the main from the critic Hanslick and the conservatory in Leipzig.

This so-called "battle of the Romantics" was indicative of two streams of thought in 19th-century music, those who followed the example of Beethoven and retained but developed the forms of Classical composers, and those who struck out in new directions. Liszt was undoubtedly in the latter camp. His highly virtuosic piano music, best exemplified by the *Etudes d'exécution transcendente* (1938) and the *Grandes études de Paganini* (a revised version of the first from 1851), revels in extremes of key relations and chords that suspended resolution of conflicts of tonality, while his radical transformation of themes and motifs during a piece is one of his greatest contributions to compositional technique. However, as well as his contribution to the piano repertory, Liszt is equally important for his development, during his time in Weimar, of the symphonic poem. Unconvinced of the need to follow existing symphonic models Liszt conceived of a one-movement form that, while retaining the barest scheme of sonata form, were structured to either tell a story or evoke an idea. While these were highly influential on later composers such as Strauss and Sibelius, who both fully developed the form, Liszt's works are rarely performed. They did, however, inform the composition of his greatest orchestral work, *Eine Faust-Symphonie* (1854–7). This three-movement description of characters from Goethe's drama contains some of his finest orchestration and most impressive transformation of motifs that, in Wagnerian fashion, represent ideas and characters.

OPERA IN ITALY AND FRANCE

Alongside the cities of Austria and Germany the other great musical centre of the 19th century was Paris. As well as being the home of the radical innovations of Berlioz, Paris was to become one of the most important European centers for opera, by both French and Italian composers. This might seem surprising given the pre-eminence of Italy in opera but until the emergence of Milan as the major Italian opera center following the *Risorgimento,* no one Italian city had a monopoly on opera production in the same way that Paris did in France. That given, Italy had long been a producer of operatic talent through its regional houses in Naples, Rome, Florence, Venice and Milan, and this was a role it was to retain throughout the 19th century, producing a number of major figures, Gioachino Rossini (1792–1868), Vincenzo Bellini (1801–35) and Gaetano Donizetti (1797–1848), whose work was to be influential on not only the later Verdi but also French opera composers. Although each of these composers was born and spent their early careers in Italy they all gravitated towards Paris and either settled or spent some of their most fruitful years in the French capital, with many of their works existing in both Italian and French versions. This confirmed the dominant position of Italian opera in the city during the early decades of the 19th century and initially French composers such as Auber and, especially, Halévy were content to steer a middle course between the long-phrased melody of Italian opera and the blurring of the distinction between *aria* and *recitative* that is characteristic of the French tradition from the works of Lully onward.

RICHARD WAGNER

Perhaps no other figure in the history of Western music has aroused so many passions as Richard Wagner (1813–83). Impossible to ignore, his innovations in operatic structure, harmony and use of motifs have left their mark on the works of almost all subsequent composers. A highly divisive figure who engaged with musicology, literature, politics and philosophy, his music and writings have attracted many followers and most controversially were used as an expression of German nationhood during the Third Reich. Never one to think on a small scale, his works range from the grand operatic spectacles of *Der fliegende Holländer* and *Tannhäuser,* inspired by composers such as Meyerbeer, to his ground-breaking, mythologically-inspired four-part music drama *Der Ring des Nibelungen*, to the sensuous mysticism of *Parsifal* subtitled *Ein Bühnenweihfestspiel* (a sacred festival drama).

Richard Wagner (1813–83),
by Max Sinz

Born in Leipzig, Wagner's early musical training was with Christian Gottlieb Müller after which, in 1831, he attended Leipzig University to study music and then went on to undertake intensive instruction in counterpoint from Christian Weinlig who was Kantor at the Thomaskirche. Wagner began to compose in earnest after he took up a post as chorus master to the theater in Würzburg in 1833. His first surviving opera *Die Feen* (1834) was written during this time and Wagner himself wrote the libretto for this work, something that he was to do for all his subsequent operas. However, it was not until he became the musical director of a traveling company that he was to see one of his own works, his second opera *Das Liebesverbot*, on the stage in 1836. During the same year he married one of the

company's singers, Minna Planer, with whom he was destined to have a stormy relationship.

In 1837 Wagner arrived in Riga to take up the post of musical director to the city's opera house. Although neither his domestic nor financial arrangements were comfortable, he found time to write the libretto and some of the music for his next project, *Rienzi*. Before this could be finished, however, Wagner's debt had accumulated to such an extent that he and Minna were forced to flee across the border under the cover of night. The couple arrived in Paris by late 1839 and there Wagner received support from Meyerbeer who gave him letters of introduction and encouraged him to finish *Rienzi*. However, the next two-and-a-half years were to be miserable for Wagner; nothing came of his introduction to the director of the Opéra. Wagner was later to blame this on the Jewish Meyerbeer in his notoriously anti-Semitic essay *Das Judentum in der Musik* (1850), although there is no evidence of any ill will on Meyerbeer's part, and it was on the latter's recommendation that *Rienzi* was accepted for a performance in Dresden during 1842.

The Wagners moved to Dresden for the performance and its success paved the way for a production of *Der Fliegende Holländer*, written in Paris, the next year. Although this work, with its darker theme of the mariner who is cursed to sail around the world for eternity, was less well received, Wagner was offered the post of Kapellmeister at the Dresden court. By this time he was working on his next project, *Tannhäuser*, subsequently performed in 1845, but arguably more influential were his performance in 1846 of Beethoven's Ninth Symphony and his reading of Greek dramatists such as Aeschylus and Sophocles, as well as the medieval epics *Tristan*, *Parzifal* and *Lohengrin* and of the poet Hans Sachs.

Wagner's *Der Ring des Nibelungen,*
set from original production at Bayreuth;
Germany; 1876

If the Greek authors were to greatly influence his concept of musical drama his next operatic project, *Lohengrin*, was to lay to foundations for one of his greatest musical innovations, the *Leitmotif*, the association of a motif with a particular idea, situation, place or character.

Wagner's work on *Lohengrin* was interrupted by the revolutions of 1848 and his active role in calling for the overthrow of the aristocracy forced him to flee when the revolutionaries were overrun by Prussian troops. In 1849 the Wagners moved to Zürich where he wrote two important essays, *Das Kunstwerk der Zukunft* (1849) and *Oper und Drama*

In 1860 the travel restrictions on Wagner were eased and he moved first to Dresden and then Vienna, although by 1863 he had accumulated such debts that he was forced to flee the Austrian capital. The composer was rescued from these desperate straits by the new King of Bavaria, Ludwig II. This ardent Wagnerian paid off the composer's debts and set Wagner up in opulent accommodation in order that he could finish *Der Ring*. However, Ludwig found it hard to sustain the expenditure and approbation of the population, particularly after the poor reception given to the premiere of *Tristan* in 1865 under Hans von Bülow.

Music example: the opening to *Tristan*

Although Wagner undoubtedly did use the Tristan chord as a pure sonority, it is also true that there is a perfectly acceptable, if rather technical, functional explanation for the harmonic progression; that it is a French 6th chord (a substitute for IV) with lower chromatic Appogiatura that resolves, as it should, upwards to V in A major, the key at which it arrives by bar 44 and the start of the long, chromatic climb to the *Höhepunkt* (climax).

(1851) in which, following his study of Greek drama and later modified by the writings of Schopenhauer, he outlined his idea for the *Gesamtkunstwerk* (total art work) that would unify all the arts into a single dramatic form that Wagner envisaged as the music-drama. *Lohengrin* was performed in Weimar by Liszt in 1850 though Wagner was by then busy with the libretto for one of his most astounding achievements, the immense cycle of *Der Ring des Nibelungen,* based on the Medieval German *Nibelungenlied* and comprising three operas, *Die Walküre, Siegfried* and *Götterdämmerung*, and a prelude, *Das Rheingold*. The cycle was not finished until 1874 and in it, the closest he came to realizing the ideal of the *Gesamtkunstwerk*, Wagner fully exploited the technique of the *Leitmotif*, producing a through-composed work in which the story is told within the music as well as through the action performed on the stage.

With little income from performances of his works, and spending most of his time concentrating on the composition of *Der Ring*, Wagner was dependent on benefactors and, in 1857, he and Minna moved into a villa provided for them by Otto Wesendonck. Wagner embarked on a love affair with Otto's wife Mathilde and the passion of this infatuation spilt over into the composition of *Tristan und Isolde*. Finished in 1859, this is one of his most influential scores, not least its opening chord whose harmonic ambiguity has seen it identified as the beginning of the abandonment of tonality. The chromatic writing, with its almost constant modulation supporting the emotional turmoil of the plot, does not rest until the consummation of Isolde's *Liebestod* ("love death") at the very end.

By now Wagner was irreconcilably separated from Minna and had taken up with von Bülow's wife Cosima, the daughter of Liszt. The couple moved to the Villa Tribschen on Lake Lucerne where Wagner pondered questions of German nationalism. The not-entirely-wholesome conclusions he came to were to inform the writing of his only comic opera *Die Meistersinger von Nürnberg* (1868) as well as his desire to create a temple to his own art where his works could be performed away from pernicious foreign influence. It was at this time that he made the acquaintance of the philosopher Friedrich Nietzsche with whom he formed a brief but intense friendship until they fell out over philosophical differences in 1876.

With the aid of patrons such as Ludwig II (who set aside earnings from the Hoftheater to pay for the enterprise), Wagner decided on the town of Bayreuth as the location of the new theater and festival. A villa, Wahnfried, was also built on the site chosen by Wagner. With Cosima, whom he had married in 1870 (Minna had died in 1866 and Cosima had divorced from Hans von Bülow in 1869), Wagner moved to this place in 1874. The first festival was held in 1876 with the first complete performance of *Der Ring des Nibelungen*.

Wagner's opera *Parsifal*, based on Wolfram von Eschenbach's medieval epic poem *Parzival*, was completed by the end of 1881 and first performed at the Bayreuth Festspielhaus in 1882. The mysticism of the Grail legend prompted Wagner to produce some of his most sublime music. This was to prove his final work and he died in Venice the following year. His body was taken back to Bayreuth and buried in the grounds of Villa Wahnfried.

The Bayreuth Festspielhaus, festival hall, 2007

5me Edition

GUILLAUME-TELL

Opéra en Quatre actes

PARTITION
RÉDUITE AU
PIANO et CHANT
PAR
L. NIEDERMEYER

Paroles de
JOUY et HIPP. BIS

MVSIQVE DE
G. ROSSINI

PRIX: 20f NET

PARIS LÉON GRUS, Editeur

Guillaume Tell, titlepage for 19th
century edition of score; published by
Leon Grus-Paris

Based on a play by Schiller this is
Rossini's largest-scale work, replete
with ballets and grand spectacle taken
straight from the French tradition.
Little performed due to the expense
and difficulty of its staging the music,
nevertheless, seems to mark a new
stage in Rossini's thought with clear,
unornamented lines and a radical
approach to harmony and orchestration
that drew the approval of Berlioz.

of *L'inganno felice* in 1812, and he had written a further five operas, predominantly farces, by early 1813. At this time, Italian opera was still in thrall to the by now stale conventions of the 18th century and to this rather moribund tradition Rossini brought a flair for melodic invention and snappy rhythm, allied to an exceptional ability for composing overtures that has made them popular works in their own right.

The period from 1813–18 was hectic for Rossini during which he produced his most famous comic operas: *L'italiana in Algeri* (1813) and its return fixture *Il turco in Italia* (1814); *Il barbiere di Siviglia* (1816), still his most popular work; and *La gazza ladra* (1818). However, he also became active in the field of *opera seria*, the first of which was *Tancredi* (1813) and this work with its famous *aria* "Di tanti palpiti" sees the emergence of a mature style. Rossini's genius lies in his ability to overcome the problem of alternating *recitative* that has a dramatic function with an *aria* that holds up the story. His solution, one that was to be generally adopted by all subsequent Italian opera composers, was to assign a dramatic function to sections of his lyrical writing, dispensing with the need for large amounts of *recitative*. To do this his *arias*, duets and ensemble pieces become larger musical conceptions in which alternating sections, distinguished by devices such as key, tempo or rhythm, contrast moments of pure lyricism with elements of dramatic action. By this time Rossini was not only writing for the stage in Venice but his operas were being performed from Milan to Naples, and between 1815–23 it was for the latter city, one of the great centers of Italian opera during the 18th century and still with a fine body of singers and instrumentalists, that he wrote most of his new works. These were predominantly *opera seria* and in a string of magnificent compositions, from *Otello* (1816) to *La donna del lago* (1819) and *Semiramide* (1823) he refined the musical techniques adopted in *Tancredi* to more fully express the actions of the drama. His ideas on the overture also changed toward the end of this time with his later operas tending to do away with the existing form and, in a move that was also to be highly influential, adopting instead a short prelude comprising elements of music from the act it introduces.

Semiramide was to be his last opera for the Italian stage and in 1824 he moved to Paris where he was to spend much of the rest of his life and from this point on his works were all for the French stage. His first commission in the city was for a celebration of Charles X, *Il viaggio a Reims* (1825), but as well as adapting some of his Neapolitan works for productions in French he also began to work on his first truly French work, an *opéra comique* of *Le*

Later in the century composers in France became more ambivalent about this Italian influence and pressure grew to develop a distinctively French style of opera composition.

However, in the early decades of the 19th century non-German opera was dominated by one figure, Rossini. Born in Pesaro, Marche, into a musical family—his father played the horn and his mother was a singer—Rossini soon began to play and sing, although his musical training did not begin in earnest until the family moved to Bologna in 1804. There, from 1806, he attended the Liceo Musicale where he acquired a love of the music of Haydn and Mozart and began to dabble in composition. Rossini also took work, directing operas from the harpsichord, through which he gained important experience of the dramatic world. His first successful foray in operatic composition, however, came in 1810 when he was asked to provide music for a one-act farce entitled *La cambiale di matrimonio* for the theater of San Moisè in Venice. This was soon followed by other commissions, especially after the success

comte Ory (1828). This was followed in 1829 by the opera which perhaps more than any other was to be influential on subsequent composers working in Paris, particularly Meyerbeer, *Guillaume Tell*. Although he was to live for another 40 years, this was to be his last operatic work and for the rest of his life Rossini produced little other music but led a contented life in the French capital where his works continued to be venerated.

Where Rossini had paved the way, two other Italian writers of opera were to follow, Bellini and Donizetti. While each of the rivals had an individual voice, both were influenced by the older composer and Donizetti was to be a formative influence on Bellini through his work *La zingara* (1822). They were to lay the ground for the most famous Italian composer of the 19th century, Guiseppe Verdi. All three composers are, however, especially associated with the *bel canto* style of singing. This particularly Italian approach to vocal performance literally means "beautiful singing" and is concerned with a far more melodic sense of the vocal line, as opposed to the declamatory styles in French and German opera. In particular it refers to the use of a flowing and light tone and a flexibility and ease in long lines of *coloratura*. This greater concentration on melody is particularly marked in the works of Donizetti and Bellini who, in contrast to Rossini who is quick to include vocal gymnastics within his *arias*, tend to leave such display to the closing sections of their duets and solo *arias*.

Like Rossini, Donizetti was equally at home in both *opera buffa* and *opera seria*, and could produce works to order in a remarkably short space of time. Born in the northern Italian city of Bergamo, his early career followed that of Rossini, from study in Bologna to working in Naples. During the 1820s Donizetti was still working towards a distinctive style and his first great success came in 1828 with *L'esule di Roma* that played in both Naples and Milan. However, international fame was to come with *Anna Bolena* (1830), the work in which a mature style can be readily identified. In this he follows Bellini in

making the work appear more through-composed, using *arioso* (lyrical passages that take the place of *recitative*) as links between the *arias* and duets. Between the premiere of *Anna Bolena* in Milan and 1838 when he moved to Paris, Donizetti wrote 25 operas that vary from the Romantic *Lucia di Lammermoor* (1835), inspired by the Walter Scott novel, to the comic *L'elisir d'amore* (1832). As with a number of Verdi's operas Donizetti too faced censorship, especially when the subject of the opera might be construed as having a political meaning, *Lucrezia Borgia* (1833) was actually banned from performance in Naples. It may have been this unconducive environment that prompted Donizetti to move to Paris. After an initial hiatus he was soon taking the Parisian opera stage by storm, writing the comic *La fille du régiment* for the Opéra-Comique in 1840 and adapting *Lucia* for Paris as *Lucie de Lammermoor* in the same year. Donizetti was also making an impact in Vienna and was even offered the job as Hofkapellmeister but before long symptoms of the syphilis that was to kill him became noticeable. From 1844 it became almost impossible for him to compose and he died at the relatively young age of 50.

Bellini was to die at an even younger age but if anything he achieved even more during his short lifetime, carving out an identifiably Romantic style of Italian opera and influencing not only Verdi but also French opera. He eschewed the comic operas of Rossini and Donizetti, preferring serious plots based around historical figures or Romantic fiction. His relatively few works, compared to Rossini and Donizetti, nevertheless quickly became hugely successful and transferred to opera stages across Europe. Part of his individuality comes from not immediately falling under the spell of Rossini during his training in Naples, where he had moved to from his birthplace in Sicily. The florid style

Bellini *Bianca e Fernando,* stage design by Alessandro Sanquirico, 1829

Bellini's early operas, such as *Bianca e Fernando* (1826), already contain musical ideas that were to run throughout his works, especially the so-called "lyric prototype". This formal scheme for vocal pieces is based on four four-bar phrases: the first four bars are repeated with slight variation, bars 9–12 are contrasting and modulate from the tonic before the final four bars return to the tonic with either a variation of the first motif or a cadential passage (AA1BA2/C).

César Franck at the console of this organ in Sainte Clothilde, by Jeanne Rongier; 1885

An important figure in 19th century France, César Franck (1822–90) was actually born in Liège in Belgium. Hailed as a prodigy, when his family moved to Paris in 1835 Franck was enrolled at the Conservatoire but initially his career failed to take off, even though one of his first sets of compositions, 3 Trios Concertantes (1839–42), was well received. In 1858 he became organist at the church of St Clothilde where he began to build a reputation as a teacher, and among his students were Vincent D'Indy and Henri Duparc. He wrote songs, organ and chamber pieces and large number of liturgical works but is perhaps best remembered today for his Symphony (1886–8). In a great deal of his harmonic writing he was influenced by Wagner, but some of his innovations in the juxtaposing of harmonies were taken up by Debussy.

Meyerbeer's *Le prophète*, Gustave
Roger in the role of Jean; Paris; 1849

The *grand opéra* par excellence, *Le
prophète* was premiered at the Paris
Opéra on April 16, 1849. Set during
the Anabaptist conflict in 16th-century
Germany, its tale of thwarted love,
religious upheaval, power and political
machination proved an auspicious mix as
the Parisian audiences flocked to see it.
Aside from spectacularly difficult roles
for Fidés, the mother of Jean de Leyde
the *prophète* of the title, and Berthe
who is in love with him, the sunrise that
occurs during Act III was the first use of
electric lighting at the Paris Opéra. The
work has one of the most spectacular
finales of any opera, as Jean's palace is
destroyed on stage.

The Palais Garnier

In 1860 it was decided to construct a new
home for the Paris Opéra, and a location
was decided on at the center of Baron
Haussmann's new grands boulevards at
the head of what is now boulevard de
l'Opéra. The competition to design the
building was won by Charles Garnier and
work started on the site in 1861. The
Baroque-revival Beaux Arts edifice was
gorgeously ornate but also incorporated
the latest in staging technology and was
ideally suited to its use. Its completion
was delayed by the Franco-Prussian
war and the ensuing Commune. The new
Opéra finally opened on January 5, 1875
with a gala performance of extracts
from *La Juive* and *Les Huguenots*. This
remained the Opéra's home until 1987
when the main stage was moved to the
new building at Bastille.

of much of Rossini's work was not appreciated in
Neapolitan academic circles and this may account
in part for Bellini's concentration on the long
melodic lines for which he became so famous.
Bellini's use of these and the "lyric prototype"
really came into its own with *Il pirata* (1827),
Bellini's first opera for the Milan stage. Its success
insured that Bellini's reputation quickly spread
and received further commissions, for which he
was paid handsomely. *Il pirata* was followed by
La straniera in 1829, a far more austere work
that is characterized by its economy of motivic
development and declamatory style of word setting.
This was to be the furthest Bellini was to push an
austere Romantic style and in subsequent works
he was to adopt more ornamented vocal lines in a
string of works including *I Capuletti e i Montecchi*
(1830), *La sonnambula* and *Norma* (both 1831).
By this time Bellini's operas were in demand from
foreign houses and from 1833 he relocated to
Paris to prepare versions of his operas in French.
While there he received a commission from the
Théâtre Italien for what would be his last opera,
I puritani (1835), in which French influence—an
exploitation of stage effects and a greater use of
the chorus—can be detected.

Italian influence on foreign composers was seen
most clearly in the works of Giacomo Meyerbeer
(1791–1864), whose large-scale pieces were to
become the exemplars of French *grand opéra*.
Born in Germany, Meyerbeer spent the first part
of his career in Italy where his operas, influenced
by Mozart and Rossini, became so popular that
even Goethe was moved to write admiringly of his

achievements. Although he had not yet developed
the style for which he was to become so influential
on figures such as Wagner, in works such as
Margherita d'Anjou (1820) and *Il crociato in
Egitto* (1824), Meyerbeer displays a great facility
for exploiting orchestral and staging effects to
enhance the drama. The popularity of these two
operas was such that he was invited to write a
work for the Paris Opéra, then the leading theater
in Europe. At the end of the 1820s there were
calls in France for a new, specifically French,

GUISEPPE VERDI

Guiseppe Verdi, born in 1813, was destined to become not only Italy's greatest musical figure of the 19th century but also a symbol of emerging Italian nationhood, to the extent that the composer is inextricably linked to the *Risorgimento* and the chorus "Va pensiero" from *Nabucco* has achieved the status of an unofficial national anthem. Verdi's legacy is a large volume of operas, many of them perennially popular, in which drama is the central concern rather than the underlying musical structures that were so much a preoccupation of Wagner.

After an early life and musical training in Busseto in Emilia-Romagna he studied with Vincenzo Lavigna, the *maestro* of the great opera house of La Scala in Milan. He returned to Busseto in 1836 to become *maestro di musica* of the local philharmonic society and it was during his time there he composed his first opera *Rocester*, given its first performance in its revised version *Oberto* at La Scala in 1839. By now Verdi had moved back to Milan and the success he achieved with *Oberto* prompted the impresario Bartolomeo Merelli to offer him a contract for a further three operas. This produced, in 1842, Verdi's greatest success to date, the opera *Nabucco*. The acclaim with which this was greeted ensured more commissions and the next decade saw a constant flow of work, including many of his most popular compositions: *Macbeth* (Florence, 1847), *Luisa Miller* (Naples, 1849), *Rigoletto* (Venice, 1851), *Il trovatore* (Rome, 1853) and *La traviata* (Venice, 1853).

The period following the premiere of *La traviata*, by which time Verdi had achieved considerable fame, saw a slowing-down in his output. He was now settled at the farmhouse at Sant'Agata near Busseto where he was to spend the rest of his life, and was living with the soprano Giuseppina Strepponi, much

to the scandal of his neighbors as they were not married (his first wife Margherita had died in 1840). As well as attending productions of his works in Paris, London, St Petersburg and Madrid, in 1861 Verdi was persuaded by Camillo Cavour, the first prime minister of Italy, to stand for parliament. This he did and he held a seat until 1865. Although he produced fewer operas, two of them were his longest scores (those written for Paris), *Les vêpres siciliennes* (1855) and *Don Carlos* (1867), and of the others *Simon Boccanegra* (1857), *Un ballo in maschera* (1859) and *La forza del destino* (1862) are among his greatest works. None, however, have remained as popular as *Aida*, first performed in Cairo in 1871. The political fervor of the times, especially following the failed revolutions of 1848, did present problems for Verdi, not least in his clashes with the operatic censor, leading him to make revisions to the scores and using historical settings for potentially subversive plots, such as that for *Don Carlos*.

The last period of Verdi's life saw no new opera until *Otello* in 1887. In between came the *Requiem* of 1874; famously described as "an opera in ecclesiastical clothes" it was written to commemorate the death of the writer Alessandro Manzoni. Verdi's long period of relative silence might be ascribed to his comfortable status and lifestyle, but also to a growing discontent with the direction that music was taking in Italy as French and German works, especially those by Wagner, gained in popularity. His last two operas *Otello* and *Falstaff* (1893) are

Verdi's *La Traviata*, Emma Bell as Violetta and Dwayne Jones as Alfredo; English National Opera; London; 2006

often seen as demonstrating the tensions that existed in Italian music at the time, between the "lyrical and declamatory", and Verdi's positioning of himself between the two but also, especially in *Falstaff*, harking back to *bel canto* and a greater use of counterpoint. His death in 1901 saw nationwide mourning, fitting for a composer who had come to so completely represent the Italian musical tradition.

Verdi, by Giovanni Boldini, 1886

One of Italy's greatest composers, Verdi's gift for melodic invention and fine sense for exploiting the musical potential of the dramatic moment raises his works above a mere progression of *recitative, aria* and *concertato* (finale), and gives them an overall coherence lacking in the works of some of his contemporaries.

Gabriel Fauré

The retiring style of much of Gabriel Fauré's (1845–1924) music tends to obscure the degree to which he was forward-thinking and the huge influence he had on French composers of the 20th century, especially Debussy and Ravel through works such as the *Ballade* (1877–9) for piano and orchestra. Through his chamber and piano music and songs he developed a personal style whose harmonic innovations included the use of the whole-tone scale, in the song *Sérénade toscane* (1878), and highly chromatic progressions with a widespread use of 7ths and 9ths that, while used in terms of pure sound, still maintain a functional purpose. Fauré's ability to sustain a melodic line built from a single motif is reminiscent of Brahms, and his use of mutable and fluid rhythm is highly characteristic of his works. One of his most original works was his only opera, *Pénélope* (1913), that builds on his mastery of song and consists predominantly of short lyrical passages with no linking *recitatives*.

Cavalleria rusticana

The call for *verismo* ("realism") in Italian opera toward the end of the 19th century was not only taken up by Puccini, but also in the works of Pietro Mascagni (1863–1945). His most successful work was only his second opera, the one-act *Cavalleria rusticana* (1890). He went on to write a large number of other works, many of them infused with the strong sense of melody so attractive in *Cavalleria*, that were also well-received but none quite caught the imagination of the public as the tale of Turiddu, a young peasant, who is killed by the husband of his lover Lola. Often paired with *Pagliacci*, another masterpiece of *verismo*, *Cavalleria rusticana* has not left the repertory since its first performance.

type of opera that brought together the lyricism of Italian vocal writing and the German use of the orchestra. The ideal model for this was seen as Rossini's *Guillaume Tell*. It was into this debate that Meyerbeer stepped with his new commission, the result of which was *Robert le diable* (1831). The impact of the work was immense, not only for its length of five acts, but the manipulation of orchestral effects and the unprecedented amount of work and detail that went into its staging. As well as the sheer spectacle of the performance and the technically impressive singing, the opera was singled out as being philosophical and psychological; for the first time opera, and the libretto, was treated as a means to present a discourse of ideas and it is in this, above all, that Meyerbeer was to be so influential. Meyerbeer was to produce a further five operas for the Paris stage during his lifetime and *Les Huguenots* (1836), *Le prophète* (1849) and *L'Africaine* (1865) in particular remained staples of the repertory until the 20th century.

Meyerbeer's influence on opera in France was profound and is seen in the stage works of the two most prominent French composers of the mid-19th century: Charles-François Gounod (1818–93) and Georges Bizet (1838–75). Both have seen much of their other music ignored, but they each produced a single opera that has remained in the repertory since its first performance and, in the case of Bizet, achieved worldwide prominence. Gounod was a prolific composer, particularly of sacred and liturgical music, who is important for establishing a French-language rival to *Lieder*, the *mélodie*, that was developed later by Gabriel Fauré and Henri Duparc (1848–1933). His *grand opéra* success came with *Faust* in 1859, an exceptional

work that runs the gamut of emotion and effect, from the cavortings of Méphistophélès to the pure religiosity of Marguerite. Bizet, who would no doubt have gone on to be one of the greatest 19th-century French composers if not for his early death at the age of 36, is generally remembered for one piece only out of his surprisingly large output, *Carmen* (1873–4). This sultry tale of sex, revenge and death, more properly seen as an *opéra comique*, is set in Spain, a country whose music became a favorite trope of French composers, most famously in Emmanuel Chabrier's (1841–94) tone poem *España* (1883). *Carmen* is perhaps the most popular opera ever written and has not been out of the repertory since its first performance. The end of the century saw the opera composer Jules Massenet (1842–1912) take center stage in France. Extraordinarily prolific and popular during his lifetime, his often highly-colored works display a thorough grasp of post-Wagnerian tonality and owe a great deal to the spectacle of the *grand opéra* of Meyerbeer. However, he also adopted lighter elements of style from *opéra comique*, seen to great effect in his work that is now most often performed, *Manon* (1884).

The story of Manon Lescaut, from the novel by Antoine-François Prévost, was also to be set by the most important Italian composer of the late-19th century, Giacomo Puccini (1858–1924). Representing the last flourish of the great Italian opera tradition, Puccini was not content to copy from the models of Verdi or Donizetti but reinvented many aspects of Italian opera through his fine orchestration and bold use of the harmonic innovations current in France, Germany and Austria. Born into a musical family, he was introduced to the scores of Verdi at a young age and his earliest compositions show this influence, as well as, interestingly, that of Wagner. His first opera, staged in Milan with help from the publisher Ricordi, was *Le villi* (1883). This was well received, including praise from members of the so-called *scapigliatura*, an intellectual bohemian movement dedicated to a renaissance in Italian culture. *Manon Lescaut*, Puccini's first mature work in which he closely knits developments in the plot to motifs and tonality, followed in 1893 and from this time on his fame was assured. Following the call of the *scapigliatura* for a greater *verismo* (realism) in Italian opera, Puccini responded with another tale of doomed love and a consumptive heroine, that of Mimì in *La bohème* (1896). However, one of his greatest achievements in *verismo* was to be in a

THE LEGACY OF WAGNER

The final decades of the 19th century saw composers from all over Europe fall under the spell of Wagner, and nowhere more so than in the German-speaking world, exemplified in the works of the Austrian symphonist Anton Bruckner (1824–96), and the German Modernist-turned-Romantic Richard Strauss. Aside from Wagner's attempts to forge a new type of music drama, his lasting influence came from his treatment of the orchestra and radical departures from traditional harmony. Wagner augmented the orchestra to a size never seen before. This not only allowed him to create overwhelming climaxes of sound at key points in the score but also to treat different instruments as discrete groups. In order to do this, the oboe and clarinet sections were made

Leoncavallo's *Pagliacci*, Zeffirelli's production for Covent Garden; London; 2003

The Italian opera composer Ruggiero Leoncavallo (1857–1919) was initially a devout Wagnerian and spent the formative years of his professional life in Paris where he unsuccessfully tried to make a living as a composer and piano teacher. The turning point came with the first performance of Mascagni's *Cavalleria rusticana* and this prompted Leoncavallo to adopt *verismo* for his greatest work, *Pagliacci* (1892), in which he displays a fine sense of orchestration and adventurous harmony. Although he received many commissions following *Pagliacci*, like Mascagni, the success of this opera of love, murder and jealousy set among a group of traveling players overshadowed the rest of Leoncavallo's career.

much later work, *Il tabarro*, one of the components of *Il trittico* (1918) a series of three one-act opera all to be performed on the same evening. Another part of the trilogy is *Gianni Schicchi*, a historical *opera buffa*. It was a historical theme that was to follow on from *La bohème*, an exploration of love, lust and power in *Tosca* (1900). Exotic locations were also to interest Puccini, and allowed him to indulge his genius for orchestral color, from the west of the United States of America in *La fanciulla del West* (1910) to Japan in *Madama Butterfly* (1904). He was to return to East Asia, this time historical China, in his final, unfinished, work *Turandot*. This had taken up the last five years of his life and in it he achieved a unity between music and drama not seen in the work of any other Italian composer and, through the integration of the staging with the other dramatic elements, came closest to realizing a non-German *Gesamtkunstwerk*.

into a quartet with the addition of a cor anglais and bass clarinet respectively. His additions to the brass voicings were more radical; new instruments were invented to add a bass to the trumpet and trombone sections (a bass trumpet at the same pitch as the trombone and a contrabass trombone pitched an octave below the rest of the section). It was the invention of the so-called Wagner tuba that made the greatest impact, and which was adopted enthusiastically by Bruckner and Strauss (the former used them memorably in his Seventh Symphony, dedicated to the memory of Wagner, and the latter in his opera *Elektra*). A quartet of these instruments, two in Bb and two in F at the same pitch as the horn, was used as a bass to the standard horn quartet (the tubas are played by extra members of the horn section).

In harmony Wagner was equally far-reaching, pushing the bounds of ambiguity to the extent that

Anton Bruckner was born in Ansfelden in Upper Austria. His father was a local school teacher who also played the organ and the young Anton also began to show a talent for the instrument. After training with his cousin Johann Weiss he joined the nearby monastery of St Florian as a chorister. This was a pivotal moment in Bruckner's life, reinforcing his strong Catholic faith and giving him a firm grounding in the liturgical repertory. During the first part of his career he was a choral instructor and organist at the monastery and wrote liturgical works for the religious institution. In 1856 he moved to Linz to take up a position in the city where he became aware of the music of Wagner, a passion that like his strong faith was to stay with him all his life. By the time he moved to Vienna in 1868 to take up a teaching position at the conservatory, he had already amassed a large volume of compositions, including symphonies. His greatest works were to follow, including the 4th ("Romantische", 1874), 5th (1875–6), 7th (1881–3) and 8th (1884–7) Symphonies.

Richard Strauss' *Salome*, title page op.54 (left); "The Climax" illustration by Aubrey Beardsley (right)

The son of Franz Strauss, one Europe's finest horn players, Richard Strauss was immersed in the musical world of Munich from an early age. He began composing at the age of 11 and, through the amateur group that Franz conducted, began to write works for orchestra. Initially his preference was for the compositions of Mendelssohn and Brahms, but in 1885, through the influence of the violinist Alexander Ritter, he became converted to the music of Wagner. From now on Wagner was to be, along with Mozart and Brahms, one of his guiding lights, and he embarked on a series of tone poems that represent the apotheosis of the genre. Although he had written an opera, *Guntram*, in 1892–3, it was with *Salome* (1905), based on the work by Oscar Wilde, that he made his mark. This was followed by *Elektra*, the work that marks the beginning of his long collaboration with the writer Hugo von Hofmannsthal (1874–1929). In their next work they were to retreat from *Elektra's* violent Modernism and produce one of their finest creations, *Der Rosenkavalier* (1909–10), a comedy set in 18th-century Vienna in which Strauss's masterly use of the waltz knits the work together. Other notable collaborations between the two artists include *Ariadne auf Naxos* (1911–12) and the Symbolist *Die Frau ohne Schatten* (1914–17), that Strauss considered his greatest work.

later composers were inclined to see some of his harmonies as exercises in pure sound rather than as functional components of a progression. This has proved controversial and debate has raged about the function of the so-called "Tristan chord",

the very first harmony encountered in *Tristan und Isolde*. That Wagner does use this collection of notes as a pure sonority is undoubtedly true; it occurs at the *Höhepunkt* (climax) of the prelude to thwart the resolution of the cadence. Indeed, the resolution of a climatic cadence is held back until the very end of the work (a V–I in B major that is disrupted so memorably at the height of the Act 2 love duet), leading one music commentator to remark that *Tristan* is a "five-hour coitus interruptus".

These innovations, along with an almost constant use of chromatic, semitonal voice leading that enables the music to easily pass from one key (or rather an implication of key) to another, were to start the eventual breakdown of tonality that occurred in the 20th century. However, for composers of the 19th century, the emotional and formal implications of being able to constantly suspend resolution—from which Wagner's music draws much of its power—were seen as operating within, not destroying, the tonal system. For Bruckner, steeped in the symphonic tradition of Beethoven, this meant using a Wagnerian harmonic language to push the formal constraints of sonata form within huge orchestral structures that followed the Romantic pattern of heroic ascent from despair to triumph. For Strauss, these techniques were first put to use in a series of tone poems, from *Don Juan* (1888–89) to *Eine Alpensinfonie* (1911–15), where the manipulation of harmony aided the musical telling of the story. Though he became famous with his opera *Salome* (1905), an adaptation of Oscar Wilde's play, it was in *Elektra* (1906–8) that Strauss took the suspension of tonality and chromatic voice-leading to an extreme, leading many to view him as an arch Modernist. However, this was a position the composer was to shy away from; none of his subsequent works are as ferociously Modern. Strauss continued working up until his death in 1948, by which time

he had become the last surviving representative of 19th century Romanticism. The late flowering of his final works, such as *Vier letzte Lieder* for soprano and orchestra, contains some of his most ravishing music.

NATIONALISM

The second half of the 19th century saw a call in France for a reinvention of a French tradition, in part a reaction against the dominance of Wagner. This had had its counterpart in Italy with the use of the works of Verdi to express Italian identity. Defeat in the Franco-Prussian War in 1870–1 brought about a change in French culture as composers absorbed the consequences of France's changed status in the world. One of the most important figures of the subsequent renaissance in French music was Camille Saint-Saëns (1835–1921), famous as an organist, composer and teacher. His musical talents had been recognized early on and he made his debut at the Salle Pleyel at the age of 10. After leaving the Conservatoire with the *premier prix* for organ, where he had already started to compose short works, he became organist at the prestigious church of the Madeleine. He also made the acquaintance of Rossini, Berlioz and Gounod, all of whom supported him, and Saint-Saëns in turn became a champion of the modern German school, particularly of the works of Wagner, but also Schumann and Liszt. He was the teacher of Fauré and was especially influential in setting up the Société Nationale de Musique in 1871 with his contemporaries such as Ernest Chausson (1855–99), a organization intent on promoting an "Ars Gallica" through performances of works by young French composers. For all that he was a great defender of young modern composers, in his own works he was a traditionalist, working largely in established genres and using strongly functional harmony, although in the late works he began to move towards a French Neoclassicism.

However, rising nationalist sentiments were not restricted to France and Italy, the assertion of national identities was particularly noticeable in Russia, Scandinavia and in non-German areas of Central Europe that were still part of the Austro-Hungarian Empire, notably Bohemia. That these ideas chimed with local élites is indicative of the twin poles of 19th-century life; bourgeois comfort versus political upheaval. In the same way that the revolutions of 1848 sprang from the middle-class respectability of the politically repressive Biedermeier period, so a rising level of material wealth led to a challenge to the dominant cultural force, that of Austro-German music. While Russia was an independent state, the rising urban middle class of the early-19th century were consumers of imported musical styles from France and Germany, and it was in Russia that the move toward a consciously national style first took place, through the works of Mikhail Glinka (1804–57).

While his early chamber music is very much still in the tradition of composers such as Haydn,

Mozart and Beethoven, Glinka was to become one of the foremost opera composers of his day, compared favorably to Bellini and Donizetti. His importance lies in being the first Russian composer to successfully take Italian and German operatic forms and to give them an identifiably Russian identity, not least through his choice of subject matter. Initially destined for a career in the civil service, a trip to Italy during 1830–3 to help his recovery from illness brought his strong interest in music to the fore and was invaluable in providing Glinka with a thorough grounding in Italian opera. This was followed by a period of instruction in harmony and counterpoint in Berlin, and on his return to Russia in 1834 Glinka was determined to ally these newfound skills with his early exposure to Russian folk music in the creation of a national

operatic style. It was to bear fruit in his first mature work, *Zhizn' za tsarya* ("A Life for the Tsar", 1836), a self-consciously laudatory work praising the sacrifice of the peasant Susanin for the ruling Romanov family. This was, obviously, not going to do any harm to Glinka's reputation with the country's rulers but more interestingly the central place of a peasant family in the drama gave him scope for the inclusion of dances and choruses with a distinctly Russian flavor.

It was this work, and the less successful *Ruslan i Lyudmila* (1842), that were to prove so important for the next generation of Russian composers, known as "The Five" or *Moguchaya kuchka* ("Mighty Handful"), who determined to continue Glinka's initial foray into musical nationalism and create a truly Russian style that covered all genres and forged a national musical language. The five

Vincent D'Indy

The fine works of composer Vincent D'Indy (1851–1931) have been somewhat overshadowed by his work as a teacher and his reputation as a right-wing Catholic polemicist. A follower of Franck, who was his teacher, and an admirer of Wagner he began composing after a period of intense study at the Conservatoire and achieved success with his *Symphonie sur un chant montagnard français* (1886) which displays his considerable talent for orchestration, also seen in his late works *Poème des rivages* (1919–21) and *Diptyque méditerranéen* (1925–6). The radical formal ideas of his works were in opposition to his ideas as a pedagogue and after his rather conservative plan to restructure the Conservatoire was turned down, he founded a separate institution, the Schola Cantorum, in 1894. Although one of its aims was to reform the Catholic liturgy by reintroducing Gregorian chant, in other respects it was surprisingly enlightened, admitting women and eschewing prizes. Among the composers to pass through its doors were Albert Roussel, Erik Satie and Edgard Varèse.

Aleksandr Skryabin

Perhaps the most individual Russian composer of the late 19th century was Aleksandr Nikoleyevitch Skryabin (1872–1915). His mystical philosophical outlook, broadly Symbolist, profoundly influenced his compositional approach in not only the programs that lay behind his works but also in his harmonic and melodic innovations. While never actually embracing atonality Skyrabin goes further than any other 19th-century composer in escaping from the tonal system and, in works such as *Le poème de l'extase* (1905–8) and his piano sonatas, in conceiving of harmony and melody as indivisible aspects of the same grouping of pitches. Characteristic of his harmonic groupings is the so-called "Mystic Chord", a union of wholetone and octatonic elements, two scales that Skryabin used extensively. Another device that crops up frequently in his works is the "resolution" of a dominant seventh chord, often with an added sixth and ninth, onto a different dominant seventh a tritone apart. Strings of these were to form the harmonic basis of many of his later works.

composers, based in St Petersburg, who were to achieve this were: Mily Balakirev (1837–1910), leader and driving force behind the group; César Cui (1835–1918) whose music, while greatly admired by his compatriots, has been relatively ignored; Aleksandr Borodin (1833–87); Modest Mussorgsky (1839–81); and Nikolay Rimsky-Korsakov (1844–1908). If it was Balakirev that provided the political and ideological drive for the movement, it is the latter three composers who were to make their mark through the quality of their music. A further, though greatly differing figure, is associated with the rise of a Russian national school, Pyotr Il'yich Tchaikovsky (1840–93). Known today for his extremely popular orchestral works, especially his Fourth, Fifth and Sixth Symphonies (1878–93), and ballets *Lebedinoe ozero* ("Swan Lake", 1877), *Spyashchaya krasavitsa* ("The Sleeping Beauty", 1889) and *Shchelkunchik* ("The Nutcracker", 1892), as well as the opera *Yevgeny Onegin* (1878), Tchaikovsky moved Russian music from one that was narrowly focused on establishing a national tradition to one that was international. This was due in part to his ease at working in a language that eschewed the modal and harmonic innovations of his contemporaries in Russia, a direction that was taken up by the pianist-composer Serge Rachmaninoff (1873–1943) who, like Strauss in Germany, was to be the last of Russia's great Romantic composers.

By contrast, Borodin employed a far more self-consciously Russian musical language, at least after his meeting with Balakirev in 1862. Seen to great effect in his Second Symphony (1876) and the tone poem *V sredney Azii* ("In Central Asia", 1880), this includes the use of modal inflections in his melodies and drones in the bass that hint at folksong, while in the latter work a chromatic second theme representing Asia is contrasted against the diatonicism of Russia. His largest work, the opera *Knyaz' Igor'* ("Prince Igor"), however, remained unfinished and was completed by Rimsky Korsakov and Aleksandr Glazunov (1865–1936). In this too he opposes a Russian diatonicism against a chromaticism that represents the Polovtsians. Borodin's explorations of musical language in the use of octatonic scales, augmented 2nds and the opposition of chords whose roots are separated by non-diatonic intervals—in particular the tritone—can be more clearly seen in the works of Musorgsky. Perhaps the greatest of the "Five", Musorgsky's uncompromising search for a way to set the speech patterns of Russian to music in an idiomatic way that did not disrupt the lyrical flow of the vocal line was realized in his great opera *Boris Godunov* (1868–9) where his earlier concern for extreme naturalism was tempered by a greater awareness of dramatic structure. A widespread use of modal inflection in his melodies and opposition of distant tonalities was to be carried through into his later works, the operas *Khovanshchina* (1872–80) and *Sorochinskaya yarmarka* ("Sorochintsï Fair", 1874–80) as well as the impressionistic piano work *Kartinki s vïstavki* ('Pictures at an Exhibition', 1874). These innovations were to make Musorgsky influential on later, ostensibly Modernist, composers such as Debussy and Ravel in France and Prokofiev and Shostakovich in Russia. The last of the "Mighty Handful", Rimsky-Korsakov, was the most prolific of the group, influential as the teacher of Igor Stravinsky and the writer of an important treatise on orchestration, of which he was a master. Of all

the Russian nationalists he was the most concerned with the inclusion of folksong into his works, often in an appropriate context as in his operas *Snegurochka* ("The Snow Maiden", 1880–1) and *Mlada* (1889–90). As well as for his own music, not least the popular tone poem *Sheherazade* (1888) that emphasizes the Russian nationalists' fascination with Asia, through his editing and promotion of his colleagues' music he was to lay the foundations for the international acceptance of a "Russian school" of composition.

In the same way that Glinka was important for the establishing of national school in Russia, it was his near contemporary Bedřich Smetana (1824–84) who was to perform the same role for the Czechs. Like Glinka, he too spent years abroad, in Weimar and Leipzig, where he was profoundly influenced by the music of Liszt, and Göteborg, although he compared this city unfavorably to the cosmopolitan musical life of Prague, before returning to the latter city to engage with building a Czech national music. This was a project that Smetana came to relatively late, up until the 1860s he spoke and wrote only in German (the language of education in Bohemia, then under the Austro-Hungarian Empire) and once he had made the decision to engage with the burgeoning nationalist movement in Prague he began to teach himself Czech. One of the events that prompted him to take this position was the opening of a Czech-language theater in Prague and a realization that opera could play an important part in the building of a national identity. Indeed, Smetana's greatest achievement was the founding of a Czech opera tradition, and his works are still at the core of the repertory of the Národní divadlo (National Theater) established in 1868 in Prague. The first of his Czech operas was *Braniboři v Čechách* ("The Brandenburgers in Bohemia", 1862–3), quickly followed after its successful premiere by *Prodaná nevěta* ("The Bartered Bride", 1866) that despite its initially unpromising reception was to become his most popular work, receiving over 100 performances during his lifetime. He went on to write a further five operas, two of them on overtly nationalist themes, *Dalibor* (1867) and *Libuše* (1872). Although there were calls to follow the musical example of Wagner, Smetana remained convinced that a national style could not be achieved through copying a supposedly international Wagnerian idiom and turned instead to Czech dance rhythms and an attempt to set the flow of the Czech language to music. This was not restricted to opera and one of his most nationalistic pieces, the programmatic cycle of tone poems *Má vlast* was first written for four-hands piano (1879–80) and then scored for full orchestra (1880–4).

Smetana's mantle was inherited by the arguably more successful composer, at least on an international stage, Antonín Dvořák (1841–1904). Although he did not turn to full-time composition until he was in his 30s, he had been principal viola player in the Provisional Theatre in Prague where he took part in performances of Smetana's operas conducted by the composer; it was Smetana who conducted the premiere of one of Dvořák's first pieces, the overture to his opera *Král a uhlíř* ("The King and the Charcoal Burner", 1871). This and a number of his other early works are heavily influenced by Wagner, however, when the extreme difficulties of this operatic score caused the first performance to be abandoned, Dvořák began to rethink his compositional style. He retained the through composition of the Wagnerian works but adopted what has been called a "new classicism",

with a clearer sense of form and a simplification of themes that incorporated elements of folk dance and song. While he was to refine these ideas throughout his life—at times incorporating more or less national elements within the music and turning to a more expressive idiom in his later works—these concerns were to remain at the heart of his style. Dvořák pursued the quest for a clearly articulated national style in a surprisingly wide number of genres, from opera to songs, and string quartets to symphonies. Like Smetana, his operas, all in Czech, range from the comic in *Šelma sedlák* ("The Cunning Peasant", 1877), to the historical and Slavic *Dimitrij* (1881–2) that was intended as a sequel to Musorgsky's *Boris Godunov*, to the fairytale of *Rusalka* (1900). Although Dvořák

Jean Sibelius at his piano,
photograph, 1940

J. Sibelius vid pianot.　Foto: Bonney.

Carl Nielsen's *Maskarade*, at the
Royal Opera House; London; 2005

Although there was less sense of the
political need to establish a musical
nationalism in Denmark than elsewhere
in Scandinavia, the end of the 19th
century did see the emergence of
a Danish national song style and
symphonic tradition through the works
of Carl Nielsen (1865–1931). He is best
known outside of the country for his six
powerful symphonies that move from a
Brahmsian Romanticism toward a starker
Neoclassicism by the end of his life.
Technically his works are characterized
by modal inflections in his melodies and
an impressive handling of progressive
tonality (an overall tonal scheme that
moves from one key at the beginning of a
work toward a different tonality for the
final cadence), but their power ultimately
derives from Nielsen's ability to forge a
formal logic that adequately presents his
personal vision of an all-encompassing
"life force".

regarded opera as central to his canon, the most
overtly nationalistic works he wrote are the two
oratorios, *Hymnus: Dědicové bílé hory* ("Hymn: the
Heirs of the White Mountain", 1872) and *Svatá
Ludmila* ("St Ludmilla", 1885–6), both dealing
with central events in Czech history. He is perhaps
best remembered today for his symphonic works,
especially the later symphonies (from the Sixth
to the Ninth, 1880–93) that display the influence
of Beethoven and Brahms in their treatment of
form and developmental technique but allied with
folkloric elements in their melody and rhythm.

Although born not long after Dvořák, Leoš
Janáček (1854–1928) belongs far more to the 20th
than the 19th century, his works standing alongside
those of composers like Gustav Mahler and Richard
Strauss. Like his two nationalist predecessors
Janáček saw opera as central to his work, although
he wrote a number instrumental pieces, two of
which have remained very popular and which first
attracted attention to his compositions outside of
the Czech lands, *Taras Bulba* (1925–7) and the
Sinfonietta (1926). The time he spent collecting
Moravian folksongs, especially those from Eastern
Moravia with their irregular rhythms, was highly
influential on his musical thinking even if this is
often at a deep level and not immediately obvious.
His writing is experimental in a number of ways,
from the chromatic harmonies akin to those used
by Strauss in *Elektra* that at times suspend any
sense of tonality, to an often astringent style of

orchestration and, especially, an idiomatic style of
vocal writing that has been described as the "sung
stylizations of the irregular patterns of everyday
speech". This was used in a string of operas from

Jenůfa (1904) to *Z mrtvého domu* ("In the House
of the Dead", 1928), including his most popular
work *Příhody Lišky Bystroušky* ("The Cunning
Little Vixen", 1923–4).

The third area in Europe that saw the emergence
of national musics during the 19th century was
Scandinavia. This took different paths in different
countries, largely through the figures of Edvard
Grieg (1843–1907) in Norway and Jean Sibelius
(1865–1957) in Finland. Both of these areas were
under the control and influence of neighboring and
more powerful countries, in the case of Norway
this was Sweden and Denmark, for Finland it
was Russia. In both cases the music of the two
composers became an important national symbol,
used as a bulwark and a rallying point against the
cultural dominance of the foreign rulers as well as
proving influential on later composers in Britain
and France.

Grieg was until 1864 immersed in Danish and
German culture, the former being the language
of the Norwegian middle-class and the latter
being the dominant musical force of the region;
Grieg had also spent the years 1858–62 at the
Leipzig conservatory where he received his
musical training. Two years after his return from
Germany, however, this was to change. He spent
the summer of 1864 with the great Norwegian
violinist Ole Bull who introduced him for the first
time to Norwegian folk music and shortly after
made the acquaintance of the young Nationalist
composer Rikard Nordraak (1842–66); from this

point on Grieg was to dedicate himself to becoming a Romantic nationalist. Many of Grieg's works are chamber pieces, either for piano, voice or string quartet, although his piano concerto (1868) and the incidental music he wrote for Ibsen's *Peer Gynt* (1874–5) have become staple works of the orchestral repertory. His earlier works have a strongly functional harmony—even if they display some of the chromaticism of Wagner—overlain with themes and rhythms derived from folk models. However, later works, and especially the string quartets (in G minor, 1877–8, and F major, 1891) point to later developments in the works of Debussy and Ravel with their breaking down of functional progressions and use of harmonic parallelism.

If Grieg was to pave the way for the technical innovations of musical Impressionism, Jean Sibelius was to be one of the greatest symphonists of the early 20th century, reinventing the form and proving an inspiration to the emerging symphonic traditions of Britain and the United States of America. In a similar way to Smetana and Grieg, Sibelius was brought up in a Swedish-speaking household and it was only later, during the 1890s, that he began to study Finnish; by that time the adoption of the majority language was seen as an act of support for self-determination and of the development of a national culture, so-called "Fennicisation". Initially a violinist, Sibelius turned to composition during the late 1880s, although his early endeavors in this direction show little hint of the individual voice he was to evolve. It was at this time that he met Armas and Eero Järnefelts, whose sister, Aino, Sibelius was to marry. These two brothers were passionate supporters of the Finnish cause and it was through them that Sibelius first became involved in the ideas and debates of national identity that were being circulated. The years 1889–91 were spent in Berlin and Vienna, where he not only acquired a more thorough understanding of counterpoint but turned toward orchestral composition, chiefly after the revelation of discovering the works of Bruckner.

Perhaps even more importantly, this was when he discovered the Finnish national epic, the *Kalevala*, from which he was to derive the programs for many of his tone poems. Sibelius became fascinated with the melodic patterns and rhyme schemes used in the recitation of the poems and, especially, the repetitive patterns operating within the span of a minor pentachord. This was a technique Sibelius was to adapt to his own music and the first of his truly Finnish works in which this can be seen to operate was the enormous *Kullervo* symphonic poem (1891–2) with chorus and soprano and baritone soloists,

based on the *Kalevala*. This had been completed on his return to Finland and once back in his native country he began to more fully explore its folk music, especially that of Karelia. The musical voice that he created from these national influences, as a rejection of German Romantic models with ostinato patterns set over long pedal notes, modal inflections with a concentration on the minor, and sharp rhythms-were to be played out during the 1890s in a series of tone poems, including *En saga* (1892) and the *Lemminkäis-sarja* ("Lemminkäinen Suite", 1896). However, it was his seven symphonies that were to prove truly radical, matching his newly-found musical language to an international form that had a wider reach than the more locally-relevant national themes of the tone poems and *Kullervo*. With

SIR EDWARD ELGAR.

their sweeping themes and sparse sense of the open spaces of the Finnish landscape, from 1899 to 1924 his symphonies show a progressive refining of the treatment of form with a Neoclassical regard for succinctness and economy of expression, from the four-movement First and Second works to the single-movement of the Seventh. It seems that by the time he had managed to compress the entire symphonic discourse into a single span of music then he felt he could achieve no more. From the mid-1920s onward he produced no new finished works and just before his death he destroyed all the sketches and scored sections of what would have been his eighth symphony, to the enduring mystery and frustration of musicologists and performers alike.

Edward Elgar

Although Sibelius was to prove influential on 20th-century British symphonists, the first successful English composer in the genre was Edward Elgar (1857–1934). His music has been sometimes unfairly dismissed as long-winded and imbued with an Edwardian nostalgia; although his control of form is sometimes idiosyncratic, much of his work shows a superb grasp of harmony that derives from the German composers he so admired, including Mendelssohn, Brahms and Wagner. Much of Elgar's best work is to be found in his lighter pieces, such as *The Wand of Youth Suites* (1907–8) or *Salut d'amour* (1889), in which the lyricism and invention of his melodic writing comes to the fore, and which were to be more influential on later British composers, such as Eric Coates (1886–1957) and Vivian Ellis (1904–96), than his ostensibly more serious works. Of these he is noted for his two symphonies (1907–8 and 1909–11) and the violin and cello concertos (1905–10 and 1918–19), as well as the oratorio *The Dream of Gerontius* (1900) that was inspired by his Catholic upbringing.

POPULAR MUSIC

MASS MUSIC FROM MASS CULTURE (SINCE 1875)

Emile Berliner with gramophone

Recordings of celebrities and singers became commercially available on cylinders in the 1890s, initially in only small numbers and at some expense. Emile Berliner's development by 1894 of the flat-disc gramophone for sound reproduction allowed for easier mass production of discs than cylinders and so gained a larger market. Electrical recording methods were developed by the 1920s and shortly after replaced mechanical ones, while the speed of discs—at first anywhere between 70 and 82 rpm—was standardized at 78 rpm, a format that lasted until the mid-1940s, when Columbia introduced the 33 1/3 rpm disc and so doubled the playing time.

"Popular" and "Pop" music as terms cover such variety of styles and ideologies that their scope is open to wide interpretation. The core elements that define them—mass dissemination, commercial focus, transience—also provoke questions of quality, cultural hierarchy and intrinsic artistic value. In practice, the broad headings as generally used of popular music along with its later developments (from the mid-1950s on) as pop represent the largest and most familiar of all musics throughout the world today; they are marked by extreme diversity and the paradox of often distinctive, localized styles that gain appreciation as part of internationally disseminated hybrids.

The key elements for the establishment of a mass popular music culture arose principally from three influences from the mid-19th century. First, a growing middle class in Western European saw an involvement in higher culture as a means of social improvement, with involvement in the arts, especially music, a leading part of such ambitions; the piano in the parlor was a significant feature of this culture. Second, increasing affluence created a large consumer market for music, initially in printed form for domestic use. Third, dissemination was furthered through technological means of mass music reproduction such as the nickelodeon, the player-piano or pianola, and most significantly the development of sound reproduction on disc which allowed not just the composition but a particular performance—and hence the performer—to become significant in their own right. The rate of technological development in conjunction with expanding wealth put America at the center of these developments and their spread into and beyond Western culture (the presence of US troops abroad during two World Wars was significant here). In consequence, the history of popular music in the 20th century has predominantly been viewed from an American perspective. The same can be said of some of the earlier years of pop, but the British contribution in the 1960s and latterly the embracing of aspects of world music and world markets have made the perspective of pop today a global one.

OPERETTA

In essence, Operetta is a popular development of opera, most prevalent and influential from the 1860s to the 1920s. The term includes a

1877: Thomas Edison invents the phonograph.

1878: Gilbert and Sullivan's *H.M.S. Pinafore* opens in London.

1912: The RMS Titanic sinks on its inaugural voyage; only 712 of its 2201 passengers and crew survive.

1919: John Alcock and Arthur Whitten Brown make the first non-stop transatlantic flight.

1927: The British Broadcasting Corporation (BBC) broadcasts its first radio programs.

1929: "Black Tuesday": on 29 October the New York Stock Exchange crashes precipitating the Great Depression in America.

1939: Hitler's invasion of Poland triggers World War II.

1943: *Oklahoma!*, Rodgers and Hammerstein's first Broadway musical, breaks Broadway records.

1945: Atom bombs dropped on the Japanese cities of Hiroshima and

Nagasaki cause Japan's surrender and bring about the end of World War II.

1948: Mahatma Ghandi is assassinated in India.

1953: Queen Elizabeth II succeeds her father King George VI to the British throne.

1958: Elvis Presley releases the single *Jailhouse Rock*, which immediately becomes no. 1 in the US charts.

1961: US troops and Cuban exiles land at Cuba's Bay of Pigs but fail to regain control of the country from President Castro.

1963: American President John F. Kennedy is assassinated.

1964: The Beatles appear on national television in the USA to an audience of 70 million viewers.

1968: American civil rights leader Martin Luther King Jr is shot dead in Memphis, Tennessee.

1969: Neil Armstrong becomes the first man to walk on the moon.

1973: America withdraws from its military involvement in Vietnam.

1974: US President Nixon resigns from office after the Watergate Affair.

Victor Herbert (1859–1924), the most prominent and influential American composer of operetta and popular song of his generation and later a founder of the American Society of Composers, Authors and Publishers.

1980: John Lennon is shot dead in New York.

1981: Pope John Paul II is shot in St Peter's Square, Rome, but survives the attack; President Sadat of Egypt is also shot, but fatally so.

1985: The charity rock concert Live Aid is broadcast simultaneously to 152 countries.

1985: A massive earthquake brings Mexico city to ruins.

1987: Thousands of students march on Tiananmen Square, Beijing, and are met with military force.

1990: South African anti-apartheid leader Nelson Mandela is released after 27 years in prison.

1991: The opening up of Russia to the West is begun by Boris Yeltsin, and South African apartheid is finally dismantled by President Frederik de Klerk.

2001: On September 11 Islamic terrorists crash planes into New York's World Trade Center.

fluid range of designations such as *opera bouffe*, *operette*, comic opera, operetta itself and, later, musical romance. The form uses 19th-century operatic conventions but in a lighter dramatic and musical framework that is overtly romantic; operatic *recitative* is mostly substituted with spoken dialogue, increasingly so as the form developed. The plots are generally concerned with troubled love (resolved happily), often set against a colorful and exotic background, typically central-European with gypsies and titled classes. The music emphasizes lyrical qualities and strong melody often in dance forms, most notably the waltz, a result of operetta's early twin geographical hearts Paris and Vienna.

Jacques Offenbach (1819–80) was the predominant French writer of operetta and developer of the form, principally as a reaction to the increasingly serious style of the Opéra Comique company in Paris. Consequently Offenbach's work burlesques its consciously serious models, and developed from single-act satiric diversions to full-length works. His extensive output created a unique identity for *opéra bouffe* apart from its operatic sources, and through the popularity of such works as *La Belle Hélène* (1864) and *Orphée aux enfers* (1858), Offenbach's influence spread most prominently to London and Vienna.

In London, the direct result was the formation of one of the leading collaborations of the comic lyric stage: William Schwenck Gilbert (1836–1911) and Sir Arthur Seymour Sullivan (1842–1900). *Trial by Jury* (1875) a one-act curtain raiser before the main operetta of the evening, Offenbach's *La Perichole*, is the earliest surviving Gilbert and Sullivan work; their next, *The Sorcerer* (1877), was full length and specifically parodied a combination of Offenbach style with Donizetti's comic opera *L'elisir d'amore*. Their works are known collectively as the "Savoy Operas" after the London theater in which from *Iolanthe* (1882) they were given their premieres. *H.M.S Pinafore* (1878), *The Mikado* (1885) and *The Pirates of Penzance* (1879) are perhaps the best known, although the entire canon has proved one of the most consistently enduring of all light lyric theater repertories, unchallenged until the works of Rodgers and Hammerstein, but not surpassed.

In Vienna, Johan Strauss II (1825–99) took his supremacy in the ballroom onto the stage with such works as *Die Fledermaus* (1874) and *Der Zigeunerbaron* (1885). An effective rival to Offenbach, Strauss also established what became a Viennese dominance of the form, especially alongside works of his contemporaries Franz von Suppé (1819-95), Carl Zeller (1842–98) and Carl

Millöcker (1842–99). Franz Lehár (1870–1948) and Emmerich Kálmán (1882–1953) consolidated Viennese operetta in the following generation. Both were of Hungarian birth and wrote across a time of political upheaval in Europe through the changing fortunes of the Austro-Hungarian empire and through to the interwar years, accounting for the themes of class, nostalgia, national identity and foreign influences that their works exhibit.

Günther–Treumann–Lehar.
Die Lustige Witwe.

Die Lustige Witwe, Louis Treumann and Mizzi Günther—the first Count Danilo and Hanna Glawari (1905)—with composer Franz Lehár

Franz Lehár's music for *Die Lustige Witwe* ("The Merry Widow") is some of the most famous of all operetta. The score includes a wealth of now-standard melodies, including "Vilja" and the "Merry Widow Waltz", and its rapid popularity throughout Europe made it influential on the whole genre, for which it still stands as an exemplar. The London production (1907) made an impact on the young Ivor Novello, who later in his career paid tribute to it through witty musical allusions to it in his own musical romance set in Vienna, *The Dancing Years* (1939).

Lehár's international successes began with *Die lustige Witwe* (1905) and continued through some 26 works from *Der Graf von Luxembourg* (1909) to *Das Land des Lächelns* (1929). Kálmán's *Die Csàrdàsfürstin* (1915), *Gräfin Mariza* (1924) and *Die Herzogin von Chicago* added 20th-century popular music styles such as the foxtrot to the by-now obligatory waltz.

The American forms of operetta are inevitably entwined with the early origins of the musical, developed through the intermediate roles possible with naturalized American composers of European descent. In the 1890s, Victor Herbert (1859–1924, of Irish birth and German education) took the lead with shows that drew on Gilbert and Sullivan along with Viennese operettas; the most well known include *Mlle Modiste* and *The Red Mill* (1905), *Babes in Toyland* (1903) and *Naughty Marietta* (1910). The operettas of Sigmund Romberg (1887–1951, of Hungarian birth) of the 1920s were transatlantic successes and represent the more pared-down style of later operettas as clearly defined musical set-pieces interpolated into a playscript. His works include most famously

The Student Prince (1924), The Desert Song (1926) and The New Moon (1928), and find a British equivalent in the musical romances of Ivor Novello (1893–1951), especially The Dancing Years (1939), Perchance to Dream (1945) and King's Rhapsody (1949). Although operetta had become effectively a historical rather than contemporary form by the 1950s, such later shows as Leonard Bernstein's Candide (1956), Stephen Sondheim's Sweeney Todd (1979) and Andrew Lloyd Webber's The Phantom of the Opera (1988) openly acknowledge the debt that the musical owes to operetta.

AMERICAN POPULAR SONG

At its simplest, the dominant forms of Western popular music evolved on the one hand from sentimental, tuneful parlor ballads and theater songs (from music hall to opera) and on the other from an injection of new rhythmic ideas in social dance. In America, the strong and lively syncopations of ragtime brought into the dominant "white" popular music some of the rhythmic

Sheet music cover Maple Leaf Rag,
1904, by Scott Joplin

Scott Joplin (b. Texas, 1867/8; d. New York, 1917), black American composer and pianist, was a leading exponent of ragtime, a style of music from the 1880s influenced by the hard syncopated rhythms of African-American music. Although common in practice, it was the formal composition and publication of piano rags that lead to their widespread popularity. Maple Leaf Rag was the second ragtime piano composition of Joplin's to be published (1899), becoming sufficiently popular to provide him with a small income from continuing royalties. The cross-rhythms of ragtime (usually the accompaniment on the beat, and the melody alternating its accent between on- and off-beats) became a significant component of American popular music at the turn of the 19th-20th century. It was incorporated into many songs, initially with explicitly black contexts, but the racial elements was soon subsumed into the broader language of popular song as in Ragtime Cowboy Joe and Waiting for the Robert E. Lee (both 1912), and not least Alexander's Ragtime Band (1911), an early important hit for Irving Berlin. Joplin's contribution to ragtime was soon forgotten, but in the 1970s his music gained renewed popularity through recordings by Joshua Rifkin and through music for the movie score to The Sting, starring Robert Redford.

vitality of minority "black" music; previous musical interchanges were shown in speciality acts in a country with strong areas of segregation by color, notably with white minstrels performing in black face to pastiches and parodies of African-American music and dance. The most significant changes came from syncopated melodic rhythms that fused with a Western style whose focus tended toward greater complexity in melody and harmony

than in rhythm. Popular dances increasingly stressed an animated duple time (for example, the cake walk and the two-step) and combined with the repeating cross-accents of ragtime and the early sounds of jazz. The approach to rhythm in popular music was fundamentally changed in the 20th century. Through the early decades of the century, to the influence of ragtime could be added the dance forms of quickstep, foxtrot and more specialized crazes such as the charleston and the lindy hop. With dance steps dictating tempo, accent and style, the popular song became the principal form of popular music, presented by a named soloist, arranged for dance band, played by jazz ensembles, and sold in printed and recorded versions suitable for domestic music making.

Popular songs were also spread through musical theater, and song writers of the period on both sides of the Atlantic tended to write for musical comedy, into which new songs could be interpolated to suit changing tastes, fashions and performers, as well as for a more general audience if necessary. Musical comedy had evolved symbiotically with operetta, sparked especially by the London shows of impresario George Edwardes at the Gaiety theater from the 1890s on and often presented subsequently in New York, most notably Florodora (1899, London; 1900, New York). Musical comedies were characterized by intimate plots, current musical styles and recognizable contemporary characters in modern dress. Several of the formative American shows were presented between 1915 and 1919 at the small Princess Theater in New York, notably Very Good Eddie (1915), Oh, Boy! and Leave it to Jane (both 1917), and several featured the script and lyric writers Guy Bolton and P.G. Wodehouse and composer Jerome Kern (1885–1945). Kern's later successes include the grander ambitions of Show Boat (1927), written with scriptwriter and lyricist Oscar Hammerstein II (1895–1960), whose expansive plot spanning several generations of a family gave the opportunity to combine operatic emotion, operetta melody and popular dance.

Hundreds of successful songwriters on both sides of the Atlantic fueled the popular song industry, commonly referred to as "Tin Pan Alley" after the Manhattan district where music publishers were concentrated and the rattling sound there of pianos demonstrating new melodies to promote sales of sheet music. With the rise of radio from the early 1930s, the importance of sheet music diminished; "Tin Pan Alley" subsequently became a generic term for popular song rather than a geographical location. The major American songwriters of this period working with consistent success in musicals for Broadway (stage) and Hollywood (movie) were Cole Porter, George and Ira Gershwin, Richard

Rodgers and Lorenz Hart; jazz-band writers and performers, such as Duke Ellington contributed other important repertory numbers. On Broadway, significant shows and songs included: for Gershwin, *Girl Crazy* (1930; including "I Got Rhythm", "But Not for Me" and "Embraceable You") and *Of Thee I Sing* (1931; including the title song); for Porter, *Gay Divorce* (1932, including "Night and Day") and *Anything Goes* (1934, including the title song, "I Get a Kick out of You" and "You're the Top"); for Rodgers and Hart, *On Your Toes* (1936; including "There's a Small Hotel"), *Babes in Arms* (1937; including "Where or When", "The Lady Is a Tramp" and "My Funny Valentine") and *Pal Joey* (1940; including "Bewitched" and "I Could Write a Book"). The status of hit songs from Broadway musicals was further boosted by their inclusion in Hollywood movie versions to an extent that the songs became a major and lasting part of shared American popular culture. These song "standards" (sometimes collectively called the "American songbook") constituted the repertory of popular and cabaret singers of the time: Frank Sinatra (1915–98) and Ella Fitzgerald (1917–96) are perhaps two of the most acclaimed. Such numbers have become the core repertory for subsequent cabaret singers and jazz musicians. Other countries had their own equivalent writers, notably Vivian Ellis in Britain, but the American repertory was and remains dominant. Even where non-American songwriters gained wider fame, as with, for example the Frenchman Charles Trenet (1913–2001), it was often through songs in translation: Trenet's song *La Mer* (1946) is probably better known in Bobby Darin's version *Beyond the Sea* from 1959, while the French

Comme d'Habitude by Claude François and Jacques Revaux only became a worldwide success when turned into English by Paul Anka as *My Way*. Such performers as Maurice Chevalier did become internationally famous (not least through his movie appearances), but usually in the context of American rather than French productions.

The spread of radio became a significant factor in the growing market for and distribution of popular music in the 1930s–50s in particular, with the favoring of some styles through patronage by radio stations or their presenters. The earliest radio musical successes came from dance bands, in England with Jack Hylton and Savoy Orpheans on the BBC, and in America with many bands across the rapidly growing number of networks. Paul Whiteman and his Orchestra was perhaps the most well known but also the most influential through its rich orchestrations and polished performance style. In addition, the band is associated with the male vocal trio the Rhythm Boys, whose style of singing close to the microphone enabled amplification rather than vocal power to make the voice audible and created a more naturalistic and intimate vocal sound called "crooning". One of the vocal trio, Bing Crosby, became one of the leading crooners and subsequently one of the most famous of all American vocalists. Of later dance bands ("big bands", as the larger ensembles are known) and their leaders, Glen Miller is the most recognizable, not least through a distinctive use of lead clarinet (instead of solely saxophone) that has made his band arrangements of such numbers as *Moonlight Serenade* and *American Patrol* iconic. The dance band sound was softened and given a more sophisticated gloss in the 1950s, especially with the use of strings, in the arrangements of Nelson Riddle, best known through classic recordings of "American songbook" numbers, notably by Sinatra and Fitzgerald.

Bessie Smith

Bessie Smith (1892/4–1937) was the most well-known blues singer of the 1920s and 30s. She began her stage career in the 1910s as a dancer and singer, and performed in black theaters (American theater was racially segregated). In 1923 she was signed as a singer by Columbia records, who nicknamed her "the Empress of the Blues", and she became famous with live performances and recordings, at one stage the highest paid black performer of her time. Her delivery was strong and personal, her vocal inflections heartfelt, influenced by her often turbulent personal life. In the 1930s she began to adopt her style to include elements of swing, but she died in 1937 as a result of her injuries in a car accident.

Paul Whiteman conducting his Orchestra, mid-1930s

Self-styled "The King of Jazz", Paul Whiteman (1890–1967) was the most famous of American bandleaders. He learned his trade first as an orchestral player, then in a navy band during World War I, and afterwards brought a new fusion of ragtime and jazz into his dance-band sound through keen rhythmic vitality and rich orchestration. Musicians who played with his band included Bix Beiderbecke, Eddie Lang and Jack Teagarden, while singers included Bing Crosby and Mildred Bailey. His sound was copied widely and his recordings of such songs as *Whispering* became standards, and through tours to Europe with his Orchestra, his sound also significantly influenced European bands. Although in the early years purists were not pleased by his fusion of popular song and jazz styles, he was significant in bringing them together in a sophisticated mix that found a natural home not just in the dance hall and in the mass media—recordings, radio and movie—but also in the concert hall. He commissioned *Rhapsody in Blue* from George Gershwin (1924) and promoted the works of such American composers as Victor Herbert and Duke Ellington.

Jazz

The evolution of the musical style known as jazz has its roots in the synthesis of the musics of European settlers and black African slaves in the southern United States of America. A dominant musical force for the first two-thirds of the 20th century, jazz made its mark on a wide number of popular and art musics particularly through its treatment of rhythm and syncopation. The great marker of the style is its use of improvisation, often based on the harmonic patterns, known as "changes", from popular songs, referred to as "standards". The name itself, originally referring to sex or to "make something lively" says much about the music as it first appeared in New Orleans during the first decades of the 20th century. At this time there were many black and Creole bands playing instrumental versions of popular ballads and dances. The bands consisted of instruments such as trumpets, cornets and trombone, with clarinets and drums. Often the music included call and response sections and elements from African musics such as growling and rasping textures were

The Original Dixieland Jazz Band (ODJB)

The Original Dixieland Jazz Band are credited with making the first jazz recording *Livery Stable Blues*, in 1917; they also recorded *Tiger Rag* in the same year. The ODJB were chiefly important for taking the music north to Chicago and New York (1916–17) and their impact was huge in disseminating the music.

used. The syncopations of blues and ragtime were also incorporated into the music played by these bands for New Orleans honky-tonks (a combination of bar, dance hall and brothel). The music itself was referred to initially as "hot", denoting its fast performance style, and based on a strong 4/4 beat over which the melody could be pulled about and given "blue" notes (flattened 3rds and 7ths).

The first true jazz musician is said to be Buddy Bolden (1877–1931), a trumpet player who lead a band playing ragtime and blues. His claim was disputed by the pianist Jelly Roll Morton (1890–1941) who is notable for being the first jazz

composer, writing pieces in the new syncretic New Orleans style. While both these musicians, and the vast majority of other early jazz players, were black it was a group of white musicians, the Original Dixieland Jazz Band (OBJB), led by cornet player Nick LaRocca (1889–1961) who made the first jazz recording, *Livery Stable Blues*, in 1917. Soon black musicians from New Orleans were taking their music to a wider audience. Notable among these was the cornet player King Oliver (1885–1938) who took his band to Chicago in 1918. In 1922 he employed another cornet player, one who was to achieve unprecedented fame for a black musician, Louis Armstrong (1901–71). His smooth tone and virtuosic technique that included a safe high register were to make him an almost instant hit. In 1925 Armstrong began a series of recordings with a group known as the Hot Five that included the trombonist and band-leader Kid Ory (c. 1886–1973). These soon became the standard to match and are important for the placing of the trumpet at the front of the ensemble as a soloist, as opposed to the generally polyphonic style that had predominated so far. A white musician from Chicago who was to be almost as influential was the trumpet player Bix Beiderbecke (1903–31).

By the late 1920s the New Orleans style began to be supplanted by a parallel style based around a larger ensemble with written scores. This more "symphonic" sound had been pioneered by the band leaders Ferde Grofé (1892–1972) and Paul Whiteman (1890–1967). They added saxophones as the main melody instruments to their bands' line-up and adopted a smoother sound than that of the New Orleans players. This form was adopted by the black band leaders Fletcher Henderson (1897–1952) and, especially, Duke Ellington (1899–1974), the greatest figure in jazz big-band history. Ellington's longevity as a band leader saw him as an influential figure in all periods up to his death and as a composer and arranger he was responsible for producing some of the great classics of the genre, such as *Black and Tan Fantasy* (1927). It was around this time that the characteristic rhythmic feel of jazz came to be known as "swing", and with a greater use of cymbals by the drummer to mark the tempo, a "comping" style articulating harmonies on the piano and the use of the bass to mark the 4/4 time, a new era began that saw the big band take center stage. Many of these were led by white musicians, including the phenomenally successful Benny Goodman (1909–86) and Artie Shaw (1910–2004), both clarinetists. Among black musicians the Ellington band and that led by Count Basie (1904–84) reigned supreme. The Basie band was important for its soloist Lester Young (1909–59) on saxophone who was to be influential on a later generation of players.

Smaller ensembles were also recording, including that led by trumpet player Roy Eldridge (1911–89)

great influence on the up-and-coming Dizzy Gillespie (1911–93). If prohibition had encouraged the New Orleans style with a general desire among people to transgress and enjoy themselves, and the

wing era saw a move to a gentler, escapist style following the Wall Street crash of 1929, then the outbreak of World War II gave a sense that the world was changing again. Based in the jazz club Minton's, after hours a small group that coalesced around Gillespie and the saxophonist Charlie Parker (1920–5) rejected the "white" style of the big bands and began experimenting with rhythm and harmony by adding extensions (7ths, 9ths, 11ths and 13ths) and substituting chords within the standards. By doing this they came up with Be-Bop, and created new melodies and improvisations over existing changes, as in pieces such as *Anthropology* (1945) based on the standard chords for *I Got Rhythm*. Allied to phenomenal displays of virtuosity this new, at the time startling, style was to sweep away that of the swing big bands and its harmonic and melodic

innovations were to be adopted by big-band leaders such as Gillespie himself.

While Dizzy Gillespie went on to introduce elements of Cuban music into jazz, bringing over the conga player Chano Pozo (1915–48), Parker continued with small groups and one of his sidemen Miles Davis (1926–91) was to take the harmonic developments of Be-Bop and give them a "cooler" feel. This was partly an attempt to introduce elements of European art music into jazz and, along with saxophonist Gerry Mulligan (1927–96) and arranger Gil Evans (1912–88) Davis recorded the "Birth of the Cool" sessions in 1949–50. These ideas were also prevalent on the West Coast with musicians such as Dave Brubeck (1920–2012). A parallel movement was Hard Bop, a development of Be-Bop with a funkier, more earthy sound inspired by Gospel. This was promoted by black musicians such as Art Blakey (1919–90), Charles Mingus (1922–79) and Sonny Rollins (1930–) as a counterpoint to the "white" style of cool. However, it was a black musician John Coltrane (1926–67) who emerged out of the Miles Davis Quintet and, after modal experiments with Davis, was to push harmonic ideas to their limit in the 1960s with a "sheets of sound" style that was overwhelming in its melodic and harmonic complexity. Further avant-garde developments came from this, in the form of a completely improvised and atonal "free jazz", explored by pianist Cecil Taylor (1929–) and saxophonist Ornette Coleman (1930–).

By the 1980s jazz had ceased to be the cultural and musical force it had once been, partly due to the loss of a wider-commercial audience. Musicians, such as keyboard players Chick Corea (1941–), Herbie Hancock (1940–) and Joe Zawinul (1932–2007), looked to pop and rock and produced a "fusion" of the musics, while other players, like trumpeter Wynton Marsalis (1961–) have looked to the past and sought to preserve and explore the jazz canon of such greats as Armstrong, Ellington and Gillespie.

Charlie Parker and Dizzy Gillespie,
on stage at Birdland, New York, 1951

The radical nature of Be-Bop, an improvisation of jazz by Parker and Gillespie, made some jazz fans turn back to an earlier form of the music, prompting a revival of "traditional" jazz in the New Orleans style.

Wynton Marsalis

Jazz trumpeter and composer Wynton Marsalis (1961–) is one of the leading performers of his day and also one of the most successful. His work spreads beyond the bounds of jazz convention, recording works by Bach and composing string quartets and movie music.

MUSICAL THEATER AFTER WORLD WAR II

The development of the modern musical is generally dated from 1943 and the premiere on Broadway of *Oklahoma!,* the first work from the collaboration of Rodgers and Hammerstein (it is now widely

accepted that *Oklahoma!* is more a representation of wider changes in musical theater than a cause of them). The qualities that the musical developed were a greater integration between music and drama than in musical comedy—the songs continued the plot or added depth to the characters—and a broadening of themes to include serious subjects. The distinctions between musical comedy, musical play, musical romance and so on increasingly became inappropriate, the single word "musical" expressing better the expanded possibilities within any single work. The music gradually developed to incorporate pop, rock and, by the 1980s, quasi-operatic styles; at the same time the origins of the most successful works, especially those by English composer Andrew Lloyd Webber, have challenged the assumption that the musical is by definition an American form.

Although new Broadway musicals with scores by Berlin were produced into the 1940s, and for Porter into the 50s, it is the partnership of Richard Rodgers and Oscar Hammerstein II that generally defines this period. Their works explore American national identity and history while creating strong on-stage characters with clearly focused and memorable songs. Several were faithfully adapted into major movies and remain mainstays of the performing canon, particularly *Oklahoma!* (19434), *Carousel* (1945), *South Pacific* (1949),

The King and I (1951) and *The Sound of Musi* (1959). If the overall effect of Rodgers's shows with Hammerstein is of a more serious and integrated drama than before, the music itself, while direc and memorable, was influenced by the convention of operetta and 1930s popular song. The nex generation of writers, particularly the lyricis and composer Jerry Herman (b.1931) and th collaboration of John Kander (b.1927) and Free Ebb (1933–2004) brought a more punchy, show sound to the theater, with the established orchestra strings and woodwind giving way to big banc orchestrations of brass, saxophones and drum kits Where Herman presented an especially flamboyan type of show in such works as *Hello, Dolly!* (1964 and *La Cage aux folles* (1983), Kander and Ebb ir *Cabaret* (1966) and *Chicago* (1975) drew on more adventurous forms that combined clear pastiche of Weimar cabaret and American Vaudeville into more dramatically inventive and less linea dramatic structures. Musicals brought some of the vibrancy of developing commercial pop music tc the stage, as with 1950s American pop in *Bye By Birdie* (1960, Charles Strouse), Latin-America sounds in *Sweet Charity* (1966, Cy Coleman), anc the light pop of *Promises, Promises* (1968, Ha David and Burt Bacharach, a formidable pop-son writing team especially through the 1960s).

The embracing of rock by musical theate brought further developments through the 1970 and 80s. In Britain, *Jesus Christ Superstar* was conceived and released as a rock album (1970) and after huge American success transferred tc stage on Broadway (1971) and London (1972). I was innovative in its combination of orchestral anc rock resources (a sign of its roots in progressive rock), controversial treatment of the final days o

Oklahoma! sidebar

Oklahoma!, Marc Platt and Katherine Sergava in the dream ballet, at the St. James Theatre, New York, 1943

Oklahoma! opened on Broadway at the St James Theatre, March 31, 1943. The music was by Richard Rodgers, with script and lyrics by Oscar Hammerstein II (after the play *Green Grow the Lilacs* by Lynn Rigg). It was praised for its music and strong story line, for the mix of comic and serious in its plot and dialogue and for the distinctive choreography by Agnes de Mille that was in some ways integrated into the action of the play. It immediately became a long-running success in New York and, after the delays caused by World War II, in foreign stagings (it opened in London in 1947). Its themes of prosperity, optimism and national identity resonated with wartime audiences in America and overseas, contributing to what has become the show's iconic status as effectively the start of the developed genre of the musical. Many of its songs became popular standards, and include "The Surrey with the Fringe on Top", "Oh! What a Beautiful Morning", "People Will Say We're in Love" and the title song itself.

Cabaret sidebar

Cabaret, poster of Liza Minnelli

Kander and Ebb's musical *Cabaret* was an unusual fusion of Broadway musical and Weimar Republic cabaret in the manner of Bertolt Brecht and Kurt Weill. The nightclub setting and satirical narrative voice of its Master of Ceremonies were used to portray a drama about the devastating personal effects of the rise of the Nazis in pre-war Germany and along with such preceding shows as *Fiddler on the Roof* (1964) and *Man of La Mancha,* demonstrate the interest in expanding the range of content and form of the musical. A hit on stage in 1966 in New York, *Cabaret* was made even more well-known through a movie (1972) that had Liza Minelli in the central role of Sally Bowles. Minelli's rendition of the title song is strongly associated with her, as is the iconic image of her in an angular pose in black stockings and a bowler hat. Only a small part of the original stage score and plot featured in the movie version, a practice that had become common in Hollywood adaptations of stage musicals in recognition of the different techniques and capabilities of the mediums of stage and movie and their respective audience expectations.

the life of Christ, and episodic presentation that also drew on the format of a rock concert. It was written by the English composer Andrew Lloyd Webber (b.1948) and lyricist Tim Rice (b.1944); their record in musical theater both together and working with others over the following 30 years has put them at the forefront of musical theater across the globe. They followed *Jesus Christ Superstar* with expanded stage revisions (1972–3) of another Biblical episode, *Joseph and the Amazing Technicolor Dreamcoat*, first conceived and staged in 1968. An album release of *Evita* followed (1976), subsequently staged (1978), in which the life of Eva Peron was depicted in a series of episodes with rock and Latin American music grafted onto popular song techniques and the continuous musicalization of opera. Lloyd Webber has also collaborated with other lyricists on works that have regularly gained records for longevity and have been produced in countries across the world. The list includes *Cats* (1981), *Starlight Express* (1984), *The Phantom of the Opera* (1986) and *Sunset Boulevard* (1993). Large-scale, romanticized and semi-operatic (through-composed) musicals provided the main successes of the 1980s and early 90s, following the example of the early icon of the form: *Les Misèrables* (1980), a French musical by Alain Boublil (b.1941) and Claude-Michel Schoenberg based on the novel by Victor Hugo.

In counterpoint to Lloyd Webber has been Stephen Sondheim, who first learned his writing skills for musicals from Oscar Hammerstein II, and developed them as a lyricist in collaboration with composers Leonard Bernstein (*West Side Story*, 1957) and Jule Styne (*Gypsy*, 1959). His works have gained critical praise through their clever manipulation of verbal and musical motifs in the service of penetrating characterization and unified scores: for example, *A Little Night Music* (1973), with the song "Send in the Clowns", is entirely based on variants of triple time. Sondheim's musicals often have themes of adult relationships and responsibilities, as in *Company* (1970) and *Into the Woods* (1987), while the diversity of his subjects is shown through *Pacific Overtures* (1976; the American involvement in the opening up of Japan) and *Sweeney Todd* (1979; Victorian melodrama).

Sondheim's more classical compositional methods (especially motivic development and rhythmic sophistication) seemed to offer an avenue for broader development of musical language, but through Sondheim's many emulators what has evolved is a distinct "musical theater" style of its own, divorced from contemporary pop music as indeed the whole genre now is. There is no longer a common contemporary and widely shared popular music vernacular upon which the musical theater can draw as it could during most of the genre's development and consolidation. The music of youth culture has increasingly led away from the narrative and strophic forms that the lyric stage requires in favor of more abstract and rhythmically-centered club/dance music, a predominance of gospel-inflected pop ballads and a myriad of specialized vernacular forms and hybrids. Through the 1990s and into the early 21st century, musical theater has as a consequence drawn on songs from a nostalgic repertory of pop songs from specific writers and groups or as pastiches of familiar but now historical styles. Commercially this has helped counter the high costs of production by tapping into a ready-made audience for the music, for example Abba's catalogue for *Mamma*

Andrew Lloyd Webber, at the Majestic Theater, New York City, January 9, 2006

Andrew Lloyd Webber (b. 1948) is one of the most successful of all composers of musicals, his work performed across the world and with record-breaking lengths of performances. Unlike many composers in musical theater, he has not worked primarily with a single librettist, although his early great successes were in collaboration with Tim Rice. His musical style is eclectic, but with a central core of strong melody and harmony that has yielded such hit songs as "I Don't Know How to Love Him" (*Jesus Christ Superstar*) and "Memory" (*Cats*). He has been attracted to themes of strong contrast that have the potential for distinctive staging; but although many of his shows have been large-scale "mega-musicals" (*Evita, The Phantom of the Opera* and *Sunset Boulevard*), others have been more intimate in theme and presentation (*Aspects of Love* and *The Beautiful Game*).

Mia! (1999). Similarly, popular movie has been annexed for stage musical adaptation, as with *Spamalot* (2005) after *Monty Python and the Holy Grail* (1975) and Mel Brooks's *The Producers* (movie 1968; musical 2001). *Hairspray* (2002), after John Waters's movie (1988), combines a cult movie with 1960s nostalgia in both story and pastiche songs. Such a return to lighter and more comic entertainment has also been a reaction to the quasi-operatic tone and serious atmosphere of the most prominent works of the 1980–90s; and although a dramatic and compositional strand has evolved in the writing and appreciation of the musical from World War II on, the more recent need to appeal to a mass audience to sustain a commercially challenging form has brought again to the fore the requirements for spectacle and diversion that mark much of the genre's early origins and success.

MOVIE MUSIC

The earliest music for movies was played live in the cinema to accompany the silent image and enhance its mood while also creating a more conventionally complete theatrical experience for the audience. Early on, the music was improvised by a pianist to accompany short, descriptive cinematic scenes and, as narrative developed in movies (principally with comedies and melodramas), indications in sound of character and carefully placed references to popular songs and familiar classical music added additional emotional and observational layers. As cinema gained in popularity 1900–14, musical accompaniment became more sophisticated and cinema organs (notably the Wurlitzer) supplanted the piano; movie companies provided cue sheets that indicated how familiar or newly composed music could be coordinated with the moving image. Fully composed movie scores gained ground after D.W. Griffith's epic *The Birth of a Nation* (1915), and by the end of the 1920s composers including Victor Herbert, Arthur Honegger, Darius Milhaud and

Al Jolson in *The Jazz Singer*

Although not immediately hailed as such at its first screenings in 1927, *The Jazz Singer* effectively signaled the change in Hollywood from silent movies to movies with synchronized sound. The plot concerned a young Jewish singer who defies his religious traditions in favor of a career as a popular entertainer; a story that provided opportunities for six songs and small sections of dialogue with synchronized sound and image, the rest of the movie silent as was the convention. Al Jolson played the title role. He was already a leading stage performer in revue and musical comedies, and his persona as a blackface performer combined with his performance technique, honed in live theater, proved suitably dramatic and emotive for introducing the new medium; his rendition of "My Mammy" in the movie's finale is one of the defining scenes of movie history.

Dimitri Shostakovich had written original scores to accompany silent movies (this geographical spread—USA, France, Russia—indicates the worldwide interest developing for movies).

The first movie to match a pre-recorded soundtrack to its image was *The Jazz Singer* (1927), in which the music sung by the lead character (a synagogue cantor, played by Al Jolson) was provided by a synchronized disc. The effect worked best when the music heard was actually part of the on-screen drama, rather than as background. Consequently, music at first played a lesser role in sound movies than with silents. The exception was for musicals, many of

which exploited the unique possibilities of movie technique, as in those choreographed by Busby Berkley, such as *Gold Diggers of 1933*, and those featuring the dance partnership of Fred Astaire and Ginger Rogers, including *Top Hat* (1935, songs by Berlin) and *Shall We Dance* (1937, songs by Gershwin).

Through the 1930s, individually composed movie scores began to reassert themselves such that the leading Hollywood studios developed full-time music staff. Such scores increasingly drew on 19th-century symphonic techniques, matching specific musical themes to characters and events, much as the leitmotif was used in programmatic and operatic music. Many of the important composers for movies at this time had brought European classical training and heritage with them as either first- or second-generation immigrants to the USA or as Jewish refugees from Nazi Germany. The most influential include: Max Steiner, whose scores include those for *King Kong* (1933, one of the first extensive movie scores), *Gone with the Wind* (1939) and *Now Voyager* (1942); Erich Korngold, with *Captain Blood* (1935), *The Adventures of Robin Hood* (1938) and *The Sea Hawk* (1940); and Franz Waxman, whose style suited horror movies, as with *The Bride of Frankenstein* (1935) and *Dr Jekyll and Mr Hyde* (1941), but also such psychological dramas as *Sunset Boulevard* (1950). The leading movie composer of this time with an exclusively American background was Alfred Newman (1900–70), influential as a composer of some 200 scores and as Music Director for 20th Century-Fox, for whom he wrote the famous ident fanfare in 1935. Some movie composers explored more dissonant qualities to reinforce the changing atmosphere rather than the distinct themes of the more symphonic style, as with Bernard Herrmann (1911–75) in movies including *Citizen Kane* (1941) and *Psycho* (1960).

Britain, France, and the Soviet Union provided the main centers of thriving non-American movies and hence movie music into the 1950s. In France, Arthur Honegger and Jacques Ibert contributed scores to movies by directors such as Jean Renoir, while George Auric wrote the scores not only for Jean Cocteau's *La belle et la bête* (1946) and *Orphée* (1949), but also several leading British comedies, such as *The Lavender Hill Mob* (1951). Composers from the concert hall, such as Ralph Vaughan Williams, Arthur Bax, William Walton and John Ireland wrote scores for British movies, but a movie specialism as seen in America was rare, with William Alwyn and Malcolm Arnold as the most prominent UK equivalents. In Russia, especially through director Sergei Eisenstein's approach to music as integral to movie making, such mainstream orchestral composers as Sergey

Prokofiev and Shostakovich brought symphonic techniques to movie in uncompromising fashion, as with Prokofiev's score for *Aleksandr Nevsky* (1938) and Shostakovich's for *The Gadfly* (1955). In the 1960s, Italian movie became prominent, and the collaborations between composer Nino Rota and directors Federico Fellini (*8 1/2*, 1963; *Casanova*, 1976), Franco Zeffirelli (*Romeo and Juliet*, 1967) and Francis Ford Coppola (*Godfather* trilogy, 1972–90) yielded notable scores that showed Rota's ability to combine distinctive melody with atmospheric effect.

From the 1960s onward, new styles of movie score tended toward either the symphonic and thematic Hollywood model or the incorporation of popular music. In the former category, John Williams's work for Hollywood blockbusters stands as an exemplar of the epic orchestral movie score, usually headed by a striking, simple and memorable theme, and include *Jaws* (1975), *Close Encounters of the Third Kind* and *Star Wars* (1977), *Raiders of the Lost Ark* (1981), *E.T.* (1982), *Jurassic Park* (1993) and the first three of the "Harry Potter" series (2001–4). John Barry (1933–2011) in his scores especially for the "James Bond" movies (for which he wrote the famous theme tune) combined thematic techniques, popular song with an established singer for the title sequence and the mixing of big band and pop with orchestra. These musical fusions in such movies as *Goldfinger* (1964), *Diamonds Are Forever* (1971) and *A View to a Kill* (1985) were influential on the action movie genre, and can be seen in more recent examples such as the taut music by John Powell for the "Jason Bourne" movies (2002–7): thematically minimal, subject to intense repetition and employing extended and well-graduated crescendos that heighten tension and drama.

The music of contemporary youth culture has often been introduced as diegetic music— actually sung or played in the course of the drama—most famously with Bill Haley and his Comets performing "Rock Around the Clock" in *Blackboard Jungle* (1955). Possibly the most extensive bridging of popular music and pop star was in the sequence of movies made by Elvis Presley, starting with *Love Me Tender* (1956) and exploiting his sexually charged persona and back-catalogue of hits. With the Beatles' movies (beginning with *A Hard Day's Night*, 1964) an entire group became both the source of soundtrack and central characters; their playful style on screen was developed further by the American youth group the Monkees through the psychedelia of sound and image in *Head* (1968). There is an inevitable overlap with the musical movie, and leading examples include the transference to screen of The Who's rock albums *Tommy* (1969; movie 1975) and *Quadrophenia* (1973; movie, 1979). Composers who have turned to movie scores from a pop perspective include Mike Oldfield (*The Exorcist*, 1979), and Giorgio Moroder (*Midnight Express*, 1978; *American Gigolo*, 1980; *Flashdance*, 1983).

Beyond the dominance of Hollywood, other countries have developed distinctive styles. Japan in particular has used indigenous references in combination with symphonic elements to retain a distinct national quality, as for example with Fumio Hayasaka's score for *The Seven Samurai* (1954) and Matsuro Sato's for *Sanjuro* (1962). In a similar but more playful vein have been the scores for the "monster" movies, beginning with Akira Ifukube's for *Godzilla* in 1953. Most significant globally have been the products of "Bollywood" (derived from the name of the city of Bombay, now Mumbai, and Hollywood), so-called to stress the Hindi-language Indian commercial movie industry's

Forbidden Planet, MGM, 1956

The soundscape score for the 1956 science fiction movie *Forbidden Planet* was innovative in being made from electronic sounds only. This befitted the movie's reworking of Shakespeare's play *The Tempest*, set on a planet whose alien culture, long dead, was technologically advanced. The score, by Louis and Bebe Barron, is distinctive in the machine-like sounds assembled into atmospheric tone pictures; it was produced electronically through such techniques as ring modulation and further treated with recording techniques.

A.R. Rahman

Most well known composer of Indian contemporary music, A.R. Rahman has sold over 100 million copies of his scores from movies. Acquiring nation-wide fame from his music for the Tamil film *Roja*, Rahman went on to compose music for a number of movies, *Rang De Basanti* being his latest claim to success. Globally, Rahman adapted his movie music (notably *Taal*, *Dil Se* and *Mudhalvan*) for the score to the stage musical *Bombay Dreams* (London, 2002, and Broadway, 2004) and also contributed to the score for the stage adaptation of J.R.R. Tolkien's *Lord of the Rings* (Toronto, 2006).

simultaneous indebtedness to and difference from its American counterpart. Most have music as a major component, not least through diegetic song and dance. Leading composers have included S. D. Burman (1906–75), whose significant movies scores include *Baazi* (1951) and *Aradhana* (1969) and most recently A.R. Rahman (b. 1966), whose hypnotic and popular strains are exemplified by *Taal* (1999).

FROM BILL HALEY TO THE SPICE GIRLS

Where popular music in the first half of the 20th century had been marked by increasing homogeneity and the establishment of core genres and markets, the second half pulled in the opposite direction: forms subdivided and intermingled in ever-complex combinations, especially across ethnic boundaries. Rather than a new form substituting an earlier one, there have been increasing numbers of smaller branches running alongside parent forms. The first major new movement was away from mainstream popular song derived from white Western culture and towards forms which reflected the black American dimension, present since the 19th century and in part absorbed in the early 20th, but that had never been commercially mainstream when set against a dominant white culture and institutional segregation. Gradual moves towards

James Brown, performing at the Jazzhouse Montmartre, Copenhagen, Denmark, September 1982

The wide acceptance of the self-given nickname of "the Godfather of Soul" gives an indication of the extent of the influence on popular music of James Brown (1933–2006). Through the 1950s and 1960s his energetic performances—physically and vocally—demonstrated the energy latent within the fusion of rhythm and blues with gospel that became soul and funk. Such hit songs as *Papa's Got a Brand New Bag* and *I Got You (I Feel Good)*, both released in 1965, are soul standards, while his later funk recordings of the 1970s introduced even freer vocalizations and intricate rhythms to an already vibrant style and which influenced rap and hip hop.

greater racial equality brought black music into the mainstream and grew financial markets to support them. Also, the earliest widely known example of rock and roll is provided by *Rock Around the Clock*, recorded in 1954 by Bill Haley (1925–1981) and his Comets, a white-singer and band from a country music background. Haley followed up this major international success with such other hits as *See You Later, Alligator* and created the

audience for Elvis Presley. Presley's initial impact was through a visceral performance that drew on black rhythm and blues and gospel characteristics in a much more personally charged way than that of Haley; presented by a young white performer, this music was challenging to the racially segregated American establishment as much as it was appealing to white youth, particularly when combined with an overtly sexual physicality in performance and rebellious subtext.

However, it is black music by black performers that contributed one of the key factors for the development of pop, the loosely related collection of styles under the label rhythm and blues. Its roots are in large part to be found in the evangelical gospel music of black churches, with its distinctive call and response forms and extreme vocal elaborations and ornamentations of single words and use of shouts and cries to convey heightened emotion. This was combined with the underpinning harmonies and inflected scales of blues and the self-expression and drive of jazz. Influential rhythm and blues performers included singers and saxophonist Louis Jordan, and the singers and instrumentalists Ray Charles, Dinah Washington, Little Richard and Chuck Berry. With the performances and recordings of James Brown (1933–2006) the key elements of soul were established, bringing the energy and ecstatic vocalizations of gospel to rhythm and blues. Rhythm and blues also spawned rock and roll in the 1950s, when it fused with white country music and Tin Pan Alley songs; such cross-racial fusion aided its rapid and widespread appeal, as did its dissemination through radio and television.

An appeal to both black and white music markets produced the most popular and commercially successful of black music identities of the 1960s, with the formation in Detroit by Berry Gordy of the Tamla record label, later Motown and also the generic name for the sound it developed through a policy of using the same musicians and record producers for a range of solo and group singers. The basis of the sound was a heavy on-the-beat version of rhythm and blues along with animated bass lines and dense instrumental sound, often strings) with rock and roll instrumentation. Artists for the record label included Martha and the Vandellas, the Supremes, Marvin Gaye, Stevie Wonder and Diana Ross; relocated to Los Angeles in the 1970s, the Motown label's success continued with the Commodores, Lionel Ritchie and the Jackson 5. Also into the early 1970s, the music of Sly & the Family Stone and the Temptations brought elements of rock and soul together to form an influential style of dance music that was to feed into the 1980s dance developments of House Music and disco.

The conventionally separate roles of singer and songwriter began to blur in the 1960s through the rise of popular song as political protest (the American military interventions in Vietnam and Korea were a particular catalyst), drawing on the biographical quality and the oral tradition of blues and especially folk song. The examples of Bob Dylan and Joan Baez, with their stress on acoustic performance and direct personal

expression, marked this seminal change in songs such as respectively *Blowin' in the Wind* and *Big Yellow Taxi*, while the works of Paul Simon and Art Garfunkel also provide a clear example of the overlap of folk material, singer-songwriter branding and widespread popular appeal.

Youth music in America and Britain in particular was not just that of rebellion and protest, but also of conspicuous consumption and leisure in response to the economic boom. The American West Coast provided a focus with on the one hand a hedonistic conformist lifestyle (surfing, cars and girls providing the major thematic tropes), and on the other the San Francisco "hippy" movement of idealized political values, communal lifestyles and a liberated attitude to sex and drug use. Musically the former was evoked typically through the "surf sound" of the Beach Boys, the latter by the experimental rock of such performers as the Grateful Dead and Frank Zappa and the Mothers of Invention. In Britain, the Beatles are the most lasting symbol of similar movements of commercially significant and confident youth expression, combined with an expression of British pop music as a major cultural force. Through their 10-year career, the Beatles' sound evolved from

a conventional rhythm-beat combination (drums, bass guitar, rhythm guitar and lead guitar) with songs on conventional themes (*She Loves You*, 1963) to self-consciously poetic imagery (*A Day in the Life*, 1967), and experimental and extended numbers in large-scale arrangements (*Hey Jude*, 1968). Of other contemporary British groups, the Kinks were influential on later songwriting, if not on the creation of the image of the global pop supergroup.

A mainstream popular sound in the 1960s and 70s still put personality singers at the forefront, with the more conventional solo singers such as Gene Pitney (*24 Hours from Tulsa*, *Something's Gotten Hold of my Heart*) and Roy Orbison (*Crying*), although the more subversive element of pop had equivalents in such singers as Dusty Springfield: her folk music background in the Springfields gave way to an interplay between white performers and black music (her recording of the gospel-influenced *Son of a Preacher Man*) along with more conventional ballads, many of continental origin and sung in translation (including *You Don't Have to Say you Love me*). The solo pop performer has continued to be a significant figure in pop music in all subsequent decades, although the tendency toward one or two hit songs rather than sustained careers has also persisted. Those who have maintained a profile over a significant period have tended to be influential as a result. Among these high-profile singers, Whitney Houston has become the exemplar of gospel-inflected, melismatic ballad singing in such numbers as *I Will Always Love You*. As a consequence, a style of melodic embellishment to represent an overt emotionalism has become ubiquitous in the genre.

At another extreme, Madonna has promoted not so much the distinctive sound of the individual musician, but rather embodied in pop

Bob Dylan, 1985

The influence of singer and songwriter Bob Dylan has spread across many areas of pop music. His works embody a combination of folk origins, social and political protest and expressive autobiography that has served as a model for singer-songwriters, and been instrumental in the fusing of music and poetry within a single role instead of following the traditional separation of writers and performers. He was born Robert Zimmerman (1941) in Duluth, USA, but later legally changed his name to Bob Dylan. His songs of the early 1960s were in the mode of the prevailing folk movement; these include *Blowin' in the Wind* and *The Times they Are a Changin'*, which caught the mood of the times in their challenges to establishment thought and poetic imagery. He found much of his musical and textual inspiration in folk-blues heritage, but also took from rock. Songs such as *Like a Rolling Stone* have become classics and important albums released include *Blonde on Blonde* (1966) and *Blood on the Tracks* (1974), although Dylan has remained committed to the creative role played by live performance.

John Travolta in *Saturday Night Fever,* with Karen Lynn Gorney, 1977

The popular dance form of disco emerged in the early 1970s as a development of soul and funk, especially associated with American Latino, African American and gay social underclasses. The main features of the style were strong on-the-beat-rhythms, rich orchestral textures, and memorable choruses with uplifting music and lyrics. It quickly spread to become the dominant club dance form, and the movie *Saturday Night Fever* (1977), with music by the Bee Gees, remains iconic in subject and sound. Performers associated with the form include singers Donna Summer, Gloria Gaynor and the group the Village People. The form also relied on creative record producers, notably Giorgio Moroder, and the skill of club DJs in creating seamless, continuous record mixes through an evening, techniques that have become the core of club dance music thereafter.

Rock

"Rock" is a contraction of "rock and roll', and its musical origins lie in a similar instrumental arrangement of lead, rhythm and bass guitar with drums and rhythm and blues musical vocabulary. It is distinguished, however, through its highly amplified presentation, heavy rhythmic patterns and reliance on distinctive riffs within often extended compositions that feature virtuosic performance. It arose in the 1960s as a more committed form of youth music that eschewed the overt commercialism of pop. Inevitably, the association with rebellion against the political and social status quo (a term appropriated with a sense of irony by one leading rock group for their name) generated its own popularity and essential commercialism. Leading exponents have been to a significant extent British, including such groups as the Rolling Stones, Genesis, Deep Purple and Pink Floyd. Later developments added to the range of rock to include: overt theatricality in glam rock (David Bowie, Queen, Alice Cooper); social commentary (Bruce Springsteen); and extremes of volume and pace in hard rock (AC/DC, The Who, Bon Jovi), even more so in heavy metal (Kiss, Black Sabbath, Judas Priest).

Many of rock's early exponents were classically trained, with the result that their formative works, now viewed as the sub-genre progressive rock, often include classical referents and display ambitions in scale and emotion beyond contemporary pop styles. Examples include: Deep Purple's *Concerto for Group and Orchestra* (1969; by Jon Lord, the group's virtuoso keyboard player), the Who's "rock opera" *Tommy* (also 1969); and the use of unorthodox time signatures in Pink Floyd's *Dark Side of the Moon* (1973). Emerson, Lake & Palmer also made rock renditions of classical works, notably Mussorgsky's *Pictures at an Exhibition* and Janáček's *Sinfonietta* (as *Knife-Edge*). Such intensions toward a higher cultural status than pop has been reinforced through a focus on the "album" as an integrated work in its own right rather than the "single" that characterizes pop, but also on the fully-staged, stadium live performance: rock's intention is not to be background for dance and club culture, but for attentive and concentrated listening.

The lives of many rock musicians have led to an association of the form with hedonistic indulgence—especially drug use to sometimes fatal effect—emphasizing further the sub-genre's anti-establishment role. Rock guitarist, singer and songwriter Jimi Hendrix (1942–70) has become symbolic of rock's artistic virtues and personal vices. Self-taught as guitarist, he became a backing guitarist for Little Richard and learned from such blues musicians as Albert King and Muddy Waters.

In 1965 he formed the Jimi Hendrix Experience, and released the first single (*Hey Joe/Stone Free*) in 1965. His compositions exploited sound treatments and unusual effects available in the recording studio and his guitar playing made great use of

the tremolo arm for bending pitches. *Purple Haze* demonstrates his distinctive sound—loud, sustained and virtuosic—and remains one of his best-known numbers. He was influenced by the songwriting of Bob Dylan and took an interest in techniques of jazz improvisation; indeed his constant search for new influences gave his music a vitality and range that have been profoundly influential on rock music. He died in London in 1970 from a probably accidental overdose of sleeping pills and alcohol.

Many of the subdivisions of rock arise not so much through strong musical differentiation as from the subject matter and language of the lyrics, from culturally self-aware to the deliberately shocking. Notably, the development of punk rock in Britain in the mid-1970s was in part an angry parody of mainstream rock which, by that stage, had been subsumed by the dominant record-company system it had ostensibly sought to avoid. Further contradictions are present in the commercially aware manipulation of punk by its primary mentor Malcolm Maclaren, manager of the most notorious punk group, the Sex Pistols, whose shock value in notoriously aggressive attitudes, language and behavior (rather than their intrinsic musical value) gained them fame and a following. Punk in itself was a short-lived musical form, with its loose collection of qualities and socio-political attitudes absorbed by the late 1970s into other emerging styles, notably the more polished New Wave.

the deliberately branded personality, creating a distinctive fusion of contemporary attitudes and values along with subversive delivery in text and image. Such an approach was furthered in the "girl power" of the British group the Spice Girls where a mild musical combination of rap styles and minimal singing was overshadowed by an idea of female independence and in which the video and stage dance and movement have been as integral to the popularity as the text and music.

COUNTRY MUSIC

Parallel with the mainstreams of popular and pop music has been the genre of country music. It has a popularity that rivals all the other forms, but receives a disproportionately small prominence in the media, possibly in response to its repeating conservative themes of a simplistic romanticism and stoicism in the face of personal adversity. As one form of black folk music is at the root of rhythm and blues and hence rock and roll, so white folk music of the southern states of the USA provides the roots of country. Essentially rural and oral as expressive song or for folk dance, the form established itself more widely with the advent of sound recording in the 1920s and performers including fiddler John Carson and singer Vernon Dalhart. Cowboy songs in particular became popular, developing in the 1930s into Western Swing, a smooth and commercialized dance-band version of country that persisted into the early 1950s; its leading early exemplars were Bob Will's Texas Playboys and Milton Brown's Musical Brothers. The rise of honky tonk in the 1940s created one of the most characteristic of country sounds: country fiddle and steel guitar over a simple, rhythm and bass accompaniment in the service of strophic songs with clear narratives. It is from this background that such performers as Hank Williams emerged in the late 1940s to become star personalities; they were helped by the combination of dedicated radio programs for the genre such as "The Louisiana Hayride" and by a market that had spread to Europe and East Asia as a result of American troop movements during World War II. The geographical center for this activity became Nashville, Tennessee, and "The Grand Ole Opry".

Rock and roll dented the youth audience for country in the 1950s, and some performers adapted to include such trends: singers Roy Orbison and the Everly Brothers were especially successful. In such a way country-rock fusions developed into the 1960s in music by the Eagles, the Byrds and Gram Parsons. In response to such musical melding, in the 1960s a developing Nashville sound returned to older styles of country music but with a modern edge in the arrangements (including choral backing), which gave mainstream country music new life. It is from this period that such well-known names emerged as Johnny Cash, along with Patsy Cline, whose popularity was also a signal for a growing number of star women singers that would include Loretta Lynn and Dolly Parton (continuing in 1980s with Emmylou Harris and the 1990s with Shania Twain and LeAnn Rimes). At a similar time a rival "outlaw" sound, centered on Austin, Texas, was developing, with such singers as Willie Nelson and Waylon Jennings returning to rougher and less glamorous elements of traditional country music themes and presentation. In the 1990s the striking success of Garth Brooks into a broader market was both a result of his adoption of certain elements of pop presentation and mild rock musical influences to extend his appeal and a symptom of the wider acceptance of country music internationally.

Johnny Cash

Country singer-songwriter Johnny Cash (1932-2003) bridged the styles of country, rock and roll and rockabilly. Always at odds with the mainstream presentation of country and western, his dark and moral songs from a strongly male perspective allied to a distinctively deep voice gained an international popularity, and his musical style remains widely influential on country performers. His delivery and subject matter was matched by a preference for dark clothing, leading to his nickname of "the Man in Black".

K.D. Lang started in band-based country, developed through polished Nashville (*Shadowlands*) and turned into a major international pop soloist with international hits from self-penned albums, showing how country music is no longer a self-contained musical world.

FROM ACOUSTIC TO ELECTRONIC

Technological innovations form a significant strand of direct influence on the development of the sound of pop music, taking it increasingly away from solely live performance toward conception and composition as a process in the sound studio. First, the growth of advanced recording techniques changed the compositional palette of pop sounds, creating the specific role of the record producer who could direct the way the sound was built up. The music of the Beach Boys exploited multi-layered textures only possible in the recording studio, including the recording of vocal tracks in sections and on top of each other for qualities of tone and density impossible in live performance without additional resources (for example, *Good Vibrations*, 1966). George Martin, record producer for the Beatles, was formative in defining the sounds of that group, especially through his use of orchestral color (he was trained as a classical oboist) as with the string ensembles of *Yesterday* and *Eleanor Rigby*. In contrast, Phil Spector's "Wall of Sound" for Motown is a dense and epic instrumental backing with heavy drum beats and full orchestral range above, given further depth with echo. It is defining of a whole era of 1960s'

American commercial pop especially associated with female singing trios such as the Crystals (*Da Doo Ron Ron* and *Then He Kissed Me*) and the Ronettes (*Be My Baby*) and such duos as Ike and Tina Turner (*River Deep, Mountain High*) and the Righteous Brothers (*You've Lost that Lovin' Feelin'*).

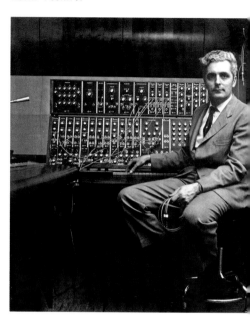

Mechanical and electric technology was introduced into popular and early pop music as a matter of course, the genre's defining aim being to represent the contemporary. "Modern" sound qualities were provided through the keyboard typically, in turn, by the distinctive tone-wheel Hammond organ (taken over into rhythm and blues from gospel music), the Mellotron (taped sounds of voice, strings and brass played through a keyboard) in progressive rock, and the synthesizer in a whole range of pop sounds and featured prominently in the music of French composer and synthesizer player Jean-Michel Jarre (b. 1948). His compositions *Equinoxe* and *Oxygene* demonstrated the subtle possibilities of synthesizer-based soundscapes, as also did the music from the groups Orchestral Manoeuvres in the Dark and Tangerine Dream.

The electric guitar, made possible by the pickup technology on guitars such as the Gibson, Les Paul, Fender Stratocaster solid body guitars and electronic sound treatments (phasers, flangers and reverb, for example), brought an instrumental power and tonal range that was essential for the development of guitar bands, most notably so in rock. But the introduction of electronically created sounds through the development of first the synthesizers, then later the automatic playing of pre-programmed musical patterns by a sequencer, and the programmable electronic drum kit changed music fundamentally. Not only did an infinite range of sounds become available to

---

Robert Moog with his Moog synthesizer, 1970

One of the leading technological advances in music in the latter half of the 20th century was that of the synthesizer, spearheaded by the American Robert Moog (1934–2005) whose main breakthrough came in combining sound treatments (such as voltage controlled oscillators, ADSR envelop generators) with a keyboard, as in the Minimoog. Initially only able to produce a single note at a time, the artistic potential of the synthesizer was demonstrated in such recordings as *Switched On Bach* by Walter (later Wendy) Carlos and interpretations of Debussy by Isao Tomita, while its potential for sound treatments made it appeal to rock musicians who could use the Minimoog as a lead instrument on stage. Moog worked closely with such musicans as John Cage in the avant garde, and the rock musicians Keith Emerson and Rick Wakeman. The development of polyphonic synthesizers (able to play several notes at a time) and digital synthesizers (beginning with the Yamaha DX7) have made the electronic generation of sound an everyday component of pop and rock.

Madonna, in "Take A Bow", 1994

Madonna (*b.* Madonna Louise Ciccone, 1958) has become the most famous of pop performers through the constant reinvention of her image and style to catch current trends. Her songs have matched contemporary musical accessibility with strong promotional videos, *Like a Prayer* and its video is typical in its use of sexual and religious imagery in a provocative combination with a catchy verse-chorus song structure. Dance, costume design and impressive staging have marked her concert appearances, and she has also acted in movies, including the title roles in *Desperately Seeking Susan* (1985) and the movie musical *Evita* (1996). The title of her song *Material Girl* (1985) has been seen as a summary of her image and its values, reflecting late 20th and early 21st century society's consumerist focus.

a group or producer, but an individual could create a dense and complete musical sound on their own, often building up the sound through successive patterns of motivic repetitions used in sequence and layered.

In Germany, Kraftwerk and the Can were some of the first to create a synthesized pop sound that took its lead from the classical avant-garde of composers such as Karlheinz Stockhausen (1928–2007) and emotionally distanced through its overt use of electronic means of production. Kraftwerk's title single from their album *Autobahn* (1975) became particularly well known in Europe and America, and their sound influenced such later groups as New Order, the Human League and Depeche Mode. This techno sound, as it was called, combined with the drive of mainstream rhythm and blues to lead directly to House Music exemplified in Afrika Bambaataa's hip hop release of 1982, *Planet Rock* and that also drew on DJ techniques (scratching and mixing), emergent rap and counter-cultural ideas linked to graffiti art and break dance. The name reputedly comes from Chicago's Warehouse club, where the resident DJ Frankie Knuckles pioneered the style, and shares many similarities with the slightly slower contemporary Garage Music.

In a different mix, House Music's rhythmic insistence combined with more conventional Western diatonic and strophic forms as disco. What all such variants have in common is a repetitive and driving rhythm for dance in clubs, a quality that enables one record to be blended directly into another to create continuous and seamless music over hours; the musical hierarchy emphasizes rhythm (and in the case of disco strong harmonic direction for choruses) over melody and clear-cut formal structure.

"Dance music" of the 1990s and early 21st century is a broader extension of house and disco, with elements of hip-hop, the nuances of local styles and fashions essentially based around a central core of techniques for sound manipulation. Acid jazz, rave, ambient house, trance, jungle, trip hop and breakbeat are just a few of the evolutions of 1980s, centered on the patterns of consumer use and the image of club culture. Besides a constant rhythmic pulse and the mixing from one track to another (elements shared by house and disco), the greatest advance was made through the technique of sampling in which a sound or phrase from an existing recording is electronically recorded ("sampled"), digitally stored and then manipulated in repetition, pitch and speed within a new musical soundscape. The technology became affordable from the mid-1980s and quickly became a feature of club music. The first significant example of the technique was *Rapper's Delight*

(1979) by the Sugarhill Gang, who used samples from the disco number *Good Times* by Chic. The use of rhythms and bass lines quickly spread into rap and more widely into dance music; popular examples include *Pump up the Volume* by M/A/R/R/S (1987). Questions of copyright aside (there have been many test cases), it is now ubiquitous in the production of club tracks. In the process, the creative artist has moved even further away from performing musician to composer and record producer, assembling the sound through entirely electronic means, whether synthesized or sampled. The creative use of samples is often one of creating a new context for known musical elements. Examples of prominent samples include those in MC Hammer's *U Can't Touch This* and Vanilla Ice's *Ice Ice Baby*, while the technique is at the root of the aesthetic of such groups as the Orb.

Beyond the creation of the music alone, technology has brought about the ever-tighter fusion of sound, image and brand in main-stream pop especially since the establishment of the dedicated pop music channel MTV in 1981 in America and the use of promotional videos for performers and their newly released singles. It was an extension of the long-established use of a constant background of recorded music in public spaces and brought about a steady demand for imagery to accompany newly released singles vying for attention in a crowded market. Inevitably, striking imagery helped record sales considerably. In 1975, the video to accompany the seven-minute *Bohemian Rhapsody* by the British rock group Queen announced the start of the pop video age, but it was the video in 1983 for the title song of the album *Thriller* by Michael Jackson, already an established performer since childhood with his brothers in the Jackson 5, that consolidated the approach as integral to pop culture. In it, Jackson combined his distinctive soul-style vocalizing, funky rhythm, slick and energetic choreography with narrative and big-budget production values. The power of the pop video can be seen in such provocative examples as that by George Michael in the video for *Outside*.

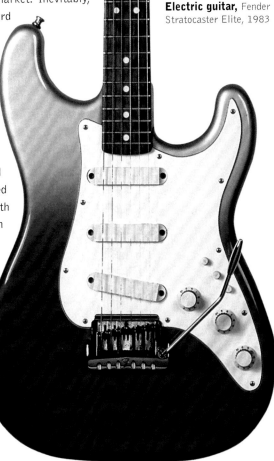

Electric guitar, Fender Stratocaster Elite, 1983

GLOBAL EXCHANGE

The history of Western popular music has followed the accretion to a central Western harmonic and melodic core of external musical influences. The

introduction of black music in rhythm along with "blues" notes provided the first main wave. In the 1920s and 30s Latin American and Caribbean sounds were introduced through dance forms, again with an influence on rhythm through the tango, rumba, mambo, samba and salsa. Spanish-Cuban bandleader Xavier Cugat (1900–90) was the prime innovator who successfully straddled the boundary of indigenous music and popular style, creating an appealing tropically styled sound; others who fed the Latin-American fusion in the following decades included Perez Prado, Ray Barretto and Willie Colón. (Leonard Bernstein's score for the successful musical *West Side Story* is indicative of how much Latin styles had become a recognizable force in American popular music in the mid-1950s, while the subject of that musical's story also indicates how it was seen in the context of exoticism rather than as indigenous.) Successful within American popular music from a similar time on was "new wave" bossa nova, whose relaxed and rhythmic sensuality is well summed up in the now-standard songs *Garota de Ipanema* and *Desafinado* by Tom Jobim, who developed the new wave sound. Singers, notably Rubén Blades, have combined the popular Latin American forms with social and political protest, while singer-songwriter Caetano Veloso has been in effect a Brazilian Bob Dylan.

Over a similar time a calypso form of Cuban origin in Jamaica, called Mento, absorbed

influences from swing and big-bands to evolv into the more specific Jamaican form of reggae at first a slow four-beat shuffle with distinctive use of a chordal reed section, trombone soloing and off-beat piano. The sound evolved on record, the Jamaican practice being for music to be played through sound systems rather than played live. As a result, producers who were in charge of such systems, became important, notably "Sir Coxone" Dodd, "Duke" Reid and "Prince" Buster. The term reggae dates from around 1968 and the single *Do the Reggay* by the group the Maytals, although characteristics of the form had emerged a shor time before in the style known as "ska", which took a fast rhythm and blues basis, but dropped on-the-beat accents to create a distinctive, repeating off-beat stress. Ska was important not just as a musical forerunner of reggae but for opening up an audience beyond Jamaica, especially through large-scale emigration at the time to the UK. As a consequence, the influence of reggae on British pop sounds has always been notable, resulting in the distinctive 1970s sound of 2 Tone, so named after the record label that represented such English groups as the Specials and Madness who drew on ska and reggae. Jamaican reggae has been subject to gradual change, as in the more aggressive, faster "rockers" style of the mid-1970s exemplified by drummer Sly Dunbar and bass player Robbie Shakespeare, such that the distinctive original style, now globally familiar, is known as "roots".

The anti-war counter-cultural stances of the 1960s prompted an interest in spiritual values, with the direct result of the annexing of elements

Bob Marley, at the Hammersmith Odeon, London, England, June 1977

Bob Marley (1945–81) is the most famous exponent of reggae. His distinctive voice and socially aware lyrics built him a worldwide following, especially in conjunction with the group the Wailers. He embraced the Rastafarian religion, which is also strongly associated with reggae, and his musical legacy remains influential across styles including rock and rap.

Youssou N'Dour, 1980

N'Dour was a national singing star by the age of 15 and gained an international following through touring in the 1980s with his own group Etoile de Dakar (later Super Etoile de Dakar). He performs Mbalax, a combination of Senegal percussion and singing mixed with Afro-Cuban sounds, into which he has intermingled hip hop, jazz and soul to create a vibrant and individual West African-Western style all his own. The extent of Western pop and rock influences on him and his influence on them in turn can be seen in the list of the people with whom he has collaborated, which includes Peter Gabriel, Bruce Springsteen, Neneh Cherry, Paul Simon, Branford Marsalis and Sting.

of non-Western philosophies of non-violence, particularly Buddhism. One resulting effect is seen in the popularity at the time of sitar player Ravi Shankar, who was invited to perform at the 1967 Monterey Pop Festival and in 1969 at the Woodstock Festival; the Beatles in particular were associated with such Indian influence philosophically if not substantially musically. In practice, certain elements of non-Western sounds have proved easier to integrate into Western pop than others. The different tunings of the scales that form the tonal basis of other musics, such as the ragas in Indian music, are not as straightforward to accommodate within Western tonality. Furthermore, the physical construction of the Western instruments used, as for example with a standard keyboard and its associated pitches, are not sufficiently adaptable. In this respect, it has tended to be either world music of sufficiently related tonality that has been used, or rhythmic elements which have fewer such constraints. For example, South Africa provided the stimulus for Paul Simon's album *Graceland* (1986), on which he collaborated with that country's black singing group Ladysmith Black Mambazo to fuse their sounds and rhythms with the musical sensibility of Western pop. He followed this in 1990 with *The Rhythm of the Saints*, drawing on Brazilian influences. Often such pop focus on the indigenous sounds from a particular part of the world has corresponded with a newsworthy geo-political focus.

However, it has been more usual for Western-based music to be adapted or even adopted wholesale in non-Western countries. Of particular significance has been the global adoption of rap, or hip hop, as a shared musical form. Its early origins lie in the toasting technique of Jamaican DJs, who would extemporize commentaries and exhortations between and over records they played, but was more directly formed from a harder edged urban sound, youth counter-cultural self-expression and electronic sound technology. It has become the predominant global form, its requirements being for a rhythmic element, however basic, over which personal commentary in rhythmic speech is added; the rapper (or MC) displays virtuosity with word-play, counter-cultural reference, rhythmic creativity and the virtuosity of speed. It coalesced as a genre in the 1970s through the example of recordings such as *Rapper's Delight* (1979) from the Sugarhill Gang, and through its adoption as a primary means of socio-political comment in the 1980s, by Public Enemy for example, fast becoming a dominant form of aggressive disaffection. Although associated at first with black American culture, rap spread quickly became more broad in its audience and performers (in the mid-1980s the white trio the Beastie Boys became prominent) and now rap

with national characteristics has developed. Of the various mainstream sub-genres, the most notable has been US gangsta rap, whose wider popularity was first marked by the N.W.A. album *Straight Outta Compton* (1988); several of gangsta rap's prominent exponents have subsequently been involved in internecine violence to fatal effect, as with Tupac Shakur and Notorious B.I.G.

A significant factor in the mass dissemination of Western recordings across countries has been the making of foreign translations of an English-language core repertory, made possible by the substitution through multi-track recording of a new-language vocal line over the original instrumental tracks. Since the early 1960s this has helped both disseminate and reinforce a Western pop hegemony within Western culture and beyond as has also the growth of English as the second-language of choice throughout much of the world. Yet technology has also helped counter such homogenizing effects, as first with the cassette tape recorder, then the introduction of home multi-track recorders and then, toward the end of the century, computer-based digital sequencers and sound recorders and the ease of burning a CD. These have put composition and recording into the home, while the establishment of the worldwide web has provided an accessible platform for self-promotion; for example, the British group the Arctic Monkeys built up a large following through internet promotion rather than through the more conventional forms of mediation by a record company. For all the multiplicity of mainstream and specialist forms of pop genres and sub-genres that now exist, the philosophical heart of pop as a "democratizing" genre in content, production and distribution has become its main defining feature today.

Snoop Dogg, at the Greek Theatre, Los Angeles, California, August 25, 2005

Snoop Dogg (born Cordozar Calvin Broadus Jr, 1971), exemplifies the stereotypical image through his subject material of violent street culture, matched in his own personal involvement with trial for murder, and prosecutions for drug and gun crime. The springboard of his early association with the influential record producer and rapper Dr Dre on the album *Doggystyle* (1993) led to him becoming one of the most famous exponents of rap with such later albums as *Tha Last Meal* (2000) and *Tha Blue Carpet Treatment* (2006).

MODERNISM

By the 1890s the ideologies that shaped 19th century Europe—a confident imperial capitalism, zealous Christianity and a connected system of ruling monarchies—were beginning to crumble under attack from scientific advances, not least the ideas of Charles Darwin, and a growing demand for social change based on universal suffrage and greater equality. The old world was not to go quietly. Its destruction took over 50 years and was accompanied by two global conflicts, demands for self-governance by areas of the world under European imperial control and radical demands—often accompanied by violent revolution—for a greater share in national wealth and political control by a previously disenfranchised majority. Against this background of change, often bewildering and isolating as long-established social networks disappeared, the musical forms and language of Romanticism began to seem inadequate to express the concerns of the newly-emerging Modern world.

While there was a great democratization of music in the commercial sphere, especially once recording technology became cheap and widely disseminated, the exploration of the themes of desolation and isolation on the one hand and preoccupation with musical language on the other led art music composers away from a mass audience. The technical developments that brought this about—atonality, rhythmic and textural complexity and the inevitable breakdown of forms that depended on functional harmonic relationships—seemed alien to a large part of the middle class audience that had proved such a willing patron throughout the 19th century. Thus, a trend began that gathered apace throughout the 20th century. Audiences for new works in the concert hall and opera house declined to a point where many composers were—and are—dependent on grants and commissions from institutions (be they arts foundations or government) rather than the proceeds from performances. This in turn created a specialist and restricted audience for new pieces, members of which had been initiated into the musical language of Modernism, requiring a certain degree of esoteric musical education. Composers themselves moved into a narrow artistic sphere by virtue of their employment, usually within universities or conservatories where their ideas and works would be treated sympathetically and from which they would derive their primary source of income.

At the same time there remained the appetite of a sizable middle class audience for the musics of the 19th century and Viennese Classicism, especially Mozart, Beethoven, Brahms and Tchaikovsky in the concert hall and Mozart, Verdi and Puccini in the opera house. And, of course, not all composers felt compelled by the avant garde imperative to constantly break new ground and dispense with all that had gone before. In terms of audience share and number of recordings, an increasingly important point of access to the Western canon as the 20th century progressed, the most successful

Nikolay Tcherepnin's (1873–1945) *Narcisse et Echo,* costume design by Leon Bakst, performed by Sergei Diaghilev's Ballets Russes

1882: Russian composer Igor Stravinsky is born.

1889: Exposition in Paris, Debussy hears and is enchanted by the Indonesian *gamelan.*

1894: Claude Debussy's *Prélude de l'aprés-midi d'un faune* has its premiere in Paris on 22 December.

1901: Queen Victoria dies.

1905: The first uprising in Russia against the Tsar.

1913: *The Rite of Spring* receives its premiere in Paris on 29 May.

1914: Gavrilo Princip assassinates Archduke Franz Ferdinand in Sarajevo; the repercussions escalate into World War I.

1917: The Tsar abdicates the Russian throne and the October revolution brings Lenin and the Bolsheviks to power.

1918: World War I ends with the signing of the Armistice in a Marshal Foch's railway carriage in France.

1925: Pierre Boulez is born in Montbrison, France, on March 26.

1933: Adolf Hitler becomes Chancellor of Germany.

1939: Sigmund Freud dies just a few weeks after the start of World War II.

1945: World War II ends.

1947: India and Pakistan gain independence from Britain.

Karlheinz Stockhausen, avant garde pioneer of electronic music

1968: Soviet troops invade Czechoslovakia in response to the liberal intentions of the country's Communist Party leader, Alexander Dubček.

1972: Arab terrorists kill 11 Israeli athletes at the Olympics in Munich.

1975: General Franco, Spanish Head of State and right-wing nationalist, dies.

1975: Russian composer Dimitri Shostakovich dies.

1986: A nuclear reactor at Chernobyl in the USSR explodes, releasing large amounts of radioactivity into the atmosphere.

2007: German avant garde composer Karlheinz Stockhausen dies.

works came from those figures still working within a broadly tonal, and in some respects Romantic, idiom: for example Dmitry Shostakovich and Sergey Prokofiev in the USSR, Ralph Vaughan Williams, William Walton and Benjamin Britten in the United Kingdom, and Aaron Copland and John Adams in the USA. This survival of a tradition of tonal composition was for a long time responsible for establishing the dominant literary and musical discourse of *fin de siècle* Paris and their ideas spilt over into related movements such as Art Nouveau. Many of the writers had the stated aim of finding a musicality in poetry, stemming from the idea that music has the ability to express pure emotional and psychological states without reference to the concrete that words often require.

The opening of Debussy's *Prélude à l'après midi d'un faune,* flute solo

overshadowed by that of the avant garde in the minds of many musicians and musicologists, due in large part to the most influential scholars and critics being attached to precisely those institutions that supported iconoclastic Modernist composers. The reign of William Glock (1908–2000) at the BBC in London was in no small way responsible for the promotion of this rather partisan view of 20th century music, giving prominence to the works of Pierre Boulez among others. With the start of the 21st century a greater awareness of the diversity of the music of the previous 100 years became more widely acknowledged, and a more insightful perspective on the work of the avant garde—due to the lapse of time—enabled a more critical appraisal of its shortcomings but also a wider recognition of the greatness of many of its practitioners.

PARIS 1890–1920

Pierre Boulez has written that Modernism in music began with the opening flute solo of Claude Debussy's (1862–1918) *Prélude à l'après-midi d'un faune* (1891–4). Based on a poem by the Symbolist Stéphane Mallarmé, the falling chromatic tritone of the opening and dreamy whole-tone and pentatonic themes that permeate this short work usher in a new sound world; one that at times dispenses with functional harmonic relations in favor of parallelism and ambiguous diminished and augmented chords. In doing this Debussy was engaged in finding a musical equivalent to the devices of the Symbolist poets Mallarmé (1842–98), Paul Verlaine (1844–96) and the Belgian Maurice Maeterlinck (1862–1949), and their great predecessor Charles Baudelaire (1821–67). Their works revel in ambiguity, sensuality and a dislocation from everyday life, as well as displaying an interest in the esoteric. Coalescing around Mallarmé, a group of artists known as the *Les Mardistes* were

Above all this was inspired by their idolizing of the works of Wagner, at the time attracting considerable interest in France, and especially the later mystical and sexually-charged *Tristan und Isolde* and *Parsifal*.

Debussy was no exception and was at first an ardent *Wagneriste*, making the pilgrimage to Bayreuth to hear *Der Ring des Nibelungen*. Although he was to refine his ideas and during the 1890s denounced the cult of Wagner, slight traces of the German composer's works were to remain in Debussy's music throughout his life, even if as tongue-in-cheek references such as the *Tristan* quotes in his piano work *Golliwog's Cake Walk* (1908). In part Debussy's ability to forge a new musical language and aesthetic stems from his literally singular education, his only formal instruction was in music at the Conservatoire in Paris where he enrolled at the age of 10. In other spheres he was able to follow his own instincts, taking inspiration as much from literature and the visual arts, especially the Symbolists, as from formal sources of learning. A confusion often arises between Impressionism in painting and aspects of Debussy's music, to which the label is often applied. Impressionism, as practised by artists such as Claude Monet (1840–1926) and Camille Pissarro (1830–1903), was a movement that sought to capture the retinal effect of light at a particular moment in time, thus requiring the artists to abandon any sense of line and to work quickly. The technique they developed to enable them to do this—taken to an extreme by Georges-Pierre Seurat (1859–91)—involved the use of myriad points of color, leading some commentators to say that it was the "impression of a scene", hence the movement's name. This has been confused with Debussy's practice of giving names to many of his works (for example "Les sons et les parfums tournent dans l'air du soir", a quote from Baudelaire used in Book 1 of his *Préludes*, 1910, or "Jeux de vagues" in *La Mer*,

1903–5). These are hints to the evocation of a mood, idea or scene, and so more akin to the ideas of the Symbolists than anything to do with the scientific investigation of light and color.

Debussy himself made it clear that he did not consider himself an Impressionist (although he also sometimes clouded the issue through a loose use of

Set design for Ravel's *Daphnis et Chloe,* by Leon Bakst; Ballet Russe production (Music by Maurice Ravel, choreography by Fokine); Scene I; June 1912

Immensely important for its contribution to the history of 20th century music, the innovative productions of the Ballets Russes, led by Serge Diaghilev, caused a great stir in Paris between 1909 and the 1920s. As well as the early ballets of Stravinsky, Diaghilev was responsible for commissioning, among others, Debussy's *Jeux* (1912–13), Dukas' *La Peri* (1911–12), Ravel's *Daphnis et Chloe* (1909–12), Satie's *Parade,* and Milhaud's *Le train bleu* (1924).

the term), and was outspoken on a number of other aesthetic issues, such as the denunciation of the worship of Wagner, largely through the mouthpiece of his literary persona M. Croche. However, the development of his own personal musical language was to prove as important for the future direction of 20th century music as the Impressionists were for 20th century art. While retaining the idea of a tonal center in much of his work, and never fully dispensing with key signatures, the concept of functional harmony and traditional key relationships were by and large discarded. Musical movement owed much more to parallel voice leading than the tensions of 19th century modulation; and through this it was possible to move to, or through, almost any other tonal center without having to set up prior expectations. Piles of intervals were used to construct sonorities, often fourths or fifths and clusters of notes derived from the pentatonic scale, major thirds that formed augmented chords derived from the wholetone scale or the minor thirds of the octatonic forming diminished chords. These sound worlds—the pentatonic, wholetone and octatonic—suspend any sense of harmonic direction, the pentatonic lacks a tritone (the interval that gives a dominant seventh its expectation of resolution), the augmented chord cannot be derived from the major or minor diatonic scale and the diminished chord, with its interlocking tritones, is endlessly restless.

Without a traditional idea of key and modulation, such as underpin sonata form, Debussy had to find new devices for musical organization on a large scale. It has been convincingly demonstrated that one of these underlying structures is the Golden Section (a division, of time or a line, whereby the ratio of the smaller part to the larger part is the same as the larger part to the whole, similar to the Fibonacci series of 0112358... where the division of 8 into units of 5 and 3—or 13 into 8 and 5, etc.—approaches that of the Golden Section). This proportion had long been used by visual artists and occurs in many places in the natural world, including sea shells and pine cones. In pieces such as the three-movement orchestral work *La Mer,* or *L'isle joyeuse* (1903–4) for piano, not only do the main climaxes fall at points of Golden Section but through subdivisions, using the same proportion, it also governs the introduction of other musical ideas such as new motifs or sudden changes in dynamic and texture. It has also been suggested that a similar use of the Golden Section as a means of formal organization can be found in the works of Erik Satie, Maurice Ravel, and Béla Bartók.

One of Debussy's most radical works, however, was his only completed opera, and the work that brought him to wider attention, *Pelléas et Mélisande* (1893–1902). His greatest expression of the Symbolist ideal, and arguably the greatest work of the entire Symbolist movement, it was based on a play by Maeterlinck and after a long period of gestation—his other dramatic projects were to be abandoned unfinished—was given its first performance at the Opéra-Comique in 1902. The opera's reception was one of bewilderment and hostility on one side and a certain amount of over-enthusiasm from Debussy's supporters on the other. The most startling aspect of the work was the vocal setting; this verges on speech, mimicking the patterns of the French text and taking declamation further than any previous composer. In this Debussy had been influenced by the vocal writing in Musorgsky's *Boris Godunov,* as he had been in developing his musical language. While there are motifs associated with individual characters, notably Pelléas, Mélisande and Golaud, these are not treated as obviously as in the Wagnerian *Leitmotif* and are hidden amongst the subtle orchestration. Debussy's approach to the timbres and sonorities of the orchestra, also seen in his piano writing, was highly individual and the care he took to score for a precise, often novel, effect shows that, for him, it was as indivisible from the composition process as a consideration of harmony, melody or form.

A composer who was also to take a Symbolist play by Maeterlinck and create out of it operatic success was Paul Dukas (1865–1935). Despite

his small output—Dukas was fiercely self-critical and destroyed many of his own works—he was to be influential on two important slightly later Austrian composers through his opera *Ariane et Barbe-bleue* (1899–1907), Alexander Zemlinsky and Alban Berg. While his music is progressive in many respects, through its harmony and especially orchestration, Dukas remained a committed Wagnerian and was also firmly rooted in the French classical tradition, influenced by, among others, Franck, Saint-Saëns and D'Indy. As well as his opera, he is best remembered for the sparkling orchestral work *L'apprenti sorcier* (1897) which tells Goethe's story of the hapless trainee sorcerer whose illicit experiment gets out of hand.

If Dukas was to represent the continuation of the post-Franco Prussian War French school, then another figure, Erik Satie (1866–1925), was to be the most radical and iconoclastic of the new generation of composers in *fin-de-siècle* Paris. Although he was sent to the Paris Conservatoire to train, he hated the formal constrictures of the institution and his teachers were not impressed with his progress. In 1877 he broke free of the middle class aspirations of his parents and moved to Montmartre, throwing himself with enthusiasm into the bohemian life of the area's cabarets and bars, later becoming a friend of Debussy who promoted his works as did Ravel. His relative lack of formal musical technique was advantageous to the extent that he was less burdened by the weight of musical knowledge that the strict training of the Conservatoire was supposed to have given him. This freed him to think outside the strictures of the canon and in doing so aimed for a simplicity in line and harmonic movement that belies its radical nature. The parallelism of works such as the *Trois sarabandes* (1887) and static modal quality of the *Trois gymnopédies* (1888) prepared the ground for

the music of Debussy, and this antique-like sense of restraint and calm was to return in later works like the symphonic drama *Socrate* (1917–18). Satie was also open to the world of cabaret and theater and his most startling piece, the ballet *Parade* (1916–17) pays homage to this world while also incorporating unusual, to say the least, instruments such as the typewriter and revolver. Although many found Satie's music easy to dismiss on the grounds of its surface simplicity, his anarchic wit and the timeless quality of many of his earlier works made him a *cause célèbre* among the avant garde and was greatly influential on composers such as John Cage and the American minimalists.

Although Debussy is often credited with many of the advances seen in French music at the beginning of the 20th century, a number of them were preshadowed by Satie and for many of the others he must share the glory with his contemporary

IGOR STRAVINSKY

Igor Stravinsky was born near St Petersburg in 1882 and over his long life he was either instrumental in creating or exploiting many of the most important musical movements of the 20th century. No other composer ran the full gamut of Modernist styles, or with such success, as Stravinsky: from the Slavic nationalism of his Russian ballets, to the Neoclassicism of the mid-century, to his startling adoption of serialism late in life. In exile from Russia for much of his life, becoming first a French then an American citizen, his material circumstances reflected the cosmopolitan nature of much of his music, and perhaps his chameleon-like ability to change and adapt to new ideas and forms of composition.

Stravinsky's father was a leading bass at the Mariinsky Theatre and was friendly with many of the leading Russian musical personalities of the day; he also, due to his work, had a large library of scores to which the young Igor had access. He had received piano lessons up until his entry to study law at university and by this time was set on a career in music and, on a visit to Germany in 1902, approached Rimsky-Korsakov who was also holidaying in the country and who took the fledgling composer under his wing. St Petersburg was home to a lively musical culture and Stravinsky had ample opportunities to hear the latest compositions from Western Europe as well as new pieces by leading Russian composers, as well as, with help from Rimsky-Korsakov, run-throughs of his student works. These display, in works such as *Feyerverk* ("Fireworks", 1908), some of the preoccupations of his later works, including use of the octatonic scale and experimental orchestration.

By 1909 Stravinsky had been brought to the attention of the ballet impresario Sergey Diaghilev (1872–1929) and was commissioned to write a ballet for the Russian folktale *Zhar'-ptitsa* ("The

Igor Stravinsky (1882–1971),
portrait by Jacques Emile Blanche; Oil on canvas; 1915; Musée d'Orsay, Paris

Firebird"). This was to have not only a huge impact on Stravinsky's life, but also the history of 20th century music. The first performance of the work in Paris in 1910, with its glittering orchestration and chromatic harmonies derived from works of Rimsky-Korsakov and Skryabin, was a huge success and opened the door to the cosmopolitan artistic life of the city where Stravinsky made the acquaintance of composers Debussy, Satie and Ravel. It also led to further commissions and in 1911, also in Paris, came *Petrushka*, again a great success with the same sure handling of the orchestra, rhythmic subtlety and chromaticism, including the tritone bitonality in C and F# of *Petrushka's* theme on two clarinets. However, nothing was to prepare the world for what was to come.

Stravinsky had been working with the Russian painter Nikolay Roerich on an idea for a ballet set in pagan Russia. *Vesna svyashchennaya* ("The Rite of Spring", 1913), which depicts the sacrifice of a young woman to the earth, was premiered at the Théâtre des Champs-Elysées on 29 May where it prompted a riot. This was as much due to the choreography of Diaghilev's star dancer Vaclav Nizhinsky (1889–1950) and the conservative audience as the music, but the event is often seen as a defining moment in the history of music. Nothing like *The Rite of Spring* had been heard before, a hugely violent and chromatic score where rhythmic ostinato patterns, often in multiple layers and acting against each other, form the principal organizing element. Modal melodic lines are set against each other at dissonant intervals, in tritones, seconds and sevenths, and the additive

Igor Stravinsky's *Rite of Spring*,
Théâtre des Champs Elysées, Paris, 1913

Costumes and Nizhinsky's choreography from the experimental and highly controversial first performance of *Le Sacre de printemps*

rhythms break down the conventional conception of the bar line (one page of the famous Sacrificial Dance from the end of the score runs 2/4, 5/16, 2/16, 3/16, 2/8, 2/16, 2/8) providing considerable difficulties for the performers. This seminal 20th century work derived some of its techniques from Stravinsky's earlier works but never before had they been worked out to such a drastic extent.

The *Rite of Spring* was soon to be heralded as a great success following subsequent performances the same year. However, with the outbreak of war in 1914 Stravinsky began to look for new ideas. Exiled in Switzerland (he was not to return to Russia until a visit to the USSR in 1962), he encountered the Italian Futurists and began work on two pieces, one *Reynard* (1915–16) follows in the Russian footsteps of his earlier ballets, the second *Les Noces*, after a substantial rescoring for four pianos, was not to be performed until 1923. The work which shows the direction he was about to move in is the *Histoire du soldat* (1918), which with its small forces (a necessity in war-torn Europe) and musical parodies of dances that included tango and ragtime shows a new lightness of touch and wit, and a willingness to reinvent existing forms. A trend strengthened by his reworkings of pieces by Pergolesi to form the ballet *Pulcinella* (1919–20). A slightly different take on this new-found paring back of forces and clarity of scoring is seen in the austere *Symphonies d'instruments à vent* (1920). The monumental sound-world of its wind and brass scoring harks back to the Russian ballets, yet here placed in a far more controlled form.

When in 1920 Stravinsky moved back to France from Switzerland he was ready to take a more ideological stand on these new ideas, which became dubbed as Neoclassicism. Music, Stravinsky had decided, should strive for an elegance and objectivity of form and language, explicitly rejecting the individualistic composer-centered Romantic ideal. The first work in which this was projected was the opera *Mavra* (1921–2), but was far more successfully realized in the woodwind and brass *Octet* (1922–3). Over the next 30 years a string of works were to follow in which Stravinsky was to modify and refine his ideas concerning Neoclassicism, but they all retained the dispassionate ideal, at least in terms of musical language and form. Notable among these works are the opera *Oedipus rex* (1926–7) in which he collaborated with the writer Jean Cocteau (1889–1963), its sense of antique austerity reinforced by commentary of the all-male chorus, and the ballet *Apollo* (1927–8) in which he collaborated with the choreographer George Balanchine (1904–83), often regarded as Stravinsky's greatest Neoclassical work and seen as an important counter-balance to the contemporary works of Schoenberg and the Vienna school.

After finishing one of his last "European" works, *Dumbarton Oaks* (1938), although for an American patron, in 1939, on the outbreak of World War II, Stravinsky left France to settle in the US. Stravinsky had traveled widely in the country on concert tours but at first he found California unfamiliar territory and his initial works, such as the *Symphony in Three Movements* (1942–5), look back to earlier musical styles. However, by the end of World War II the composer had begun to find his footing and had absorbed some of the local musical color, writing the *Ebony Concerto* (1945) for the jazz musician Woody Herman (1913–87), and following this with two flawless late-Neoclassical works, the ballet *Orpheus* (1947) and the opera *The Rake's Progress* (1947–51).

Chorus from Stravinsky's *The Rake's Progress*, Opera Australia Chorus, at the Sydney Opera House, 2006, Sydney, Australia

It was after the success of *The Rake's Progress* that he was to spring a further great surprise on the musical world; after previously decrying the works of Schoenberg he produced two works that used that composer's serial technique, albeit in a modified form. It may have been a waning of interest among young composers in his work that prompted this move, but it was one in which he was to stamp the technique with his own personal style. In the *Septet* (1953) Stravinsky uses a 16- rather than 12-tone note row that implies a tonality and *In memoriam Dylan Thomas* (1954) a five-note cell, but this time far more chromatic. The composer went on to adopt 12-note rows in his subsequent works, including the ballet *Agon* (1953–7) and his late religious pieces, such as *The Flood* (1961–2) and *Abraham and Isaac* (1962–3), although never submitting to rigidity or orthodoxy in its treatment up to the end of his life in 1971.

Edgard Varèse (1883–1965)

During the 1920s this French-born composer was to write a series of works that went further than any others in subsuming the compositional process within the effects of rhythm and timbre. The radical nature of *Hyperprism* (1923), *Octandre* (1924) and *Intégrales* (1924–5) are notable not only for their orchestration in which untuned and tuned percussion take precedence over other instrumental groupings, but also the extent to which they embrace atonality. His work for solo flute, *Density 21.5* (1936) shows his ability to logically organize atonal works, in this case within the constraints of a symmetrical division of the octave. During the 1950s he was again to be in the vanguard of musical development, constructing some of the earliest works for magnetic tape.

The futurist artist Luigi Russolo with his noise machine

The most radical ideas in the treatment of sound were to come not from France or Germany but Italy and Russia, and then the Soviet Union, through the Futurists. Initially led by the Italian Filippo Marinetti (1876–1944) who issued a manifesto in 1909 calling for an art that would attack traditionalism and embrace and celebrate the power of the machine, this was taken up by the composer Francesco Pratella (1880–1955) and the painter Luigi Russolo (1885–1947), the latter publishing a Futurist musical manifesto, *L'arte dei rumori* (1913), that called for noise in all its forms to be the basis for composition—an early *musique concrète*. To this end he constructed a series of *intonarumori* ("noise machines") whose first outing in Milan in 1914 provoked a riot, rivaling that which greeted *La sacre du printemps* a year earlier.

Maurice Ravel (1875–1937). Ravel can appear the less progressive figure due to his continued adherence to tonality, rarely dispensing with clear and strong bass lines or a sense of where the music is moving, as well as retaining an affection for, and continuing to write using the models of, the music of the French tradition in a way that neither Debussy or Satie did. His homage to earlier composers was made explicit through works such as *A la manière de...Chabrier* (1913) or *Le tombeau de Couperin* (1914–17), both for piano. However, Ravel made extensive use of chords with added 7ths, 9ths and 11ths and experimented with bitonality (the sounding of two diatonic key centers at the same time), often in advance of similar explorations by Debussy or Igor Stravinsky. He was also quick to absorb the syncopated rhythms and modal inflections of jazz into his music, especially during the 1920s, and in doing so was an influence on composers such as Les Six. His music is never anything other than beautifully crafted, especially in its orchestration, and here too he diverges from Debussy. While both composers had a highly refined sense of instrumental sound, for Ravel it was less integral to the compositional process; for him the essentials were melody and harmony, and especially in his piano works the interweaving of the two so that at times the melody emerges from a harmonic foreground.

Like Satie, Ravel did not fare well at the Conservatoire, after an initially promising start failing to win any major prizes, famously submitting works five times for the Prix de Rome without success; and this was while his music was beginning to be noticed favorably outside of the institution. However, in 1902 Ravel joined Les Apaches, a musical and literary society that also included Stravinsky and Manuel da Falla, giving him ample opportunity to keep up with the latest

artistic developments in *fin-de-siècle* Paris and also widening his general education. One piece that was to emerge from this milieu was the song cycle *Shéhérazade* (1903) for mezzo-soprano and orchestra in which a contemporary taste for the exotic takes flight with some ravishing orchestration but which also demonstrates Ravel's keen sense for the rhythms of the French language, pushing the vocal setting toward an even more idiomatic declamation than Debussy did in *Pelléas et Mélisande*. His departures from the norm, as laid down by the self-proclaimed guardians of French music at the Schola Cantorum, were attacked by conservative critics and spats in the press between himself and supporters of Debussy led Ravel to help found the Société Musicale Indépendent in 1909 where he had a platform to promote his own and other composers' music (including that of Debussy and Satie). Around this time he finished the opera *L'heure espagnole* (1907–9) which along with a later operatic work *L'enfant et les sortilèges* (1920–5) contains some of his most charming music, the former work giving full flight to his interest in Spanish music, and both expose his fascination with mechanical devices; Ravel was famously described by Stravinsky as a "Swiss watchmaker", a reference to not only his frequent use of repetition and ostinato but also his exquisite and obsessive skill as a musical craftsman.

NEOCLASSICISM AND NATIONALISM

During World War I a new generation of composers began to emerge in France, less constrained and in awe of the past and determined to fully engage with the newly emerging Modern world, including

its popular music styles, particularly jazz, and the mechanization of everyday life. These were particularly associated with the group known as "Les Six", identified as such by the critic Henri Collet, its members were: Georges Auric (1899–1983), Louis Durey (1888–1979), Arthur Honegger (1892–1955), Darius Milhaud (1892–1974), Francis Poulenc (1899–1963) and Germaine Tailleferre (1892–1983). Within the group there was a wide diversity of methods and ideas and by the mid-1920s they had effectively disbanded. However, under the guiding hand of Jean Cocteau who was calling for a purely "French" music, away from the insidious influence of Wagner in particular that was still felt in the works of Debussy, and one that embraced the everyday world, the group engaged with the sounds of machines and jazz but carried this out with a witty and detached air. The natural predecessor of Les Six was Erik Satie and *Parade* in particular, on which he had collaborated with Cocteau, was a source of inspiration. Although they were dismissive of foreign composers, especially the Germans but also including Stravinsky, their continued adherence to a form of tonality (albeit one that embraced modes and bitonality as well the inflections of jazz and other popular musics) and use of parody places much of their work close to the Neoclassicism of Stravinsky, and their music is sometimes described under this rubric.

Before they disbanded Les Six had collaborated on staging concerts to promote their and other contemporary composers' music, a volume of piano works (*Album des Six*, 1919) and (without Durey) an experimental work by Cocteau, *Les mariés de la tour Eiffel* (1921). Of the original six composers Auric would go on to write music for films, especially for those made by Cocteau, and Durey began to engage with political causes, writing pieces for massed choirs and bands as well as joining the resistance during World War II. Germaine Tailleferre continued to work in a broadly Neo-classical idiom, especially in her piano concertos (1923–4, 1933–4 and 1951), retaining a light, witty style, although a difficult domestic situation curtailed her activities during the middle of her career. Perhaps the three best-known names of the group are Poulenc, Honeger and Milhaud. Of these Honeger had perhaps the least sympathy with the detached parody that was one of the identifiers of Les Six, antithetical as it was to his serious, contrapuntally-driven works that are often gritty and delight in dissonant chromaticism, concerns that were to dominate a series of five symphonies (written between 1929–50). He did, however, write one of the most popular homages to the age of the railway, the orchestral work *Pacific 231* (1923; this evocation of the steel, steam and speed of the railway engine was a common preoccupation of composers during the mid-century, including Vivian Ellis's *Coronation Scott*, 1948, and Benjamin Britten's music for the documentary *Night Mail*, 1935–6).

Poulenc and Milhaud, along with a composer often associated with Les Six for his wit and flair Jacques Ibert (1890–1962), were to remain broadly wedded to the ideas of parody and inclusivity (be that of material, influence or audience) for their whole careers. Milhaud's works are extraordinarily diverse, covering everything from symphonies to ballet and chamber music to songs, however, through all of them runs an eclectic appropriation of styles from jazz, in *La création du monde* (1923), to Brazilian folk music in *La boeuf sur la toit* (1919). Poulenc was to steer an equally independent course from the mainstream

Henri Dutilleux (1916–), during rehearsal with the London Philharmonic Orchestra, 2002

This fiercely self-critical composer initially fell under the spell of Debussy, Ravel and Albert Roussell before discovering the works of Messiaen and Bartók during the 1940s. Often working in large-scale forms, his music treads a fine line between tonality, polytonality and atonality through which he has developed a distinctive personal style, heard in the serious First and Second symphonies (1950–1 and 1955–9) and the orchestral work *Timbres, espace, mouvement* (1976–8).

avant garde that was to emerge from the German-speaking world. Perhaps his major contribution to the canon of French music is the over 90 *mélodies* (songs) composed for the baritone Pierre Bernac (1899–1979) with whom he enjoyed a long and fruitful collaboration. His skill in writing for voice can also be seen in his substantial body of religious works and his operas, including *Les mamelles de Tirésias* (1939–44), *La voix humaine* (1958) and *Dialogues des Carmélites* (1953–6), the latter in particular remaining in the repertory. Jacques Ibert is probably best known for his delightfully anarchic *Divertissement* (1929–30) that includes a police whistle and quotes from *An der schönen blauen Donau* and Mendelssohn's wedding march from *A Midsummer Night's Dream*. However, his large output also includes notable operas, *Persée et Andromède* (1929) and *Angélique* (1926), and

Nadia Boulanger (1887–1979)

Not only was she and her sister, Lili (1893–1918), one of the foremost female French composers of the 20th century Nadia Boulanger was also one of its most important teachers of composition, working at both the Ecole Normale de Musique and the Conservatoire. Especially associated with American music she taught, among others, Leonard Bernstein, Elliott Carter, Aaron Copland and Virgil Thomson.

Albert Ketèlbey's *In a Monastery Garden,* piano solo; Score cover; Published by J.H. Larway, London, 1915

From the 1900s to 1950s Britain produced a stream of successful "light music" composers whose works reached a wide audience through their tuneful melodies, deft orchestration and solid tonal harmony, often with nods toward jazz and popular music. Many of their pieces have been, and still are, used for radio, television and movies and have become part of the national musical consciousness in a way that music by other, perhaps more self-consciously "serious" composers has never been embraced. Notable figures include Eric Coates (1886–1957), writer of *Calling all Workers* (1940), *By the Sleepy Lagoon* (1930) and *The Dambusters* (1954); Albert Ketèlbey (1875–1959), who composed *In a Monastery Garden* (1915) and *In a Persian Market* (1920); and the Canadian-born Robert Farnon (1917–2005) whose popular works include *Jumping Bean* (1947), *Portrait of a Flirt* (1947) and *The Westminster Waltz* (1955).

the tone poems *Escales* (1922) and *Symphonie marine* (1931), as well as a great deal of music for movies.

A more utilitarian and less self-consciously detached form of Neoclassicism took hold in 1920s Germany. The most prominent representative of this was Paul Hindemith (1895–1963), who, after pursuing a post-Romantic style in works

that pushed at the limits of tonality, repudiated this excess of expression in the 1920s and embraced the aims of the Neue Sachlichkeit ("new objectivity") movement. Concerned that an avant garde imperative was pushing composers away from speaking to a wider public, Hindemith, among others, formulated the idea of *Gebrauchsmusik* ("music for use") whose chief aim was to communicate. In the works of Ernst Krenek (1900–91) and Kurt Weill (1900–50) this took the form of musical theater, especially in the former's *Jonny spielt auf* (1927) and from the latter's *Royal Palace* (1925–6) to *Die Dreigroschenoper* (1928). (Weill was to emigrate to the United States of America where he turned away from his earlier Weimar style and produced a string of immensely popular, and arguably more successful, musical theater works in an American popular idiom.) Hindemith initially concentrated on a purely instrumental repertory, displaying great technical skill in tailoring each work to the characteristics of its instrumentation, although still at times demanding virtuoso performers. In works such as the *Kammermusiken* (1922–7) and *Concerto for Orchestra* (1925) he adopts a neo-Baroque idiom, taking the concertano idea of setting a soloist or group of solo players against a larger group, and aiming for a clarity in scoring and texture that is sometimes obscured by dense contrapuntal writing. Also an influential teacher and theorist (proposing a hierarchical system of

near and distant pitches and harmonies through which to order compositions) he encountered difficulties once the National Socialists came to power in 1933, and left Germany for Switzerland in 1938. It was during the 1930s that he wrote one of his greatest works, the opera *Mathis der Maler* (1933–5) in which he sets out the case for a more emotional and essential approach to art than had been advocated by the Neue Sachlichkeit.

A style closer to that of the French Neoclassicists was initially adopted by the English composer William Walton (1902–83). Under the patronage of the Sitwell family he was exposed to the music of Stravinsky, Gershwin and early jazz, these influences coalescing in the music for *Façade* (1922–9), in which a skilful mix of the Modernist techniques of bitonality and irregular rhythm with parody and popular music forms a witty backdrop to the poems of Edith Sitwell. Walton was to go on to become one of the most innovative and flexible of English 20th century musicians, his style ranging from overtly serious pieces like the powerful *First Symphony* (1931–5) to displaying an almost pagan delight in rhythm and orchestral color in the choral work *Belshazzar's Feast* (1930–1).

However, Walton remained to a certain extent outside the newly emerged English school that had sought to create a national music from folksong and by reaching back to earlier English composers such as Tallis, Byrd and Purcell. Sometimes disparagingly dismissed as "cowpat" music (a reference to the widespread use of modal inflection—often Dorian or Mixolydian—derived from rural traditional musics that was to become almost an English cliché), in the hands of its best practitioners such as Ralph Vaughan

CHARACTERISTIC
INTERMEZZO

Williams (1872–1958) and Gustav Holst (1874–1934) it is not only capable of conjuring up visions of mythologized rural idylls but, as in the case of Holst's *The Planets* (1914–16), was to combine the harmonic and rhythmic innovations of continental composers with a recognizably English idiom to create works of genuinely popular appeal. It was in the works of Vaughan Williams, however, that England was to acquire the basis of a national repertory. These range from his early works influenced by both his collecting of English folksong with Cecil Sharpe (1859–1924) and his period of study with Ravel in Paris, notably in his Second and Fifth symphonies (1911–13 and 1938–43), to the harsher and more harmonically adventurous denunciations of the horrors of war in his Third, Fourth and Sixth symphonies (1921, 1931–4 and 1944–7 respectively) in which he uses biting chromaticism (the semitonal clash of the opening of the Fourth, C/D flat, and the bitonal F minor/E minor of the Sixth), parody (in the first movement of the Sixth) and a desolate sense of floating modality (especially in the last movements of the Third and Sixth). Frederick Delius (1862–1934) was an earlier English composer acquainted with Maurice Ravel. His work, relatively ignored in his native country and due for a wider reappraisal, displays a keen harmonic sense and feel for orchestral color.

Although Vaughan Williams and Holst had both written operas, it was a later figure, Benjamin Britten (1913–76), who was to produce a body of operatic work that was to remain in the repertory. After studying with the composer Frank Bridge (1879–1941) at the Royal College of Music, where he felt more drawn to the work of Austrian composers such as Gustav Mahler and Alban Berg rather than Vaughan Williams, he initially worked at the General Post Office Film Unit writing the music for documentaries under the direction of the great motion picture maker John Grierson (1898–1972). However, it was in 1945 that his first major success came with the opera *Peter Grimes*. Notable for the way in which an apparently new life had been breathed into the form while remaining firmly in a tonal idiom, and especially the evocative orchestral interludes that separate the acts, this portrayal of a tragic and misunderstood outsider has remained in repertory ever since its first performance. A string of works followed, including, *Albert Herring* (1946–7), *Billy Budd* (1950–1) and *The Turn of the Screw* (1954), that confirmed his place, along with that of Michael Tippett, as one of England's greatest opera composers. Many of his works contain central roles for his partner, the tenor Peter Pears (1910–86), and much has been written—although without shedding much light on the music—on the

role Britten's homosexuality may have played in his compositions.

A musically more radical approach to the development of a national style took place in Hungary. In a similar fashion to Vaughan Williams and Sharp, the composers Zoltán Kodály (1882–1967) and Béla Bartók (1881–1945) spent time collecting folk music, and both were greatly influenced by the musics they encountered, not just in Hungary but elsewhere in Eastern Europe and the Balkans. Bartók was to turn this early influence into one of the most individual musical voices of the 20th century. This very individuality means that he was not destined to be as influential as Stravinsky or Schoenberg but his handling of a highly chromatic and at times unsettling musical language, some of it derived from folk modes, that still retains a sense of a tonal center (or centers, often a tritone apart) left a body of work that contains some of the greatest string quartets since those of Beethoven and pieces with the dazzling rhythms of Eastern European and Balkan folk dance, for example the *Music for Strings Percussion and Celesta* (1936). Some of his

Michael Tippett (1905–98)

Alongside Benjamin Britten, Michael Tippett is the most important 20th-century English opera composer, although he also excelled in writing rhythmically vibrant and harmonicially adventurous orchestral music, including four symphonies (1944–5, 1956–7, 1970–2 and 1976–7 respectively), the *Concerto for Double String Orchestra* (1938–9) and the *Fantasia concertante on a Theme of Corelli* (1953) for strings. In many ways he was far more progressive than his contemporary Britten, willing to embrace a far more experimental, although always broadly tonal, musical language, especially after his ground-breaking allegorical opera *The Midsummer Marriage* (1946–52), and the later operatic works *King Priam* (1958–61) and *Knot Garden* (1966–9) contain some especially fine writing.

works are more "uncompromising" than others, the Third and Fourth String Quartets (1927 and 1928) contain particularly astringent writing, and it has tended to be his more approachable pieces that have made their way regularly into concert programs, including the extraordinary early operas *A Kékszakállú herceg vára* ("Bluebeard's Castle", 1911), the ballet score *A csodálatos mandarin* ("The Miraculous Mandarin", 1918–19) and the *Concerto for Orchestra* (1943).

The Bolshevik revolution of 1917 was to mean that one of Russia's brightest stars, Stravinsky (who came from a semi-noble family), was to remain outside of the country, but this did not mean that music was neglected under the new Soviet government. Indeed, at first St Petersburg and Moscow in particular became cauldrons of artistic innovation and it was only when Joseph Stalin seized power in 1927 that these activities began to be curtailed. It was during Stalin's regime that the two greatest composers of the Soviet era, Dmitry Shostakovich (1906–75) and Sergey Prokofiev (1891–1953), were to make their names; although debate continues to rage over to what extent they were effected by or supported the diktats of the nomenklatura and, particularly, how much of this might be discerned in their music.

Shostakovich is now best remembered for his cycle of 15 symphonies, although his string quartets are widely performed and his operas such as *Nos* ("The Nose", 1927–8) and *Ledi Makbet Mtsenskogo uyezda* ("Lady Macbeth of Mtsensk", 1930–2) are beginning to receive greater recognition. During the Cold War Shostakovitch was seen by many musicologists in the West as a symbol of artistic subversion against the Soviet regime, and much effort went

Prokofiev's *Romeo and Juliet*, by the Bolshoi Ballet (with Maria Alexandrova as Juliet and Denis Savin as Romeo), Covent Garden, London, July 2004

into reading an underlying dissatisfaction into his music, in particular identifying seemingly sardonic melodies (in what was perceived as slight to the Soviet authorities in the light-hearted, end-of-war *Ninth Symphony*, 1945) or pomp that was thought to be tongue-in-cheek (the end to the *Fifth Symphony*, 1937). The truth of all this is more likely to be a complex mixture of emotion and intent, with certain works either displaying a sense of fun and sheer musical technique (as in the *First Piano Concerto*, 1933, with its accompanying solo trumpet part, or his orchestration of Vincent Youmans' *Tea for Two*, 1927) or, because of their historical situation, a genuine attempt to speak to the Soviet people with a patriotic voice (the

Seventh Symphony, 1941, written while Leningrad was under siege during World War II). Prokofiev, on the other hand, remained abroad from the time of the revolution to 1936, when he returned to what was now the USSR, although he had never broken off links with his homeland in the same way as Stravinsky had done. Spending much of his time in France, his music bears a great deal in common with that of Les Six, with an essentially Neoclassical outlook tempered with a skill for wit and parody seen to great advantage in his comic opera *Lyubov' k tryom apel'sinam* ("The Love for Three Oranges", 1919). Prolific in many genres, including operas, concertos, symphonies and movie music, much of his music has retained its place in the concert hall and his music for the ballet *Romeo i Dzhuletta* ("Romeo and Juliet", 1935–6) has become in its many stage interpretations and in the concert hall one of the most often performed of all 20th century ballet scores.

VIENNA 1890–1920

Aside from Paris, the second great musical center of the turn of the 20th century was the Austro-Hungarian capital, Vienna. With the huge weight of the 19th century Austro-German tradition, many of whose greatest composers worked in the city, bearing down on musicians it is not surprising that many of the new directions that were to come out of its fertile intellectual atmosphere were to develop from the musical language of late-Romanticism. Indeed, it is broadly possible to identify two streams in 20th century music history, one that might be described as "French" with a retention of a vestige of tonal harmony but which is also concerned with instrumental color and external references to the evocation of landscape or elements of popular music. The second might be loosely defined as "German", seeing a historical progression from the musical language of late- or post-Romanticism into atonality and then the technical means of ordering this new language. Where references are made to ideas external to those of musical technique they tend to be internalized features within a composer's—or opera characters'—psychology or subconscious, reflecting the strong influence of the rise of psychoanalysis and investigation of the mind, and so the internalization of many facets of outward behavior, by figures such as Sigmund Freud (1856–1939) and Carl Gustav Jung (1875–1961).

In Vienna the development of new ways of musical thinking were aided by the high quality of performance and education to be found in the city, boasting one of Europe's finest orchestras and one of its greatest opera houses. Where Symbolism

OLIVIER MESSIAEN

The French composer Olivier Messiaen (1908–92) was not only one of the most individual musical voices of the 20th century, forging a distinct language from influences as disparate as Mussorgsky, Debussy and Stravinsky, Indian and Indonesian music, and birdsong, but was one of the century's greatest organists and one of the most influential teachers of his time, numbering among his students Pierre Boulez and Karlheinz Stockhausen. Inspired greatly by a mystical Catholic faith, many of his works aspire to the sublime, made plain in their meditative titles. Often including birdsongs that he transcribed in the field in his music (Messiaen was a notable ornathologist), he extended his religious vision to birds, likening them to angels.

Attending the Paris Conservatoire from 1919 he progressed quickly and won numerous premier prix for his classes, including piano, composition and organ and improvisation. Paris at the time was dominated by the music of Debussy, Stravinsky and Les Six and Messiaen was to take elements from each of these, developing a highly personal modal style by the time of his first published work, *Le banquet céleste* (1928) for organ. In 1931 he took up the post of organist at La Trinité and was to remain there for the rest of his life. He continued to compose, mostly works for organ with an explicitly Christian message. However, there were also works for orchestra, including *Poèmes pour Mi* (1937) and he also wrote *Fête des belles eaux* (1937), a piece for six ondes martenot, one of the very earliest electronic instruments with a keyboard and a "ribbon" with which it was possible to play glissandos. The ondes martenot was to reappear in several of his works, and it plays a central role in his monumental *Turangalîla-symphonie* (1946–8).

Messiaen was captured and imprisoned during World War II, and while in a prison camp wrote one of his only chamber works and one of his clearest expositions of his musical language to date (explicitly codified in his book *Technique de mon language musical,* 1944). The *Quatuor pour la fin du temps* (1940–1) for clarinet, violin, cello and piano (the musicians available to him in the camp) shows his individual use of harmony, triadic constructions that avoid functionality through their relationship to what Messiaen called his "modes of limited transposition"; so-called as they can only be transposed a small number of times before they replicate the same group of notes, including the whole-tone and octatonic scales he took from his studies of Debussy and Stravinsky. Also important is his treatment of rhythm, again influenced by the Stravinsky of *The Rite of Spring*, using the overlaying of additive and palindromic rhythmic structures as formal devices.

He was released to work at the Paris Conservatoire, teaching composition and analysis, and after the war began to work on one of his largest pieces, the *Turangalîla,* a huge orchestral essay on the universe and sensual love. This work in particular was to be influential on his students, including

Olivier Messiaen

Boulez and Stockhausen as they worked out their ideas of total serialism, as sections apply serial methods to rhythmic structures. In the later work *Mode de valeurs et d'intensités* (1949) he extends the serial notion to not just rhythmic values but also dynamics. He did not proceed any further down this path, from this point concentrating on the place of birdsong in his compositions and embarked on the piano work *Catalogue d'oiseaux* (1956–8). The songs themselves were overlain on the musical language he had already developed, and were at times incorporated into it. The piano and a large array of tuned percussion were the composer's favored means of portraying the birdsong, seen in *Oiseaux exotiques* (1955–6) and *Couleurs de la Cité Céleste* (1963). It was perhaps inevitable that Messiaen's crowning work would combine birdsong and his Catholic faith; both came to the fore in his opera *Saint François d'Assise* (1975–83), especially in the Bird Sermon scene where the birdsongs float above the rest of the score with little reference to the music underneath.

had dominated 1880s–90s Paris, in 1890s Vienna it was the Secession, artists led by Gustav Klimt (1862–1918) who "succeeded" from the Künstlerhaus, rejecting its academic Classicism and Realism to pursue a "new art" of dream-like allegory. This was the world that Gustav Mahler

Sigmund Freud, photo by Princess Eugenie of Greece, daughter of Marie Bonaparte, 1937

Shown here in his study in Vienna, the "father of psychoanalysis" was to have a profound impact on the intellectual landscape of the 20th century. Through works such as *Die Traumdeutung*, his explorations of the subconscious, a seemingly chaotic web of emotions, behaviors and influences that lies beneath the everyday exterior of "normal" life, were not only to add to a growing sense of dislocation within society but also lead artists toward the expression of both the underlying structures of their works and an internalized vision of the world.

Max Reger (1873–1916)

This German composer, unlike many of his generation, preferred to work on a small scale producing beautifully constructed chamber and solo works. Not only does his music look toward that of the 20th-century Modernists with its chromatic late-Romantic musical language that nonetheless contains a certain Classical severity, but also, in his numerous organ and orchestral works, prefigures the Gebrauchtsmusik of Hindemith in the retention of traditional forms, such as the theme and variation and Lutheran chorale.

(1860–1911) found himself at the center of as director of the Hofoper. Originally from Bohemia but trained at the Vienna conservatory, Mahler had spent the 1880s and 90s working as a conductor across the German-speaking world, from Prague to Hamburg, before taking up a post in Vienna in 1897, although he had by then developed the practice of spending each summer in Austria to compose. It was during the 1880s he began producing his first of these compositions, the song cycles *Lieder eines fahrenden Gesellen* (1883–5), out of which grew the *First Symphony* (1884–8), and *Des Knaben Wunderhorn* (1887–90).

Already in these works he was exploring ideas that were to run throughout his compositions. These early vocal works, at least up until the *Fourth Symphony* (1899–1900), would often provide the basis for entire symphonic movements, and there is some justification for seeing parallels between the texts of the songs and the philosophical worlds of the symphonies into which they are incorporated. It is telling that when he and Sibelius were to meet in Helsinki in 1907, the Finnish composer was insistent that the symphony should be "profoundly logical" and stand on its own terms needing no other justificiation than its own internal coherence. Mahler, conversely, was adamant that the symphony must "be like the world [and] embrace everything", and in a sense this is what his huge spans of symphonic time attempt. Although much of his music is life-affirming, especially the Second and Third symphonies (1888–94 and 1893–6) with their progressions from darkness to salvation,

Mahler's music often projects a troubled view of the human condition and some commentators have seen this as not only an expression of the sense of a disappearing world but also of the discrimination he faced as a Jewish musician in the anti-Semitic environment of bourgeois Vienna.

Elements of irony and parody in the appropriation of popular and military music are often in Mahler's works associated with a world-weary sense of despair, or, when taken from folk music, especially *Ländler*, can be used for moments of repose or to represent a rural escape from the desolation of modern, urban existence. The miracle of Mahler's music lies in its ability to speak directly to a contemporary audience and articulate the Modernist concerns of isolation and resignation, but in doing so does not resort to the linguistic devices deemed necessary by subsequent generations, even though its creator died before the final collapse of the old order represented by the Austro-Hungarian Empire and the horrors of the two Europe-wide conflicts that so defined the 20th century. The techniques he uses are firmly rooted in late-Romantic tonality, but even the straightforward suspension of the submediant above the dominant can, in Mahler's hands, be stretched to the limits of its expressive potential, becoming especially refined in his later works the *Rückert Lieder* (1901–2), *Das Lied von der Erde* (1908–9) and the *Ninth Symphony* (1908–9).

Similar concerns and techniques permeate the works of Alexander Zemlinsky (1871–1942) and the early career of his pupil Arnold Schoenberg (1874–1951). Zemlinsky was to push tonality to its expressive limit (although, unlike Schoenberg, was never to transgress its boundaries) and his

Max Reger

work shows considerable skill in motivic variation as well as an inspirational feel for orchestration (heard in such touches as the pianissimo trombone glissandos that mark the final resolution of his meltingly Romantic *Lyrische Symphonie*, 1922–3). This piece, for soprano and baritone, also displays his considerable gifts for vocal composition, and of his other works the songs and opera *Der Zwerg* (1920–1) in particular stand out. Schoenberg also started out writing intensely emotional pieces couched in a beautifully handled late-Romantic tonality which revels in extended harmonies and the suspension of their resolution. Still among the most frequently performed of his works, these include the string sextet *Verklärte Nacht* (1899) and the immense *Gurre-Lieder* (1900–1) for voices, chorus and orchestra.

THE POST-WAR AVANT GARDE

After the upheaval and destruction of World War II many of the composers who had seemed at the cutting edge of European music now appeared part of a world that had gone for ever. Many important figures, such as Stravinsky and Schoenberg, had moved, or were to move, to the US, now the dominant power in the West as the European empires began to be dismantled. There they would encounter a growing musical culture that was less inclined to look to the past, its roots lying in either the experimental fusion of European and American culture that typified the music of Charles Ives (1874–1954), such as the multi-layered *Central Park in the Dark* (1906–9) and *The Holiday Symphony* (1912–18), or the more urbane

***Palestrina* by Hans Pfitzner (1869–1949),** ROH production; January 1997; Dress rehersal

The most famous work by this German composer is the opera he wrote in 1911–15 based on the life of the famous Renaissance composer, in which he invokes an earlier sound world through pastiche. A musical and social conservative, he was prolific in almost all the major genres of his time and through a late-Romantic musical language tinged with chromaticisms and the use of modality produced some fine *Lieder* as well as symphonic works. Like Richard Strauss, his reputation has suffered since World War II because of his involvement with the National Socialist Party and his overt espousal of extreme nationalist views stands in contrast to Strauss, who was not anti-Semitic, and whose unwilling acceptance of the directorship of the Reichsmusikkammer owes more to naïvety and the weariness of an old man than to any malicious intent.

However, by 1908 Schoenberg had reached a point in his song cycle *Das Buch der hängenden Gärten* where he felt that his use of dissonance was valid in its own terms and did not require resolution: the result being that tonality is suspended as no harmony provides a resting place. This breakthrough can also be seen in his Second String Quartet (1907–8) and is even more noticeable in the following *Fünf Orchesterstücke* (1909) where the dislocation of harmony also includes that of rhythm as Schoenberg tries to free himself from motifs, the pieces moving forward through contrast rather than a traditional conception of harmony and melody. From this point on he threw himself into the composition of atonal music—that which lacks any sense of tonality or a tonal center—firstly through a series of Expressionist works and then through the new method of serialism.

style of Aaron Copland (1900–90) that took in jazz and American folk music, in either the *Clarinet Concerto* (1947–8) or the ballet *Appalachian Spring* (1943–4). There was also a greater sense that experimentation should lead away from the normative structures of the European canon, and so composers emerged such as Conlon Nancarrow (1912–97) who wrote works of great contrapuntal complexity for player-pianos, or the collage-like works of Virgil Thomson (1896–1989) that drew on a wide variety of popular styles, and the later Milton Babbitt (1916–2011) who was to be so influential on the post-war conception of serial technique and early electronic composition. A similar process was seen in Australia where the composer Peter Sculthorpe (1929–) turned to Aboriginal and East Asian music in creating a national style.

In Europe there was a similar desire among younger composers to do away with everything

THE SECOND
VIENNESE SCHOOL

The label given to the music of Arnold Schoenberg and his two students Alban Berg (1885–1935) and Anton Webern (1883–1945) is of a "Second Viennese School", in contrast to an imagined first Classical Viennese school comprising Haydn, Mozart and Beethoven.

The "emancipation of dissonance" Schoenberg came to in 1908 gave rise to what are described as his Expressionist works, named after the Central European movement in the visual arts that sought to expose the hidden emotional and psychological layers beneath the surface image. Here the comparison with a painterly technique is more valid than in the case of Debussy and Impressionism, in that Schoenberg attempts to portray a psychological state through a seemingly non-rational and disordered collage of sound. Interest in the subconscious and psychology were, of course, dominant themes in the arts and sciences of *fin-de-siècle* Vienna. The work in which Schoenberg first achieved this intense portrayal of the inner psychological state was *Erwartung* (1909), described as a monodrama for soprano and orchestra. In this a woman walks on her own in a forest and discovers her lover's dead body and

Arnold Schoenberg, painting by Richard Gerstl, 1905; Oil on canvas

the music follows the nightmarish meanderings of her mind, making for at times uncomfortable listening. *Erwartung* was followed by another stage work, *Die glückliche Hand* (1909–13), and then in 1912 *Pierrot lunaire*, settings of poems by Belgian Symbolist Albert Giraud (1860–1929). Here Schoenberg is more subtle in the treatment of

the psychological state of his central character, the Pierrot who recites in *Sprechstimme*, a musically notated "speech-song". The counterpoint and instrumental color Schoenberg conjures up from the small ensemble of flute, oboe, violin, cello and piano is exceptional.

Although Schoenberg began to sketch out a huge orchestral and choral score that was eventually to become the abandoned *Die Jakobsleiter*, it was becoming evident to him that a new musical language would be required to give his emancipation of dissonance a coherence and one that would fit the Classical forms to which he felt compelled to return. The technique he devised to realize this was serialism, sometimes referred to as twelve-tone or dodecaphonic music. In this, all 12 notes of the chromatic scale are given equal weight, so theoretically preventing any one of them acquiring the status of a tonal center, although this was at times manipulated by composers, especially Alban Berg, to give clear impressions of tonality. The basic technique consists of the 12 notes arranged in a "tone row" and in the composition they must appear in order, one after the other or sounding simultaneously. This basic row can then be transposed (each of the 12 notes is moved up or down by the same interval), played backwards (in "retrograde"), inverted (where the intervals are given their mirror image, e.g. if an interval rises by a minor 3rd in the original row then it falls by a minor 3rd in the inversion), or played in retrograde inversion (the inversion played backwards), and each of these versions of the original row can be transposed giving a vast number of permutations on the basic material.

Schoenberg was to use this technique in many of his works from the 1920s onwards, first seen in the piano works *Suite* (1921–3) and *Fünf Klavierstücke* of 1920–3. While the *Suite* drew loosely on the forms of the Baroque dance suite there then followed a string of works that were to exploit Classical forms alongside the new dodecophony, the *Wind Quintet* (1923–4), *Suite* for seven instruments (1925–6), *Variationen für Orchester* (1926) and *Third String Quartet* (1927), though perhaps finding its ultimate expression in the unfinished opera *Moses und Aron* (1926–32). Schoenberg was not, however, to totally abandon tonality and returned to it in later works such as the *Kammersymphonie no.2* (1909–39) and the setting of the Jewish prayer *Kol nidre* (1938).

It was left to Schoenberg's two great pupils to develop his dodecaphonic technique. Alban Berg is often viewed as the Romantic in opposition to Anton Webern's Modernism, though it might be more appropriate to see his works through the prism of Expressionism as many of them are concerned with an interior psychology, be that of an apparently abstract work such as a violin concerto or of the characters within an opera. It is true that Berg continued to work in traditional forms and in a seemingly miraculous fashion incorporated within his 12-tone works hints toward the musical worlds of Wagner and Mahler, at times even quoting directly from other composers' tonal works, and for this reason his music is more approachable than that of Webern and it has tended to receive more performances than those of his contemporaries.

Berg's early works, composed under the guidance of Schoenberg, show a firm grasp of the ambiguous post-Romantic musical language that led to the eventual break down of tonality, but it was once he had broken free from the older composer just before World War I (the teacher and student had an uneasy relationship) that he began to find his own distinctive voice. This was first seen in the song-cycle *Fünf Orchesterlieder nach Ansichkartentexten von Peter Altenberg* (1912), notable for their imaginative orchestration, but it was in the following *Drei Orchesterstücke* (1914–15) that his organizational genius centered on the variations of small motivic cells comes to the fore. The next five years were taken up by one of Berg's greatest achievements, the opera *Wozzeck* (1917–22) in which continuing variation and his ability to organize all the musical parameters of a work (including dynamics and contrapuntal

layers) are melded to a system of *Leitmotifs*. In this work some elements of 12-tone composition can be detected, but these were to be more fully explored in the subsequent *Kammerkonzert* (1923–5) and *Lyrische Suite* (1925–6) where he shows off his considerable ability to explore intervallic relationships. Aside from the unfinished opera *Lulu* (the orchestration was completed by Friedrich Cerha), Berg's most enduring work is his *Violin Concerto* (1935). Composed as an elegy to Manon Gropius (the daughter of Alma Mahler and the architect Walter Gropius) Berg weaves into the 12-tone language folksong, a Viennese waltz and a Bach chorale (*Es ist genug*). Berg was to die soon after, without hearing the work, and it stands as a fitting elegy for the composer himself.

Anton Weber could not have been more different; his relationship with Schoenberg was easier, perhaps because of an abiding concern with the formal logic of Classical structures and a desire to replicate them within the constraints of a new musical language. The supreme musical miniaturist, he was the first composer to exclusively dedicate himself to 12-tone technique and in his almost obsessive control of all aspects of the work, including rhythm, dynamics and orchestral color, was to lay the ground for post-World War II "total serialism". After early post-Romantic works and the atonal songs that he worked on during the period 1908–20, Webern took up dodecophony in the early 1920s and during 1924–6 produced a series of songs (op.17–19) using the method, refining his approach as he worked through them. It was, however, with the *String Trio* (1926–7) that he turned to the purely instrumental style that was to dominate the works of the next few years. In these, including the *Symphony* (1927–8), *Quartet* (1928–30) and *Concerto* (1931–4), he arrives at the means whereby the pitches of the tone rows make sense only in relation to themselves, no possible external reference being possible, often achieved using the device of pairs of semitones within his tone rows. The sense of dislocation from what had gone before also comes through in the sparse and spatially disjointed scoring of instrumental color, his *Klangfarbenmelodie*, so characteristic of Webern's mature works. During the 1930s Webern returned to settings for voice, bringing to it the explorations of his instrumental works but also including canons and symmetrical structures that are intense feats of technical skill, preserving as they do a strict adherence to dodecaphonic method.

Alban Berg (left) and Anton Webern, at Pregelhof in 1912

Tone row from Webern's *Streichquartett* (1936–8)

Note the pairs of semitones that comprise the dominant interval class of the arrangement of 12 notes—an important way in which Webern ensured that his works did not give any hint of a tonal center—and also the way that the first four notes spell-out BACH (H is the German notation for B natural, B stands for B flat), in homage to the earlier composer.

that had happened before, and initially this was to center itself on the Darmstadt School, named after the town where an influential summer course in composition was held during the 1950s. The four major figures associated with Darmstadt are Pierre Boulez (1925–), Karlheinz Stockhausen (1928–2007), Luigi Nono (1924–90) and Bruno

Musique), dedicated to furthering advances in electro-acoustic music and which was to be used by Boulez to realize *Repons* (1981–4) and *Dialogue de l'ombre double* (1985). Younger composers who have taken advantage of the Paris-based facility include Tristan Murail (1947–) and George Benjamin (1960–).

The desk of Iannis Xenakis,

showing the complex working-out of one of his scores

As composers began to experiment further with a sense of abstract sound they began, in the case of musicians such as Brian Ferneyhough (1943–), Iannis Xenakis (1922–2001) and Harrison Birtwistle (1934–), to move toward a texture of extreme complexity where the musical effect comes from the spectrum or weight of sound as much from the individual elements of musical material. Quite aside from the sheer technical difficulty of performance their scores became so complex that they pushed at the extremes of traditional notation. Facing these constraints, and particularly when confronted with electronic music, composers began to devise different solutions. One was to write a "graphic" score that sought to convey through diagrams and images the idea of the work as much as the control of the individual musical piches.

Witold Lutosławski (1913–94)

A different solution to the problem of notating complex textures was devised by the Polish avant garde composer Witold Lutosławski. He reasoned that only a certain degree of control was needed by the conductor and composer to create the sort of texture that had previously required a high degree of virtuosic technique to both write and play. Through a system of repeating cells, played *ad libitum* by the musicians but whose duration of repetition was controlled by the conductor, he manages to control the ptich classes (and so the harmonic structure) of a passage of music but at the same time create highly complex surface textures whose overall timbre is controlled through careful orchestration. This technique of "aleatoric counterpoint" is combined with his fondness for the manipulation of the intervallic characteristics of 12-note chords to produce highly attractive and convincing works such as *Jeux vénitiens* (1960–1), *Symphony Three* (1981–3) and *Chain 3* (1986).

Maderna (1920–73). Each of these composers was to adopt and refine the techniques of serialism derived from the works of Schoenberg and, in particular, Webern. Not content with restricting the concept to pitch structure, they were to apply the technique to all the musical parameters that could be controlled by the composer, including rhythm, dynamic and attack, to avoid any repetition that might enable the listener to posit a hierarchy within any aspect of the music. Dubbed "total serialism" this was first to be realized in *Structures I* (1951–2) for piano by Boulez, but similar concerns underlie works by Stockhausen, including *Kreuzspiel* (1951).

Boulez pursued his interest in total serialism in his theoretical writings and a string of works that were to become classics of the post-war avant garde, including *Le marteau sans maître* (1953–5), *Structures II* (1956–61) and *Pli selon pli* (1957–62). He went on to explore the possibilities of the spatial distribution of sound, and open-ended structures that could be, theoretically, continued indefinitely (problematic as a number of works have remained "in progress" for many years). Influential as a teacher, he has also remained at the heart of the European avant garde through his setting up and directorship of IRCAM (the Institute de Recherche et Coordination Acoustique/

Whereas Boulez has never fully embraced electronic music this was to prove an abiding interest of Stockhausen who produced some of the first purely electronic works in his *Konkrete Etüde* (1952) and *Elektronische Studien* (1953–4). (Earlier, *musique concrète* had been produced in Paris by Pierre Schaeffer, 1910–95, using sounds sourced from non-electronic acoustic sources.) Electronic sound is integral to many

of Stockhausen's later works, including the monumental seven-opera cycle *Licht* (1977–2004), through electronic pieces such as *Gesang der Jünglinge* (1955–6) and *Kontakte* (1958–60) he was to be influential on musicians beyond the avant garde, particularly in popular music. Stockhausen took the notation of instrumental works to their most fully worked-out in *Gruppen* (1955–7) for three orchestras, and thereafter began to explore the aleatoric ("chance", from the Latin for dice) ideas of American composer John Cage (1912–92). After his works for "prepared piano" (where items are inserted between the piano strings to change the timbre) and his notorious experiment in silence (*4'33"*, 1952), along with Morton Feldman (1926–87) Cage had begun to devise ways of letting the performers have much greater control over the choice of musical material. Stockhausen responded to this with works such as *Klavierstück XI* (1956) and *Zyklus* (1959) where the performer can start at any point they wish.

The increasing dominance of the Darmstadt avant garde was rejected by two important figures of the late-20th century, György Ligeti (1923–2006) and Elliott Carter (1908–2012). Both composers have, in their own way, responded to the challenges of establishing a personal yet contemporary style against a dominant school, eschewing total serialism, by using their considerable musical sensibilities to create works that have complex surface textures, particularly in terms of rhythm, yet retain a clarity of language, in the case of Carter that of a dedicated atonal Modernist in works such as *Concerto for Orchestra* (1969) and *Symphonia* (1994–7). After early works such as *Atmosphères* (1961) in which Ligeti experimented with clusters (semitonal or even microtonal conglomerations of notes, also a characteristic of the early work of Krysztof Penderecki, 1933–), he was to bring these ideas along with elements of quotation and pastiche into his seminal work, the opera *Le Grand Macabre* (1974–7). This collage of techniques and sources was also to prove fertile ground for another composer from outside the Darmstadt school, Luciano Berio (1925–2003). Although he was to lead the electro-acoustic section of IRCAM from 1974–80 and compose many operatic and instrumental works (including the solo instrumental *Sequenzas*), it was his *Sinfonia* (1968–9) that was to become his most widely recognized piece. With its quotations from Mahler's *Second Symphony* and live amplified voices it both referenced the European canon and paid tribute to popular musics. This breaking free of the rigid avant garde was in time itself to become as predictable as the total serialism of the Darmstadt School had been. The Postmodern incorporation of elements of popular music, and the allusion to or quotation of works of

the canon, became ubiquitous in the music of a new generation of composers, from the religious neo-Romanticism of composers such as Henryk Górecki (1933–2010), and to the driving rhythms and brutal music of Mark-Anthony Turnage (1960–), or the somewhat anemic offerings of younger figures like Thomas Adès (1971–).

In previous centuries audiences were dependent on the choice of either a select group of patrons or composers themselves staging live works of contemporary provenance that were written to fulfill a need, be that for commerce, ritual or entertainment. This situation has now been drastically revised through the influence of technology. Recording has wrought a major change in the way that audiences select the music they listen to, and through that choice have largely stuck to the music of the past, predominantly that of the 18th and 19th centuries with the inclusion of certain 20th-century composers who retained a sense of history in their works, and especially musical language, rather than those who have sought to erase all traces of what had gone before them. The story of music is slow to emerge and much of the astringent music of the last 50 years, and the retreat into the academy that has accompanied it, still awaits a sufficiently distanced evaluation to see if it will become accepted by a wider audience in the same way that musics from the Middle Ages to the early decades of the 20th century continue to bring inspiration and pleasure into people's lives.

Philip Glass

From the mid-1960s to the 80s a group of composers, mainly based on the West Coast of the USA, evolved a musical style that challenged the complex atonal style of the mainstream avant garde. Taking their cue from the musical experiments of La Monte Young (1935–) as well as the influence of Indonesian *gamelan* and the drumming traditions of Sub-Saharan Africa, the works were initially concerned with the manipulation of rhythmic cells that repeated over and over again and whose subtle variation would only become evident as the pieces unfolded over a long period of time, as in Reich's *Drumming* (1970–1) or *Music for Pieces of Wood* (1973). The main exponents of the style that became known as Minimalism, Steve Reich (1936–) and Philip Glass (1937–), generally worked in a straightforward tonal idiom (often in simple triadic harmony), yet managed to produce works that sounded fresh and exciting. A more sophisticated approach has been adopted by John Adams (1947–), who has used a broadly Minimalist style in orchestral works (such as *Shaker Loops*, 1978, and *Harmonium*, 1980–1) and operas. The best of his dramatic works have taken contemporary political themes such as *Nixon in China* (1985) and the controversial *Death of Klinghoffer* (1989–91).

GLOSSARY

Accompaniment The supporting layers of the music to the dominant line, texture or harmony, theoretically subordinate to that line but often complementary, playing an almost equal role (as with the piano accompaniments for *Lieder*).

Aerophones Instruments whose sound is produced by air passing through a tube.

Aleatoric Music left to chance, requiring the performers to improvise or make choices of passages, pitches, dynamics or tempos from which to play.

Aleatoric counterpoint A technique developed by Witold Lutosławski in which *ad libitum* repeating cells are played simultaneously to create complex textures without the need for overly-complex notation.

Allegro Literally "happy", a tempo marking generally denoting a moderately fast speed.

Alto A low female voice or the line or vocal part lying between the tenor and soprano in four-part harmony.

Antiphony An effect in which groups of singers or instrumentalists in groups, are placed in different areas of a performance space, and whose physical groupings are heightened by contrasts of dynamic, texture or material. Sometimes described as "call and response" due to the characteristic alternating focus of the music.

Appogiatura A note, not of the parent harmony against which it sounds, one step above or below the harmony note to which it falls.

Arco An indication that string instruments should be played with bows rather than plucked.

Aria A lyrical section of an opera in closed form that reflects on emotions rather than drives forward the action; often as the *da capo aria*, in ABA form.

Arioso "Like a song," the term in opera for *recitative*-like passages part way between song and declamation, often associated with Donizetti and 19th-century French opera.

Atonal The absence or avoidance of tonality achieved through a variety of techniques including serialism.

Augmented An interval that has been extended by a semitone (hence an augmented fourth has one more semitone). Also a major chord whose fifth has been increased by semitone to produce two superimposed major thirds.

Ballet Western classical dance derived from the theatrical French dance of the 17th and 18th centuries.

Bass A low male voice or the lowest line or vocal part, that below the tenor, in four-part harmony.

Bel canto Literally means "beautiful singing"; an Italian approach to vocal performance and composition concerned with an intensely lyrical melodic line.

Bitonal The sounding of two diatonic key centers at the same time.

Brass Either a term used to describe aerophones made from metal (usually brass) and played using vibrating the lips in a cup- or conical-shaped mouthpiece. Or, that part of the orchestra consisting of the horn, trumpet, trombone and tuba sections.

Cadence A harmonic pattern of two different chords that brings a musical section to a close. The three most common cadences are: perfect cadence (chord V to I), plagal cadence (chord IV to I), and interrupted cadence (chord V to a chord other than chord I, commonly vi).

Cantus firmus The melody used as the basis for a polyphonic composition in Medieval and Renaissance music.

Cantata A work for voices and orchestra, predominantly of the Baroque, often setting a religious text.

Canon The exact repetition of a melodic line in another voice, played or sung, from the first one and starting after the first line has begun.

Chant A term generally used in the West for the single unmeasured line of music to which sections of the Christian liturgy are sung.

Choir An ensemble of singers.

Chorale A hymn of the Lutheran church whose simple soprano melody is supported by three lower homophonic parts.

Chordophones Stringed instruments that are plucked, bowed or struck.

Chorus Used as "choir" but more usually denoting a group of singers in an opera separate from the solo roles. Also used to describe the refrain of a strophic composition.

Chromatic From the Greek for "colored"; describing notes foreign to the underlying tonality of a musical section.

Chromatic scale The collection of all 12 semitones contained in a Western scale.

Cluster A tightly arranged grouping of notes, separated only by tones or semitones (even microtones); used extensively by a number of avant garde composers.

Concertato A leading concept of the Baroque in which contrasting musical ideas or groups of singers or instrumentalists are used in opposing groups.

Concerto An instrumental work where a soloist or body of soloists is set against a larger ensemble. In the 19th century this came to mean a work exclusively for a single soloist and orchestra that demands virtuosity from the solo performer.

Concerto grosso A work for two bodies of (usually) string players, supported by a *continuo* generally on harpsichord. These groups are the *ripieno* soloists (usually two violins and a cello) and the *concertino* (a larger body of musicians).

Consort A small instrumental ensemble of the Renaissance.

Continuo Also known as *basso continuo*. An accompanying part in Baroque music played on harpsichord, cello or theorbo derived from figured bass.

Continuous variation Coined by Schoenberg to describe Brahms' compositional technique of constantly varying the basic melodic material of a work to provide the piece's motivic drive.

Counterpoint Polyphonic music that follows a set of formal rules, as in fugue.

Declamation A musical vocal that emulates the pitch and rhythms of speech.

Diatonic Music derived from a system of seven notes spaced within an octave, for example the major and minor scales or seven Church modes.

Diminished The reduction of an interval by a semitone (thus the diminished fifth has one less semitone than the perfect fifth). Also a chord consisting of superimposed minor thirds.

Dissonance The opposite of consonance, used to describe notes that produce a clash or tension when sounded together. Dissonant intervals include the major and minor second, major and minor seventh and tritone.

Dominant The fifth degree of the major or minor scale and the triadic chord built on that note. One of the strongest degrees of the tonal system as it contains a leading note that in traditional harmony must be resolved upward onto the tonic. The dominant seventh is a triad built on the fifth degree of the diatonic scale with an added minor seventh above the root; the unstable interval of a tritone in this chord creates a tension that demands resolution by step onto the tonic and third of the tonic chord.

Duet A work for two soloists, usually with accompaniment.

Dynamic The degree of loudness or softness of a musical passage or note, usually denoted by the Italian terms (from quietest to loudest): *pianissimo, piano, mezzopiano, mezzoforte, forte, fortissimo.*

Electro-acoustic Music consisting of electronically created or recorded sounds played back to an audience via magnetic tape or digital recording equipment.

False relation Semitonal chromatic contradiction between different voices in polyphony.

Figured bass Numbers under notes in a bass line that indicate the harmonic progression, for example, 5-3 denotes a root position triad and 6-3 indicates a first inversion.

Form The organization of the structural units of a work denoted by shifts of harmony (as in sonata form) or the alternation of musical material (as in the AB scheme of binary form).

Fugue An advanced contrapuntal form that overlays thematic material by introducing a basic subject (theme) in each successive voice, alternating tonic and dominant entries (known as the subject and answer).

Gebrauchsmusik Literally "music for use", a term coined by such composers as Hindemith to describe their broadly tonal, Neoclassical works that were intended to appeal to a wider audience than that of the avant garde.

Gesamtkunstwerk The "total art work" envisioned by Wagner for his music dramas in which music, poetry, drama and the visual aspect of set and costume design are integrated into a single creative work.

Glissando From the French *glisser* "to slide", the rapid passage through consecutive notes, either by quickly catching each note as in a harp glissando or in a true *portamento* achieved by the trombone or strings where the passage is seamless.

Grand opéra A style of opera current in 19th century France, characterized by historical settings, opulent sets, virtuosic vocal writing and dramatic plots.

Harmonic Either pertaining to the use of harmony or referring to one of the overtones of the naturally occurring harmonic series.

Harmony The study of, or the simultaneously sounding of notes to produce chords, the juxtaposition of which results in chord progressions. Functional harmony refers to the traditional Western tonal system of harmonic movement in which notes within the harmony are assigned specific functions and act according to a set of rules in establishing and moving from key to key.

Heterophony The simultaneous variation of a melodic line by two or more performers.

Homophony Where all the lines of a work move together in the same rhythm to form block-like harmonies.

Hymn A term used to denote a song that is used in the worship of a deity.

Idée fixe A device used by Berlioz that associates a particular theme to an idea or character in his music, influential in Wagner's conception of the *Leitmotif*.

Idiophones Instruments that produce the sound from their own body, usually by being struck, shaken or scraped.

Imitation The copying of all of, or elements of, a melodic line in another voice from the original one.

Improvisation The creation of a piece of music as it is being performed, associated particularly in the West with jazz and some works of the avant garde.

Interval The degree of separation between two pitches, the smallest of which, in the traditional Western tuning system, is the semitone. In increments of a semitone within the octave they are: semitone, tone, minor third, major third, perfect fourth, augmented fourth/tritone (i.e. three tones)/diminished fifth, perfect fifth, minor sixth, major sixth, minor seventh, major seventh and octave.

Isorhythm The repetition of a rhythmic pattern but with varying pitches or melodic material.

Key A concept of tonality where a hierarchy of notes acts to privilege one above all others as a tonal center.

Keyboard A set of keys or levers that when depressed either cause a string to be plucked or struck (as in the harpsichord and piano) or open a pipe enabling air to pass through (as in the organ), or activate electric or electronic production of the relevant pitches (as in the synthesizer).

Klangfarbenmelodie A term used by Webern to describe the varying instrumental colors that forms a parallel unfolding to that of the musical material.

Leading note The seventh degree of a diatonic scale that in traditional harmony rises by semitonal voice leading to the tonic.

Leitmotif The association of a musical motif with a particular idea, situation, place or character, the motif returns whenever that idea, situation or character occurs in the plot.

Libretto The verbal text of an opera.

Lieder German art song of the 19th century, from the German *Leid* for song.

Lyric prototype A formal scheme for vocal pieces based on four four-bar phrases: the first four bars are repeated for bars 5–8 with slight variation, bars 9–12 contrast and modulate from the tonic before the final bars 13–16 return to the tonic with either a variation of the first motif or a cadential passage (AA1BA2/C).

Madrigal A form of secular polyphony for between three and six voices popular in the 16th–17th century.

Mass Used to denote the main liturgical service of the Christian church, often including the eucharist.

Mediant The third degree of a diatonic scale.

Melody A musical line that corresponds most closely in the West to the concept of a "tune".

Mélodie French art song of the late-19th and 20th century.

Membranophones Instruments with stretched skins that are beaten to produce the sound.

Microtone An interval of less than a semitone, often a quartertone (that is, half a semitone) used by a number of avant garde 20th century composers.

Mode A collection of pitches, either relating to a melody or arranged in a scale, that are held to behave in a certain fashion to imply a hierarchy in which one pitch is the final (first or last note of the scale) or tonic.

Modes of limited transposition A term given by Olivier Messiaen to scales, widely used in his own music, that can be transposed only a limited number of times before they reproduce the first collection of pitches.

Modulation The process of moving from one key or tonal center to another.

Monody An innovation of the early Italian Baroque where, thinking to invoke the earlier practices of the ancient Greeks, a single melodic line that clearly annunciates the text was set against a homophonic accompaniment, in contrast to dominant polyphonic style that had preceded it.

Motet A polyphonic vocal genre that was the dominant form of medieval and Renaissance music.

Motif A small collection of notes with a distinctive harmony, melodic shape or rhythm.

Music drama The term used by Wagner to describe his operas that aspired to the *Gesamtkunstwerk*.

Musique concrète Ambient sounds, such as birdsong, traffic or non-musical artifacts being struck, compiled on tape or digitally to create a piece of music.

Neoclassicism A compositional style of the first half of the 20th century that retained a broadly tonal idiom and traditional forms, seeing itself as an alternative to the experimentation of the avant garde.

Note The name or sound of a specific pitch.

Octatonic A scale in which semitones and tones alternate. There are very few variations of the scale's two forms—the first starting with a semitone, the second with a tone—as each can only be transposed by semitone once before repeating the same collection of pitches.

Octave An interval whose two notes are seven diatonic notes away from another one, are given the same pitch name and in which the upper pitch is double the frequency of the lower.

Opera A staged dramatic work that is in full or in large part sung.

Opera buffa or *opéra comique* "Comic" opera, generally light-hearted, on domestic themes and with spoken sections between musical numbers.

Opera seria Literally "serious opera" that dealt with tragedy and heroic themes, often derived from antiquity.

Oratorio A setting of a religious text for chorus, soloists and orchestra for performance in the concert hall rather than during the liturgy.

Orchestra A large group of musicians, in the West usually comprising four main bodies of musicians, the strings, percussion, brass and woodwind.

Orchestration The technique and practice of assigning music to individual instruments and groups of instruments to create particular instrumental colors and effects.

Organ An aerophone in which the passage of air through fixed-pitch rows of pipes is controlled by a keyboard.

Organum The name given to medieval polyphony.

Overture An instrumental work before the first act of an opera or musical, usually drawn from musical themes that appear in various acts. Also used for a descriptive orchestral work that is not connected to a dramatic work but which follows the general scheme of the operatic overture.

Parallelism The movement of all parts of a harmony in the same direction, characteristic of the works of Debussy.

Passacaglia, chaconne or **ground bass** A formal device where a repeated melodic pattern, usually in the bass, provides the unifying principle of the work.

Passion Choral works with self-contained narratives recounting Biblical events such as the birth of Christ.

Pentatonic A collection of five notes arranged in a scale that does not contain a tritone, for example C–D–E–G–A.

Percussion The section of the orchestra given over to the membranophones and idiophones. This can include a large number of different instruments, both tuned and untuned, such as: timpani (large tuned kettle drums), bass drum, side drum, triangle, cymbals, tam tam (gong), marimba (a large wooden xylophone with resonators), tubular bells and glockenspiel (high-pitched, tuned metal bars).

Phrase A musical unit longer than a motif but shorter than an entire melody, typically the units into which a melody can be broken down.

Pitch The frequency of a sound given a position in relation to other sounds by a note name, for instance A (at 440 hertz the standard tuning for Western music).

Pizzicato An indication for string instruments to be played by plucking rather than bowing the string.

Plainchant See Chant.

Polyphony Literally "many voices", music in which two or more voices (lines of music, often vocal) act independently but sound at the same time. Also the name given to the predominant style of Renaissance vocal writing.

Polytonal An extension of bitonality in music, where different voices, lines or harmonies in more than two keys sound simultaneously.

Progression The harmonic and temporal juxtaposition of chords. Cadences are a form of progression.

Psalm A term denoting Biblical or ancient West Asian religious song, generally referring to the texts of the book of Psalms in the Bible.

Recitative A passage in an opera in which the vocal setting approaches that of speech, and through which the plot is advanced.

Register A particular section of the range of a voice or instrument (often "high" or "low").

Rhythm The temporal organization of sound, often by alternating weak and strong elements. In the West rhythm has been traditionally conceptualized as the division of beats within bars (divisions of a set number of beats) that act as cells within a larger framework.

Riff A short musical idea used as the subject for later variation or improvisation, particularly in jazz and rock.

Ritornello A term used to describe music that "returns" to or repeats an earlier section of music.

Rondo A formal device where alternating sections return to an original passage of music, for example in the formal scheme, ABACADA etc.

Scale A series of notes organized in order of ascending or descending pitch, often within an octave or associated with a mode or tonality.

Scherzo From the German for "joke". A movement characterized by a fast tempo and witty or comic elements that takes the place of a minuet in a symphony or sonata.

Score The manuscript or printed form of music that contains all the notated elements of a work.

Serialism A compositional technique, also known as dodecophony or 12-tone composition, whereby the 12 notes of the chromatic scale are arranged in a "tone row". In the composition they must appear in order, one after the other or sounding simultaneously. The row can be played backwards (in "retrograde"), inverted (where the intervals are given their mirror image), or played in retrograde inversion (the inversion played backwards); each of these can be transposed.

Sonata A solo or chamber instrumental piece that in the late-18th and 19th centuries usually consists of several movements, of which the first uses sonata form.

Sonata form A system of musical organization that depends upon the juxtaposition of two main blocks of music of contrasting material and key that are "developed" and then restated at the end in a way that reinforces the tonic. The first section of a sonata form movement is the exposition—sometimes preceded by a slow introduction—in which the first subject group (of one or more ideas, the most important of which is called the first subject) in the tonic key is set against the contrasting second subject group in a different key, most usually the dominant. The development section follows in which the musical ideas of the exposition are explored and taken through a series of more distant modulations before returning to the material of the exposition for the recapitulation. The recapitulation begins with the first subject group in the tonic and then a restatement of the second subject group, this time also in the tonic. The piece either ends with a tonic cadence at the end of the exposition material or a short coda, also in the tonic.

Song A work of music for solo voice, with or without accompaniment.

Soprano A high female voice or the highest line or vocal part, above the alto, in four-part harmony.

Staff or stave A group of five horizontal lines on which variations in pitch and the passing of musical time can be shown. They form the basis of the Western notation.

String quartet Either a group of four instrumentalists comprising two violinists, a viola and a cello player, or a work written for such an ensemble.

Strings The main body of the orchestra, consisting of the bowed chordophones: the violins (divided into "first" and "second" sections), violas, cellos and double basses.

Strophic Vocal works in which all the stanzas of text are sung to the same repeating music.

Subdominant The fourth degree of a diatonic scale.

Submediant The sixth degree of a diatonic scale.

Suite A collection of works based on dance rhythms, usually including an *allemande* in duple time that acted as an "introduction" to suite in general, a *courante* in triple time and either fast, in an Italian suite, or slow and stately in the French version, a *sarabande* again in triple time and with a fast and slow version and a *gigue*, a fast lively movement often in duple compound time.

Supertonic The second degree of a diatonic scale.

Suspension Similar to an appoggiatura, a non-harmony note that falls to the harmony note one step below. Suspensions must be prepared by the note that "suspends" the resolution to the harmony note appearing in the previous harmony. Suspensions often involve the fourth or sixth degree above the root of the chord falling to the third and fifth respectively.

Symphony A large-scale, generally abstract, work for orchestra usually in several movements. The first movement of the Classical and Romantic symphony was invariably in sonata form, followed by a slow movement, a minuet or scherzo and a finale, usually also in sonata form.

Temperament The way in which a scale or notes are tuned in relation to each other. Equal temperament proposes that the octave is divided into 12 equal semitones.

Tempo The speed, or indication of speed, of the music. These are represented: by an indication of the number of rhythmic units (often a crotchet or dotted crotchet) that can be played within a minute; or by a variety of, usually Italian, terms (from slow to fast: *largo, lento, andante, moderato, allegro, presto* and *prestissimo*).

Tenor A high male voice or the line or vocal part lying between the bass and alto in four-part harmony. It derives from the principal line of Medieval organum, from the Latin *tenere* "to hold".

Theme The principal melody or a tune or motif on which a piece of music is based.

Time signature A means of conveying how many beats to a bar a particular section of a work has, where 4 conventionally stands for crotchets, 8 for quavers and 16 for semiquavers, thus 4/4 indicates there are four crotchets to a bar or 6/8 six quavers.

Timbre The quality of a sound expressed by the difference between instruments or voices.

Toccata A work of music, usually for keyboard, which is virtuosic.

Tonality The concept of key and tonal relations or the key in which a piece is written.

Tone poem An orchestral work that seeks to describe such extra-musical ideas as landscapes, narratives or emotions.

Tone row The arrangement of the 12 notes of the chromatic scale used in serialism.

Tonic The first note of a diatonic scale or the triad built upon that note, it also denotes the "home" pitch of the tonality, thus C is the tonic of C major.

Treatise A work concerned with the philosophy or technical aspects of music.

Triad A chord consisting of two superimposed thirds, either a major triad that consists, from the root, of a major and minor third, a minor triad with a minor then major third, a diminished triad of two minor thirds, or an augmented triad of two major thirds.

Tritone The interval of either an augmented fourth or diminished fifth, consisting literally of "three tones". Dissonant and inherently unstable it is the driving force behind the resolution of the dominant seventh. Because of its dissonance it was traditionally associated with the Devil.

Tuning Either related to the idea of temperament or the adjusting of an instrument, though tightening strings or extending or reducing the lengths of tubes to bring it into concord with the other instruments of an ensemble.

Valve A device whereby brass instruments can change the basic fundamental of the overall tube, enabling a different harmonic series to come into play. A combination of three valves (increasing the length of the tube by a tone, semitone and minor third respectively) gives the player access to the whole chromatic scale.

Variation The technique of developing the ideas latent in a particular passage of music. Also used to refer to the second part of the form of theme and variations where after the initial statement of a theme the musical ideas (such as harmonies, interval patterns and textures) are singled out and explored more fully.

Whole tone Either a tone comprising two semitones, or a six-note scale that comprises only tones.

Woodwind A term that either designates aerophones, including flutes (where the sound is produced by the passage of air over an edge, either a sharply cut opening or a duct), oboes (where the sound is produced by the passage of air through two bound reeds) or clarinets (where the air passes over a single beating reed). Or, a description of that part of the orchestra that includes the flute, oboe, clarinet and bassoon sections.

COMPOSERS

Pages mentioned in *italics* indicate pictures

Adams, John (1947–) American Minimalist composer noted for his operas on contemporary themes. 95, 111

Adès, Thomas (1971–) British composer, fêted from a young age, whose works adopt a variety of eclectic styles. 111

Albinoni, Tomaso (1671–1750/1) Italian composer of instrumental and vocal works known for his cheerful and straightforward style. 31, 37

Albrechtsberger, Johann (1736–1809) Austrian composer and teacher whose pupils included Beethoven. 45, 50

Arcadelt, Jacques (c. 1507–68) Franco-Flemish composer of madrigals. 22

Aristoxenus (c. 368 BC–?) Ancient Greek musical theorist. 6, 10

Armstrong, Louis (1901–71) Black American jazz trumpeter. 80, 81

Arne, Thomas (1710–78) English composer, violinist and keyboard player, associated with theater music in London. *35*

Artusi, Giovanni Maria (1540–1613) Italian music theoretician with a conservative approach to innovation. 26, 28

Auber, Daniel-François-Esprit (1782–1871) Leading French composer of *opéra comique* during the early 19th century. 61, *61*

Auric, Georges (1899–1983) French composer, member of Les Six, who also wrote music for movies. 84, 101

Babbitt, Milton (1916–2011) American serial composer and theorist, also noted for his early work on electronic music. 107

Bach, Carl Philipp Emanuel (1714–88) German composer, son of J.S. Bach, active in Berlin and Hamburg, noted for his highly individual symphonic works. 44

Bach, Johann Christian (1735–82) German composer, son of J.S. Bach, active in London, admired by Mozart. 42, 44, *44*, 46

Bach, Johann Sebastian (1685–1750) German composer and keyboard player active in almost all main musical genres, both religious and secular. His collected works provide the summation and pinnacle of Baroque music and are of supreme importance to the Western musical canon. 24, 25, 32, 33, 34, 35, 36, 37, 38–39, *38*

Bacharach, Burt (1928–) American songwriter whose early sophisticated style is iconic of the 1960s urban chic. 82

Baez, Joan (1941–) American singer-songwriter from a folk tradition but with long-lasting popular appeal. 87

Balakirev, Mily (1837–1910) Russian nationalist composer. 72

Barretto, Ray (1929–2006) Puerto Rican Latin jazz musician. 92

Barry, John (1933–2011) Prolific British composer of movie scores. 85

Bartók, Béla (1881–1945) Hungarian composer of highly rhythmic and adventurous music incorporating elements of folk melody and dance rhythms. 96, 101, 103

Basie, "Count" [William] (1904–84) Black American jazz pianist and bandleader. 80

Beach Boys, The American pop group, known for the "surf sound" of the 1960s. 87, 90

Beatles, The British pop group of the 1960s and 70s. 76, 85, 87, 90, 93

Beethoven, Ludwig van (1770–1827) German composer, one of the greatest figures of Western music; spans the gap between Classicism and Romanticism. 40, 41, 42, 43, 45, 49, 50–51, *50*, 52, 53, 54, 55, 56, 57, 58, 59, 61, 63, 70, 71, 74, 94, 103, 108

Bellini, Vincenzo (1801–35) Italian opera composer, who established an Italian Romantic style with *bel canto* writing. 60, 61, 65, 66, 71

Benjamin, George (1960–) English composer, a student of Olivier Messiaen. 110

Berio, Luciano (1925–2003) A post-war Italian Modernist, known for his *Sinfonia* that quotes other composers' works. 111

Berg, Alban (1885–1935) An Austrian composer, one of the Second Vienna School. He adapted serialism to produce his own emotional style. 97, 103, 108, 109, *109*

Berlin, Irving (1888–1989) American songwriter of the 20th century. 78, 82, 84

Berlioz, Hector (1803–69) French Romantic composer whose radical orchestration and approach to the symphony forged a new path for 19th-century music. 52, 53, 54, 55, *55*, 56, 58, 60, 61, 64, 71

Bernstein, Leonard (1918–90) American composer and conductor, active across a diverse range of classical and popular music styles and forms. 78, 83, 92, 102

Berry, Chuck (1926–) Black American rock and roll singer-songwriter. 86

Biederbecke, Bix (1903–31) American jazz trumpeter. 79

Binchois [Gilles de Bin] (c. 1400–60) Franco-Flemish Renaissance composer. 19

Birtwistle, Harrison (1934–) English Modernist composer known for his uncompromising style. 110

Bizet, Georges (1838–75) French composer known for his opera *Carmen*. 68

Black Sabbath British heavy metal rock band. 88

Blades, Rubén (1948–) Panamanian salsa singer and songwriter. 92

Blakey, Art (1919–90) Black American jazz drummer and bandleader. 81

Boccherini, Luigi (1743–1805) Italian-born composer of symphonies who spent much of his working life in Spain. 44

Boethius (c. 480–c. 524) Italian music theorist. 10, 12, 15, *15*

Bolden, Buddy (1877–1931) Early Black American jazz trumpeter. 80

Borodin, Aleksandr (1833–87) Russian Nationalist composer of The Five. 72

Boulanger, Lili (1893–1918) Sister of Nadia and one of France's most promising composers up to her early death. 102

Boulanger, Nadia (1887–1979) French composer and one of the 20th century's most important teachers of composition. *102*

Boulez, Pierre (1925–) French Modernist composer, member of the "Darmstadt School", noted for his development of "total serialism" as well as his conducting and founding of IRCAM in Paris. 56, 94, 95, 105, *105*, 110

Bowie, David (1947–) British rock singer and songwriter. 88

Brahms, Johannes (1833–97) German Romantic composer, seen as the heir to Beethoven due to his grasp of compositional technique and adherence to Classical forms. 56, 57, 58, 59, 61, 68, 70, 74, 75, 94

Brioschi, Antonio (fl. c. 1725–50) Early Italian composer of symphonies. 43

Britten, Benjamin (1913–76) English composer who is often credited with establishing an indigenous repertory of opera in English. 95, 101, 103

Brooks, Garth (1962–) American country singer-songwriter whose adoption of elements of rock has proved widely popular. 89

Brown, James (1933–2006) Black American Soul singer. 86, *86*

Brubeck, Dave (1920–2012) American jazz pianist and composer who uses unusual time signatures and classical references. 81

Bruckner, Anton (1824–96) Austrian Romantic composer. A follower of Wagner he produced monumental symphonies that represent the summation of the Austrian Romantic tradition. 56, 69, 70, *70*, 75

Bull, John (1562/3–1628) English composer of Renaissance keyboard works. 23

Bull, Ole (1810–80) Norwegian violinist, whose championing of Norwegian folk music was a great influence on Grieg. 59, 74

Busnoys, Antoine (c. 1430–before 1492) Flemish Renaissance composer. 19

Buxtehude, Dieterich (1637–1707) German or Danish composer and organist, a forerunner of J.S. Bach and known best for his keyboard works. 34, 36, 37, 38

Byrd, William (c. 1540–1623) An English composer of Renaissance polyphony. 23, 102

Caccini, Giulio (1551–1618) Italian composer and singer, significant for his solo songs with basso continuo. 24, 25

Cage, John (1912–92) American avant garde composer whose experiments led him to consider silence and ambient sound as part of his music. 90, 97, 111

Cambert, Robert (c. 1628–77) French composer and organist, significant in the establishment of early French opera. 29

Cara, Marco (d. 1525) Italian composer of *frottole*. 22

Carissimi, Giacomo (1605–74) Italian composer and teacher based in Rome important to the development of oratorio, motets and cantatas. 33

Carson, "Fiddlin'" Johnny (1868–1949) American folk fiddle player. 89

Carter, Elliott (1908–2012) Committed Modernist American composer whose works display subtle and complex textures. 102, 111

Cash, Johnny (1932–2003) Popular and rebellious American country singer. 89, *89*

Cavalieri, Emilio de' (c. 1550–1602) Italian organist and composer of the earliest surviving example of a play set entirely to music. 32

Cavalli, Francesco (1602–76) Leading Venetian performer and composer, especially of opera, of his day. 28

Cesti, Antonio (1623–69) Italian singer and organist who developed early *bel canto*. 28

Chabrier, Emmanuel (1841–94) French 19th-century composer whose orchestration and use of vibrant musical color look forward to that of Debussy. 68

Charles, Ray (1930–2004) Black American rhythm and blues singer and pianist. 86

Charpentier, Marc-Antoine (1643–1704) French composer of a wide range of religious and theatrical works and chamber pieces, a repertory overshadowed during his life by the works of Lully. 33

Chausson, Ernest (1855–99) French composer, a key figure in the French renaissance after 1870. 71

Cherubini, Luigi (1760–1842) Italian-born composer who was the most important writer of opera in France during the Revolution. As head of the Conservatoire, he introduced important reforms. 49, *49*, 51, 53, 61

Chopin, Fryderyk (1810–49) Polish composer and pianist, one of the foremost vituosos of his day and known for his harmonically advanced and technically difficult compositions for the piano. 56, *58*, 59, 60

Ciconia, Johannes (c. 1370–1412) Italian composer of Ars Nova. 18

Cimarosa, Domenico (1749–1801) Italian composer of Classical *opera buffa*. 48

Clementi, Muzio (1752–1832) Italian pianist, teacher and composer. 47

Cline, Patsy (1932–63) American country singer of the 1950s "Nashville sound". 89

Hancock, Herbie (1940–) American jazz pianist, exponent of jazz fusion. 81

Handel, George Frederick (1685–1759) Prolific English composer of German birth, significant in every genre of his time. He is noted for developing the dramatic forms of oratorio which he invented, and opera, of which his finest examples are still core repertory. 25, 32, 34, *34*, 35, 36, 37, 40

Hanslick, Eduard (1825–1904) Austrian music critic whose defense of the tradition of Beethoven and Brahms enraged the supporters of Wagner and Bruckner. *56*, 61

Harrer, Gottlob (1703–55) German composer, one of the first musicians north of the Alps to write symphonies. 44

Harris, Emmylou (1947–) American country and alternative rock singer. 89

Hasse, Johann (1699–1783) German composer of *opera seria*. 32

Haydn, Joseph (1732–1809) Austrian composer who spent much of his life working for the Esterházy family. One of the greatest musical figures of the 18th century, he is known for developing the symphony and string quartet. 40, 42, 43, 45, *45*, 46, 50, 57, 59, 64, 71, 109

Haydn, Michael (1737–1806) Austrian composer, younger brother of Joseph, noted for his liturgical works. *48*, 53

Henderson, Fletcher (1897–1952) Black American bandleader. 80

Hendrix, Jimi (1942–70) American virtuoso rock guitarist, singer-songwriter. 88, *88*

Herbert, Victor (1859–1924) American composer, conductor and cellist of Irish birth, noted for his light lyrical style and many successful operettas. *76*, 77, 79, 84

Herman, Jerry (1931–) American composer and lyricist for Broadway musicals. 82

Herrmann, Bernard (1911–75) American composer of Hollywood movie scores, many for Alfred Hitchcock. 84

Hindemith, Paul (1865–1963) German theorist and composer of *Gebrauchsmusik* during the 1920s and 30s whose tonal works were a counterbalance to the innovations of the Second Vienna School. 102, 106

Hofmann, Leopold (1738–93) Austrian Classical composer of symphonies. 45

Holst, Gustav (1874–1934) English composer important in the "English Renaissance" of music during the early 20th century. 103

Honegger, Arthur (1892–1955) French composer of Les Six who wrote a number of challenging symphonies. 84, 101

Houston, Whitney (1963–2012) Black American popular singer of the 1980s and 90s. 87

Ibert, Jacques (1890–1962) French composer whose music bears something in common with the aims of the Les Six. His works are characterized by a ready wit and fine ear for orchestral color. 84, 101

Ireland, John (1879–1962) English composer of songs and instrumental works in a late Romantic style. 84

Ives, Charles (1874–1954) American composer whose early works were ahead of their time, noted for their simultaneous layering of contrasting musical elements and quotation from popular works. 107

Jackson, Michael (1958–2009) Black American pop singer, first as a child in the Motown group the Jackson Five and later solo. 91

Janáček, Leoš (1854–1928) Czech composer whose works look forward to the developments of the 20th century. He is particularly regarded for his operas that set the text in a manner close to speech. 74, 88

Jarre, Jean-Michel (1948–) French popular composer who specializes in synthesizer based instrumental music. 90

Joachim, Joseph (1831–1907) Austro-Hungarian violinist, for whom both Schumann and Brahms wrote works. 59, *59*

Jobim, Tom [Antônio] (1927–94) Brazilian composer and songwriter, innovator of the "new wave" bossa nova. 92

Jolson, Al (1886–1950) American singer noted for his "black face" minstrel style and highly impassioned delivery. 84, *84*

Jordan, Louis (1908–75) Black American singer-songwriter especially popular in the swing era for his lively style of jazz and rhythm and blues. 86

Judas Priest British heavy metal rock band. 88

Kálmán, Emmerich (1882–1953) Hungarian composer of especially melodic and successful operetta. 77

Kander, John (1927–) American writer of musicals in partnership with Fred Ebb. 82

Keiser, Reinhard (1674–1739) German composer of Baroque opera whose focus on pairing text with music and on the importance of *recitatives* made him the foremost opera composer of his day. 31

Kern, Jerome (1885–1945) American popular songwriter influential on the development of the musical. 78

Ketèlbey, Albert (1875–1959) English composer of light music. 102

Kinks, The British pop group led by singer-songwriter Ray Davies (1944–). 86

Kodály, Zoltán (1882–1967) Hungarian composer and ethnomusicologist whose works stand alongside those of Bartók in creating a national style. 103

Korngold, Erich (1897–1957) Austrian composer of dramatic and orchestral works, but known from the mid-1930s on for his scores for Hollywood movies. 84

Kraftwerk German pop group whose use of electronic sounds and recording techniques helped establish the techno style. 91

Křenek, Ernst (1900–91) Austrian composer, worked in a variety of idioms but remembered for tonal operas that were influenced by the Neue Sachlichkeit. 93, 102

Ladysmith Black Mambazo South African male choral group founded in 1960. 93

Lassus, Orlande de (1530/2–94) Franco-Flemish composer who worked in Munich and wrote motets and madrigals. 18, 22

Legrenzi, Giovanni (1626–90) Italian composer and organist whose clear music and defined harmony represent the best of late Baroque style. 36

Lehár, Franz (1870–1948) Austrian composer of operettas whose *Die lustige Witwe* is the prime exemplar of the form. 77, *77*

Leoncavallo, Ruggero (1857–1919) Italian *verismo* composer, best known for his one-act opera *Pagliacci*. 69

Leoninus (*fl.* 1150–*c.* 1200) Influential French composer of the Notre Dame school, putative author of the *Magnus liber*. 15

Ligeti, György (1923–2006) Hungarian composer who lived and worked in Vienna for much of his life. His works range from early avant garde pieces using clusters to the opera *Le Grand Macabre*. 111

Liszt, Franz (1811–86) Hungarian composer and pianist. The greatest virtuoso of his time, he is influential for his piano works, noted for their difficulty, and the harmonic innovations of his tone poems. 54, 55, 57, 58, 59, 60, *60*, 61, 63, 71, 73

Lloyd Webber, Andrew (*b.*1948) Leading British composer of musicals in collaboration with several lyricists, most notably Tim Rice and Don Black. 78, 82–83, *83*

Little Richard [Richard Wayne Penniman] (1932–) Influential black American singer in the development of rock and roll from rhythm and blues. 86, 88

Locatelli, Pietro (1695–1764) Italian composer and violinist, significant in the development of a virtuoso violin style. 37

Loewe, Carl (1796–1869) German composer of *Lieder*. 57

Lully, Jean-Baptiste (1632–87) Italian composer, a powerful figure in French music of his day, known for his stage works, mainly operas. 24, 25, 29, *29*, 30, 32, 33, 37, 61

Luther, Martin (1483–1546) German religious thinker who started Reformation and also composed chorales. 18, 20, *20*, 21

Lutosławski, Witold (1913–94) Polish Modernist composer who developed the technique of aleatoric counterpoint. 110

Lynn, Loretta (1935–) American country singer from the 1960s onward. 82

Machaut, Guillaume de (*c.* 1300–1377) French composer important for the development of the motet. 12, 16, 17, *17*

Maderna, Bruno (1920–73) Italian avant garde composer, a member of the "Darmstadt school". 110

Madonna [Madonna Louise Ciccone] (1958–) American popular performer successful for marrying performance skills with promotional image. 87, *90*

Mahler, Gustav (1860–1911) Bohemian composer whose songs and symphonies look forward to the abiding concerns of the 20th century. Also a notable conductor, carrying out reforms at the Hofoper in Vienna. 41, 56, 74, 103, 106, 111

Malipiero, Gian Francesco (1882–1973) Italian Modernist composer. 97

Marais, Marin (1656–1728) Leading viol player of the French Baroque. 37, *37*

Marini, Biagio (1594–1663) Italian composer and instrumentalist, known particularly for his sonatas and sinfonias for one or two violins and continuo. 24, 35

Marley, Bob (1945–81) Jamaican singer and songwriter of reggae. *92*

Marsalis, Wynton (1961–) Black American trumpeter and composer, active across the jazz, popular and classical fields. 81, *81*

Marschner, Heinrich August (1795–1861) Early German Romantic composer whose operas influenced Wagner. *54*

Martin, George (1926–) British composer and record producer associated with developing the Beatles' sound. 90

Mascagni, Pietro (1863–1945) Italian *verismo* composer best known for his one-act opera *Cavalleria rusticana*. 68, 69

Massenet, Jules (1842–1912) The most popular composer of French opera at the end of the 19th century. 68

Mendelssohn, Fanny (1805–47) Sister of Felix, she was a successful composer, writing numerous *Lieder*. 55, 56, 57

Mendelssohn, Felix (1809–47) German Romantic composer noted for his symphonies and overtures, and also his championing of Bach. 55, 56, 57, 58, 59, 61, 70, 75

Messiaen, Olivier (1908–92) Twentieth century French avant garde composer whose Catholic faith informs his works, notable for its intensely personal musical language that incorporates birdsong. 101, 105, *105*

Meyerbeer, Giacomo (1791–1864) German-born composer, made a mark in Paris with the first *grand opéra*. 52, 55, 62, 65, 66, 68

Miller, Glen (1904–44) American jazz musician and bandleader. 79

Millöcker, Carl (1842–99) Austrian conductor and composer of operettas, especially of the 1880s. 77

Milhaud, Darius (1892–1974) French composer and member of Les Six, his work is noted for its use of percussion and draws on eclectic influences including jazz and Brazilian music. 84, 96, 101

Mingus, Charles (1922–79) Black American jazz bass player. 81

Monteverdi, Claudio (1567–1643) Italian composer of preeminent position in Italian Baroque music, known for his operas, collections of madrigals and sacred music and wide range of techniques—contrapuntal, harmonic and instrumental and formal. 24, 26–27, *26*, 28, 32, 48

Morales, Cristóbal de (*c.* 1500–53) Spanish composer whose sacred works influenced Palestrina. 20, 21

Morley, Thomas (1557/8–1602) English madrigal composer. 22, 23

Moroder, Giorgio (1940–) Italian composer, songwriter and record producer associated with disco and techno music of the 1980s and 90s. 85, 87

Morton, Jelly Roll [Ferdinand] (1890–1941) American jazz pianist and bandleader. 80

Mozart, Leopold (1719–87) Austrian composer and violinist. 46, *46*, 47

Mozart, Wolfgang Amadeus (1756–91) Austrian composer, perhaps the most famous and loved figure of Western music. His works cover the full range of contemporary genres. 28, 31, 40, 41, 42, *42*, 43, 44, 45, 46–47, *46*, *47*, 49, 50, 52, 53, 54, 56, 57, 60, 61, 64, 66, 70, 71, 94, 108

Mulligan, Gerry (1927–96) American Cool jazz saxophonist. 81

Murail, Tristan (1947–) French avant garde composer whose works include the use of electronics. 110

Mussorgsky, Modest (1839–81) The most radical of The Five, his word setting and harmony influenced many figures. 72, 73, *73*, 96, 105

Nancarrow, Conlon (1912–97) American avant garde composer of works of great contrapuntal complexity for player piano. 107

N'Dour, Youssou (1959–) Singer and percussionist from Senegal who has integrated indigenous and international styles into a unique cross-over style. *92*

Newman, Alfred (1900–70) American composer of Hollywood movie scores. 84

Nielsen, Carl (1865–1931) Danish composer of the late-19th century known for his powerful symphonies. 74

Nono, Luigi (1924–90) Italian avant garde composer of the ''Darmstadt school''. 110

Nordraak, Rikard (1842–66) Norwegian Nationalist composer. 74

Novello, Ivor (1893–1951) British songwriter noted for his musical romances of the 1930s and 40s. 77, 78

Obrecht, Jacob (1457/8–1505) Netherlandish composer, a contemporary of Josquin des Prez, he was an important writer of motets, masses and songs. 20

Ockeghem, Jean de (c. 1410–97) Franco-Flemish composer who worked at the Nôtre Dame in Paris. 19, 20

Offenbach, Jacques (1819–80) German-born composer who worked in France producing popular operettas noted for their wit and gentle satire. 48, 77

Oldfield, Mike (1953–) British instrumentalist and composer of complex music that draws on world, folk, classical and electronic influences. 85

Oliver, King (1885–1938) American jazz cornettist and band leader. 80

Orbison, Roy (1936–88) American popular singer-songwriter influential in the development of rock and roll. 87, 89

Original Dixieland Jazz Band [ODJB] Early promoters of jazz, led by cornet player Nick LaRocca (1889–1961). 80, *80*

Ory, Kid [Edward] (c. 1890–1923) American jazz trombonist. 80

Pachelbel, Johann (1653–1706) German composer of church and chamber works, known for his innovative organ and keyboard music. 34, 37

Paganini, Nicolò (1782–1840) Italian violinist and composer whose works are distinguished by virtuosity. 54, *58*, 59, 61

Palestrina, Giovanni Pierluigi da (1525/6–94) Italian composer, the greatest musical figure of the Counter Reformation. His polyphonic liturgical works are considered

the models for strict diatonic counterpoint. 18, 20, 21, 22, 23, 28, 32, 33

Parker, Charlie (1920–55). Virtuoso American jazz saxophonist, especially associated with be-bop. 81, *81*

Parton, Dolly (1946–) A very successful American country singer. 89

Penderecki, Krzysztof (1933–) Polish composer whose early avant garde works explore the sound potentials of semi- and micro-tonal clusters. 111

Pergolesi, Giovanni Battista (1710–36) Leading Italian composer in the rise of 18th-century opera; also produced instrumental, chamber and sacred works. 24, 31, 44, 48, 99

Peri, Jacopo (1561–1633) Italian composer and singer significant in the development of dramatic *recitative* and composer of the earliest opera, *Euridice* (1600). 25

Perotinus (fl. c. 1200) French composer and member of the Notre Dame school who revised the *Magnus liber*. 12, 15, 16

Perugia, Matteo da (fl. 1400–16) Italian composer of Ars Nova. 18

Petrassi, Goffredo (1904–2003) Italian avant garde composer noted as a teacher; his works display an individual voice within a Modernist aesthetic. 97

Petrucci, Ottaviano (1466–1539) Italian publisher of Renaissance music. 18, 20

Pfitzner, Hans (1869–1949) German 20th-century Romantic composer whose close link to the National Socialist Party has overshadowed his prolific output. 107

Piccinni, Niccòlo (1728–1800) Italian opera composer. 48, 49

Pink Floyd British pyschadelic and later progressive rock group. 88

Pitney, Gene (1940–2006) American popular singer and songwriter. 87

Porpora, Nicola (1686–1768) Italian opera composer. 31, 45

Porter, Cole (1881–1964) American composer and lyricist of popular songs and musicals (on stage and screen). 78, 79, 82

Poulenc, Francis (1899–1963) French composer and member of Les Six; his skill at vocal writing is seen in his operas, songs and liturgical works. 101

Powell, John (1963–) British composer of Hollywood movie scores. 85

Power, Leonel (d. 1445) English composer of the early Renaissance. 19

Prado, Perez (1916–89) Cuban bandleader and composer noted for mambo style. 92

Praetorius, Michael (1551–1621) German organist and composer of sacred works based on Protestant hymns. 24, *33*, 34

Pratella, Francesco (1880–1955) Italian Futurist composer who collaborated with Luigi Russolo. 100

Prez, Josquin des (c. 1450/5–1521) French composer, regarded as the greatest musical figure of the Renaissance. 19, 20

Prokofiev, Sergey (1891–1953) Soviet composer who excelled in many genres,

mainly opera and ballet. 72, 85, 95, 104

Ptolemy (c. 83 AD–161 AD) Greek music theorist who brought the ideas of Aristoxenus and Pythagoras together. 10

Puccini, Giacomo (1858–1924) The most important Italian opera composer of the late-19th century who incorporated the innovations of the German school within the Italian tradition. 68, 69, 94

Purcell, Henry (1659–95) English composer, one of the most individual figures of the Baroque, best known for his operatic works and songs. 24, 32, 35, 102

Pythagoras (fl. c. 550–500 BC) Greek philosopher and theorist. 6, 9, 10, 14, 15

Queen British rock group led by flamboyant Freddie Mercury (1946–91). 88, 91

Rachmaninoff, Serge (1873–1943) Russian composer and pianist whose finely crafted works represent the last gasp of the Russian Romantic school. 72

Rahman, A.R. (1966–) Influential and prolific Indian composer of popular songs and scores for Indian movies. *85*, 86

Rameau, Jean-Philippe (1683–1764) French composer, prolific in all musical genres. Along with those of Lully and Gluck, his operas are considered the finest of their time. 29, *29*, 30, 37, 41, 49, 53

Ravel, Maurice (1875–1937) French composer. A contemporary of Debussy with whom he shares the credit for many 20th century innovations. 68, 72, 75, 96, 97, 98, 100, 101, 103

Reger, Max (1873–1916) German composer whose late-Romantic works look forward to 20th-century Neoclassicism. *106*

Reich, Steve (1936–) American Minimalist composer, whose pieces for percussion are some of the most successful. 111

Reincken, J.A. (1624–1722) German organist and composer. 38

Respighi, Ottorino (1879–1936) Italian composer who, although influenced by contemporary French music, initiated a 20th century Italian orchestral style. 97

Riddle, Nelson (1921–85). American bandleader, arranger and orchestrator, especially for popular songs and leading popular singers of the 1950s and 60s. 79

Rimes, LeAnn (1982–) American country singer. 89

Rimsky-Korsakov, Nikolay (1844–1908) Russian Nationalist composer, member of The Five, with an exceptional facility for orchestration. 72, 96, 97, 98

Ritchie, Lionel (1949–) Black American pop singer and songwriter. 86

Rodgers, Richard (1902–79) American composer of musicals, in collaboration with first lyricist Lorenz Hart then Oscar Hammerstein II. 76, 77, 79, 82

Rodrigo, Joaquín (1901–99) Spanish composer who followed in the footsteps of da Falla in creating a national style. *97*

Rolling Stones, The Internationally influential British rock group that developed from rhythm and blues and rock and roll origins in the 1960s. 88, *88*

Rollins, Sonny (1930–) Black American jazz saxophonist. 81

Romberg, Sigmund (1887–1951) American composer of Hungarian birth, noted for his operettas. 77

Rore, Cipriano de (1515/16–65) Netherlandish composer, one of the most noted writers of madrigals. 22

Ross, Diana (1944–) Black American pop singer, solo and with the Supremes. 86

Rossini, Gioachino (1792–1868) The most important Italian opera composer of the early-19th century. He revolutionized opera in Italy and France and initiated *grand opéra* with *Guillaume Tell*. 61, 64, 65, 66, 68, 71

Rossi, Luigi (1597/8–1653) Italian composer of vocal music, notably canzonettas, cantatas and operas. 33

Rossi, Salamone (1570–1630) Italian composer of trio sonatas. 35

Rota, Nino (1911–79). Prolific Italian composer, noted for his movie scores. 85

Roussel, Albert (1869–1937) French composer whose work ranges from fin-de-siècle Debussy-inspired pieces to those in a Neoclassical style. 71, 101

Russolo, Luigi (1885–1947) Italian Futurist painter and performer who advocated the creation of works based on noises. He is the inventor of the *intonarumori*. 100

Saint-Saëns, Camille (1835–1921) French composer, organist and teacher, an important figure in the renaissance of French music after 1871. 71, 97

Sammartini, Giovanni (1700/1–75) Italian composer, important for his early-Classical symphonies. 43, *43*, 49

Satie, Erik (1866–1925) French composer whose deceptively simple works were revolutionary and had a great influence on later avant garde composers. 71, 96, 97, 98, 100, 101

Scarlatti, Alessandro (1660–1725) Prolific Italian composer of sacred and secular works. 31, 32, 33, 43

Scarlatti, Domenico (1685–1757) Son of Alessandro, he is noted for his keyboard sonatas and operas. 25, *36*, 39

Schaeffer, Pierre (1910–95) French composer who was the first to produce *musique concrète* on tape. 110

Scheidemann, Heinrich (1595–1663) German organist and composer, noted for his works based on chorales. 36

Scheidt, Samuel (1587–1654) German organist and composer who also drew on Italian influences. 34

Schein, Johann (1586–1630) German composer who combined German Lutheran church music with Italian styles of concerto, madrigal and monody. 34

Schoenberg, Arnold (1874–1951) Austrian composer, theorist and teacher, member of the Second Vienna School and inventor of the serial technique of musical organization. 99, 103, 106, 107, 108, 109, 110

Schubert, Franz (1779–1828) Austrian composer, a major figure of the Romantic era and a prolific composer of *Lieder*. 51, 52, 54, 55, 56, 57, *57*, 58, 59

Schumann, Robert (1810–56) German Romantic composer whose sensitive vision manifests itself in piano works, symphonies and *Lieder*. 55, 56, 57, 58, 59, 61, 71

Schütz, Heinrich (1585–1672) German composer, trained in Italy, acclaimed internationally in his time. 28, 34, 36

Sculthorpe, Peter (1929–) Australian composer whose personal vision of an Australian music, inspired by that country's landscape and history, draws on Aboriginal and East Asian musics. 107

Sex Pistols British punk rock band of the 1970s. 88

Shankar, Ravi (1920–2012) Indian sitar player and composer. 93

Shaw, Artie (1910–2004) American jazz clarinettist, bandleader and composer. 80

Shostakovich, Dmitry (1906–75) Russian/Soviet composer noted for his brooding and monumental symphonies. 72, 84, 85, 94, 95, 104

Sibelius, Jean (1865–1957) Finnish composer, one of the greatest writers of post-Romantic symphonies whose grasp of form and concise motivic development is exceptional. 61, 74, *74*, 75, 106

Sinatra, Frank (1915–98) American popular singer noted for his personal style and distinctive phrasing. 79

Skryabin, Aleksandr Nikoleyavitch (1872–1915) Russian composer of the late-19th century, known for mystical programs and adventurous harmonic language that verges on atonality. *72*, 98

Sly & the Family Stone Black American rock and soul group of the 1970s, influential in the emergence of disco. 86

Smetana, Bedřich (1824–84) Czech composer who established a Czech national style through operas. *72*, 73, 75

Smith, Bessie (1892/4–1937) Black American blues singer, nicknamed the "Empress of the Blues". *79*

Snoop Dogg [Cordozar Calvin Broadus Jr.] (1971-) Leading American exponent of gangsta rap. *93*

Sondheim, Stephen (1930–) American composer of Broadway musicals. 78, 83

Spector, Phil (1939–) American record producer who developed the distinctive 1960s "wall of sound". 90

Springfield, Dusty (1939–99) British popular singer influenced by many styles, notably country and soul. 87

Springsteen, Bruce (1949–) American rock and pop singer-songwriter of socially and politically aware songs. 88, *92*

Stamitz, Johann (1717–57) Bohemian composer of symphonies who worked at the court of Mannheim and created the finest orchestra of its day. 40, 44, *44*

Steffani, Agostino (1654–1728) Italian composer, based in northern Germany, important for secular chamber duets. 31

Steiner, Max (1888–1971) American composer of Austrian birth for Hollywood movie scores of the 1930s–60s. 84

Stockhausen, Karlheinz (1928–2007) German avant garde composer of the "Darmstadt school" who initally concentrated on total serialism and electronic music, in which he was a pioneer, before pursuing his personal vision through the *Licht* operas. 91, 94, *94*, 104, 110

Strauss, Johann [II] (1825–99) Viennese composer and conductor, who exceeded his father's reputation for ballroom music and wrote many operettas. 77

Strauss, Richard (1864–1949) Late-Romantic German composer noted for his tone poems and operas; initially an arch-Modernist, he later reverted to a nostalgic language. 55, 57, 69, 70, 72, 74, 107

Stravinsky, Igor (1882–1971) Russian composer, one of the greatest musical figures of the 20th century. His early ballet *Le sacre du printemps* was the most forward-looking work of its time. He later turned to Neoclassicism and, toward the end of his life, serialism. 50, 72, 94, 98, *98*, 100, 101, 102, 103, 104, 107

Strouse, Charles (1928–) American composer and lyricist for Broadway musicals. 82

Sturgeon, Nicholas (d. 1454) English composer of the early Renaissance. 19

Sugarhill Gang, The American hip-hop group influential on early rap. 91, 93

Sullivan, Arthur Seymour (1842–1900) British classical composer and conductor, significant for the series of comic operas written with librettist W.S. Gilbert. 77

Suppé, Franz von (1819-95) Austrian composer for the light operatic stage. 77

Sweelinck, Jan (1562–1621) Dutch composer and organist, noted for keyboard compositions and vocal music. 36, 38

Tailleferre, Germaine (1892–1983) French composer, member of Les Six. 101

Tallis, Thomas (c. 1505–85) English composer of polyphony, one of the greatest musicians of his day. 23, 102

Tartini, Giuseppe (1692–1770) Italian composer and violinist, influential as a teacher and through his violin concertos and sonatas. 37

Taylor, Cecil (1929–) Black American jazz pianist associated with free jazz. 81

Tchaikovsky, Pyotr Il'yich (1840–93) Russian Romantic composer known for his symphonies and ballets. 72, 94

Telemann, Georg Philipp (1681–1767) Prolific German composer important to the transition from Baroque to Classical aesthetics and techniques. 31, 34, 37, 39

Temptations, The Black American rhythm and blues and soul quintet who emerged from Motown to influence 1970s and 80s dance music. 86

Theile, Johann (1646–1724) German composer of sacred music. 29

Thomson, Virgil (1896–1989) American composer whose works drew on popular music and church styles. 102, 107

Tinctoris, Johannes (c. 1435–before 1511) Flemish composer and theorist. 19

Tippett, Michael (1905–1998) English composer notable for his highly individual style in opera and orchestral music. 103, *103*

Torelli, Guiseppe (1658–1709) Italian composer who contributed to the development of the concerto. 36, 42

Trenet, Charles (1913–2001) French singer-songwriter, many of whose songs became international standards in English translation. 79

Tromboncino, Bartolomeo (*d. c.* 1534) Italian composer of *frottole*. 22

Turnage, Mark-Anthony (1960–) Modernist English composer known for his uncompromising works. 111

Vanhal, Johann (1739–1814) Bavarian composer of Classical symphonies. 45

Varèse, Edgard (1883–1965) French-born composer who worked in the USA, important for his early experiments in atonality and rhythm. 71, *100*

Vaughan Williams, Ralph (1872–1958) English composer, the leading light of the English musical renaissance of the first half of the 20th century. 75, 84, 102, 103

Veloso, Caetano (1942–) Brazilian singer and songwriter. 92

Verdelot, Phillipe (c. 1480–1532) Dutch composer active in Italy, one of the earliest writers of madrigals. 22

Verdi, Guiseppe (1813–1901) The greatest Italian composer of the 19th century whose operas form the core of the Italian opera repertory. 61, 65, 66, 67, *67*, 68, 69, 71, 94

Victoria, Tomás Luis de (1548–1611) Sapnish composer of sacred music, one of the greatest figures of his time. 21

Vitali, Giovanni (1632–92) Italian composer of trio sonatas. 35

de Vitry, Philippe (1291–1361) French composer and theorist whose works look forward to the Renaissance. 12, 16

Vivaldi, Antonio (1678–1741) Prolific Italian composer important in the development of the Baroque concerto and its instrumentation. 31, 37, 42

Vogelweide, Walther von der (c. 1200) German Minnesinger. 17

Wagenseil, Georg (1715–77) Austrian composer of symphonies and opera. 45

Wagner, Richard (1813–83) German Romantic composer, the most important figure of the last 150 years for his ideas on drama and musical language through his conception of the *Gesamtkunstwerk*, advanced harmony and technique of the *Leitmotif*. 17, 50, 52, 53, 54, 55, 56, 57, 58, 59, 60, 61, 62–63, *62*, 65, 66, 67, 68, 69, 70, 71, 73, 75, 95, 96, 97, 101, 109

Walton, William (1902–83) English composer noted for his rhythmic, and at times playful, musical style. 84, 95, 102

Washington, Dinah (1924–63) Black American popular singer known for an emotive blues style. 86

Waxman, Franz (1906–67) Jewish German composer of movie scores. 84

Weber, Carl Maria von (1786–1826) German Romantic composer, his opera *Der Freischütz* was one of the most influential works of the early 19th century. 48, 52, 53, 54, 55, 60

Webern, Anton (1883–1945) Austrian serialist composer, he was a member of the Second Vienna School. His compositions were greatly influential on the post-war avant garde. 108, 109, *109*, 110

Weckman, Matthias (?1616–74) German composer and organist, and a pupil of Schütz. 36

Weelkes, Thomas (1576–1623) English madrigal composer. 22

Weill, Kurt (1900–50) German composer who moved to the USA. 82, 102

Wert, Giaches de (1535–96) Flemish composer, principally of sacred music, who worked mainly in Italy. 26

Whiteman, Paul (1890–1967) Bandleader and arranger of the 1920s–40s, known as "the King of Jazz". 79, *79*, 80

Who, The British rock group formed in 1964. 85, 88

Wieck, Clara (1819–96) German composer and pianist, one of the most successful of her generation, she was married to Schumann and was a friend of Brahms. 56

Wilbye, John (1574–1638) English madrigal composer. 22

Willaert, Adrian (c. 1490–1562) Netherlandish composer who worked in Italy, one of the most important writers of madrigals. *21*, 22

Williams, John (1932–) American composer of Hollywood scores. 85

Wolf, Hugo (1860–1903) Austrian composer who almost exclusively wrote *Lieder* to which he brings a highly expressive musical language. 57

Wonder, Stevie (1950–) Black American singer, pianist and songwriter associated with the Motown style. 86

Xenakis, Iannis (1922–2001) Greek Modernist composer who was born in Romania and worked in France, noted for his dramatic use of clusters and uncompromising musical language. 110

Young, La Monte (1935–) American composer, one of the pioneers of Minimalism. 111

Young, Lester (1909–59) American jazz saxophonist. 80

Zappa, Frank (1940–93) American pop composer and performer, associated with an individual and eclectic fusion of music styles. 87

Zawinul, Joe (1932–2007) Austrian jazz pianist, exponent of jazz fusion. 81

Zeller, Carl (1842–98) Austrian composer of operettas. 77

Zemlinsky, Alexander (1871–1942) Austrian composer and conductor whose works are noted for fine orchestration and late-Romantic musical language. 97, 106

PICTURE CREDITS

a-above, b-below, l-left, r-right, t-top, m-middle